ANDREW LANG

PORTRAIT OF ANDREW LANG
by
SIR W. B. RICHMOND, R.A.

ANDREW LANG

A CRITICAL BIOGRAPHY

WITH
A SHORT-TITLE BIBLIOGRAPHY OF
THE WORKS OF ANDREW LANG

ROGER LANCELYN GREEN
M.A., B.Litt.

EDMUND WARD
16 NEW STREET, LEICESTER, ENGLAND

First published October, 1946

This book is set in Imprint Old Style
11 on 12 pt., printed and bound at the
De Montfort Press, Leicester.

CONTENTS

To
A. E. W. MASON,
this account of
his friend and collaborator
ANDREW LANG
is humbly inscribed, in acknowledgement
of a more than thirty-fold debt of gratitude,
and as a token of much esteem.

Preface

THE fact that more than thirty years have passed since Andrew Lang's death, and that this is the first book which has been written about him, needs a word or two of explanation. Literary fame is notoriously short-lived, and yet when Lang died he was still one of the most important figures in contemporary letters: nor, though his fame has suffered an unmerited eclipse, is his name altogether forgotten now, even among the younger generation.

Children, we are told, do not care now for fairy-tales as devotedly as we did in our own younger days—and yet to mention Andrew Lang is still to call forth some kindly recollection of *The Blue Fairy Book* or of the *Red*, the *Green* and the *Yellow*. Nor are the young readers of today quite oblivious to the charms of Lang's own original tales: the bookshops at Christmas 1943 displayed whole shelves of the latest reprint of *Chronicles of Pantouflia*—shelves that were not full for many days; while 1945 had exhausted the newly-illustrated edition of *Prince Prigio* some months before the year's end.

Not a few readers, both young and old, who still delight in the unending enchantment of Rider Haggard's romances, number *The World's Desire* among their favourites, and in so doing pay tribute to Andrew Lang its part author; not only the students of St. Andrew's remember "Almæ Matres" and certain other poems; and if "Butcher and Lang" is still the favourite "crib" to Homer, it has also its admirers still among the Greekless, and with Homer the name of Andrew Lang is as fondly and inseparably linked as is that of Gilbert Murray with Euripides.

A fair meed of remembrance this, perhaps, for a versatile Victorian and Edwardian critic who tried his hand in many mediums; for a learned and meticulous historian who indulged also in lighter literary pursuits; and yet not enough.

Andrew Lang, "the divine amateur of letters," who wrote indeed only and ever of the things that he loved, brought forth out of that deep love, and out of that elusive quality which we are fain to call genius, writings in poetry and in prose that are most shamefully underrated. In poetry his name is listed unintelligently with the names of Henley and Stevenson, Dobson and Gosse—and as a poet he is least known of any save perhaps only Gosse. Yet Lang's poetry, which is so little known and so unduly neglected, should have set him at the head of this group, beside, if not above, both Stevenson and Henley.

As a critic in the 'eighties and the 'nineties, Andrew Lang held a position that has no parallel today: authors of high standing have told of how they would fly of a morning to the *Daily News* or *The Morning Post*, and how, if there was a leader by Lang (signed or unsigned, it mattered not to the initiate), their day was made. To journalism, as to all else, Lang, the most professional of writers, brought that secret of love which touched all that he wrote with the magic of true literature, and which earned for him from Henley the nickname of "the divine amateur," using that much-abused word in its true and original sense.

Andrew Lang, then, was a poet: that he might have been a great poet was held by such eminent critics as George Saintsbury and Professor Blyth Webster, but even the promise of greatness is a quality possessed by few of the minor poets whose works are still read. Also he was a translator, who combined keen scholarship with one of the most perfect literary styles of a period that produced such stylists as Walter Pater, Stevenson and Kenneth Grahame: the *Odyssey*, the *Iliad*, and the Greek Bucolic poets being not his only triumphs in this field, for his version of the old French song-story *Aucassin and Nicolete*, in prose and verse, is probably the most perfect of all Lang's works.

And besides adding to our literary heritage some few undoubted poems and unsurpassed translations, Andrew Lang wrote also at least one other book that should hold a secure place in literature—his fairy-tale *Prince Prigio*. This is less known even than his poems and translations, and perhaps I am the first to propose it seriously for immortality: and yet a long and detailed study of the important branch of literature to which it belongs leaves me no choice but to rank it among the half-dozen or so of books that includes *Alice* and *The Rose and the Ring*.

When we come to see how rich and bright a legacy Andrew Lang has left to us, it seems even stranger that he is so little known, so grudgingly remembered. Even the fortuitous circumstances of the violent changes in literary taste that have happened since his death—or, again of the fact that no reasonable edition of his poems has appeared—do not fully account for this neglect.

It is probably true that to the absence of any life or critical study of Andrew Lang is largely due his present lack of recognition. Of late years the excellent lectures delivered at St. Andrew's and published separately by the Oxford University Press have done much to reinstate Lang in certain branches of his extensive labours, but only one lecture so far

(that on Lang's poetry by Professor Blyth Webster) has dealt with any
but his more learned and specialized works; and no attempt has been
made, at any length beyond that of a magazine article, to present Lang
as a literary figure and as a personality for the general reader.

There has been no biography of Lang, and, in the ordinary sense of
the word, it is probable that there never will be. Lang was one of the
shyest and most reserved of men, and the idea of having the little
privacies of his life laid bare for casual observation and criticism was so
abhorrent to him that he left strict injunctions that no "official biography" or collection of his letters was to appear. "Let us fellow-
labourers make biographies of ourselves taboo," he wrote indignantly
after reading Mrs. Coghill's book on Mrs. Oliphant in 1899. "If we have
nothing else to leave, let us leave our malison on those who publish our
lives and letters. Think what letters are: hasty, indiscreet, inaccurate
. . . authors ought to write nothing and burn everything in the way of
letters." This outburst, which was caused by Mrs. Coghill's inclusion in
her book of a "hasty, indiscreet and inaccurate" letter from Lang to
Mrs. Oliphant, shows Lang's attitude to the "official biography" which
was then even more of a depressing institution than at present.

> "But now the dentist cannot die
> And leave his forceps as of old,
> But round him, ere he yet be cold,
> Begins the vast biography"—

Lang is said to have written in derision of the popular craze for intimate
lives that reached such a height in the last twenty years of his own
career.

In obedience to his wish, no life of Lang was written, nor was any
collection of his letters made. Lang's widow obeyed her husband's
behest with heart-rending completeness, and it is said that she used to
complain that her wrists ached for weeks and weeks after tearing up
Andrew's papers; while such intimate friends as Florence MacCunn
followed her example as religiously.

The only biography to appear was the short sketch by George
Gordon in the *Dictionary of National Biography* ; but Rider Haggard,
Lang's closest friend, wrote extensively of Lang and included many of
his letters in his own autobiography, *The Days of My Life* ; and Ella
Christie and Alice King Stewart, in their recent book of memoirs,
A Long Look at Life, have added many delightful details.

After what has been said, this present book requires a word or two of
explanation. How reverently one is bound to obey the wishes of a writer
thirty-odd years dead is a question that will admit of much discussion,

and which, as the case of Thackeray has shown, may be interpreted in many ways. On the one hand, the affection and the reverence that many years of study among his writings has produced urges me to respect his wishes to the letter; and on the other hand, the complete absence of all biographical materials of a personal and intimate nature, make one's course fairly clear.

The present work was undertaken with the sanction and approval, indeed, with the encouragement, of the older members of the Lang family, amongst whom I should like to mention with gratitude Miss T. B. Alleyne, Mrs. John Lang and Lady Fayrer. But this book did not and does not set out to be a biography of Andrew Lang. To study a man's works is to a great extent to study the man himself; to understand and appreciate them is to appreciate and understand him; and so a critical study becomes a critical biography almost by the nature of the work involved.

The nucleus upon which this book is founded was a Dissertation on Lang's imaginative writings submitted a few years ago for the Degree of Bachelor of Letters at Oxford; and my gratitude to Professor D. Nichol Smith and Professor J. R. R. Tolkien for their unfailing guidance and encouragement leaves with me a debt that can never adequately be repaid.

The chief materials for a book on Andrew Lang are of necessity his own works: and their quantity is more astonishingly great than may readily be estimated. George Saintsbury reckoned that two hundred volumes of a "library" edition would scarcely contain them, and my own computation would put it at nearer three hundred—even excluding the great amount of Lang's work that is lost to us in the anonymous files of forgotten daily papers. From this great mass of literature a number of grains of evidence have been sifted—after diligent search, for Lang was not at all an autobiographic author, differing from Stevenson in this respect to a marked degree; and the biographies of his friends and acquaintances have also yielded much of interest.

All such material, being already published, needs no excuse to the ghost of Andrew Lang when collected together: and of unpublished material there is relatively little. Miss Lilias Rider Haggard has allowed me to examine the large collection of Lang's letters to her father, still preserved at Ditchingham House, and from these much has been gleaned to amplify the account given by Haggard of the writing of *The World's Desire*.

To Miss Haggard's kindness must also be added that of the librarian of the Norwich Castle Museum, where the manuscript of *The World's Desire* is preserved.

Some personal recollections have also been placed at my disposal and much kind interest taken in this book by such friends and acquaintances of Lang as Mr. Bernard Shaw, Professor Gilbert Murray, Mrs. Harrison, the Hon. Mrs. Eustace Hills, and others. And in this connection I should like to express a more particular debt of gratitude to Mr. A. E. W. Mason for his unfailing kindness and encouragement.

Thus around the critical study of the literary works of Andrew Lang (and the scholarly consideration of his classical, historical, anthropological and biographical works has been accomplished already in the "Lang Lectures" by acknowledged experts in these diverse fields) some semblance of a biography has grown up ; some attempt to present the man as he was and to arrive at an understanding and an appreciation of the mind that produced the rich variety of his books. To go thus far— and further one could scarcely go, even if one were prepared absolutely to disregard Lang's wishes—cannot be to incur the posthumous displeasure of one who in these many years of study has come to seem more close and intimate a friend than many who still walk upon the earth.

Writing this in the library of Merton College, where Lang himself worked and wrote more than seventy-five years ago, I cannot better end these few words of explanation and acknowledgment, than by adding to those names already mentioned in gratitude, all those members of this College who have helped and encouraged me in this study of a past Fellow of Merton, making particular mention of Professor Nichol Smith, Professor H. W. Garrod, and Mr. Edmund Blunden.

ROGER LANCELYN GREEN.

Merton College,
    2nd November, 1945.

To Andrew Lang

Merton: 31 March, 1944

Here in this quiet spot, where the March sun falls
Its hesitant fingers over the trim green lawn,
I am near to you, and your footsteps pace with my own
On the crisp brown walks and the crocus-blossoming grass:
Back and forth together we pass and repass;
And only Time is between us, a curtain drawn
To hide from our eyes,—discovering all to my heart.

Here, where the unbloomed roses climb on the walls,
The Singing Rose that you sought in a by-gone day,
I am near to the friend whom I may not meet on this earth.
Nearest of all today, when the magic fingers of time
Stretch to the octave-span, and the day of his birth
Links through a hundred years to the long grey house
Where ringing Tweed winds on through a land of dreams.

In the "fair, forsaken place" that you loved and left,
That I love so well, and yet may not call my own;
Here, through the pang of regret, as the sad, sweet chime
Strikes to the heart with the stab of remorseless thought,
Let us wander still, forgetting the world together;
Remembering only the quest of the Singing Rose,
That leads us on through the halls of a Fairy Court
To the Tweed-side keep, or the fane of the World's Desire;
Remembering how you sang to my heart in the clear Spring
       weather,
And how you sing to my soul at the Summer's close.

CHAPTER I

A Border Boyhood

THE Scottish Border, that land of old discord and lingering romance, has for its heart the ancient little country town of Selkirk, set around and above the joining of Yarrow and Ettrick, the "many-fabled streams" of ballad literature.

"Immediately after passing Ettrickbank, the road, coming suddenly out from a clump of trees, breaks into view of a wide and pleasant valley, with a goodly prospect of wood and heathery hill stretched far to the west and south. Down this valley sweeps the gravelly bed of Ettrick; on its further bank, on the flat haugh, stand a long line of mills, and the station of a branch line of railway. Above, rising abruptly, tier upon tier in cheerful succession, trees and houses that blend into the smiling face of Selkirk."[1] It was thus that Andrew Lang last saw his native town in 1912, the year of his death; and, except for the railway and the mills, the general appearance of the place must not have seemed very different when he was born in the long grey house of Viewfield on the hillside on March 31, 1844.

The Langs had dwelt at Selkirk for many generations, though they came of a simple enough stock of peasant descent. Like most Scots, Lang could boast of a long and complicated genealogy; but of this he tells us only that "for all that I could ever hear, could ever read in any book, I have only two or three upper-class ancestors, and am but very distantly connected with Robert de Comyn, who, in 1069, was created Earl of Northumberland, and then had his throat cut. *Bourgeois je suis!*[2]" He could also trace his descent from one Beathoch of the ancient Scottish blood royal, though his family seems never to have boasted any coat of arms.[3] It pleased him, however, to remember that he "came of Harden's line," in common with Robert Louis Stevenson, and that "he and I had a common forbear with Sir Walter Scott, and were hundredth cousins of each other."[4]

It was said that the Langs were of gipsy blood, and though no
evidence is forthcoming, Andrew seems to have believed in this
legend to some extent, for he writes in his poem "Pen and Ink,"[5]

> "Ye wanderers that were my sires,
>   Who read men's fortunes in the hand,
> Who voyaged with your smithy fires
>   From waste to waste across the land—
> Why did you leave for garth and town
>   Your life by heath and river's brink ?
> Why lay your gipsy freedom down
>   And doom your child to pen and ink ? "*

However this might be, Andrew Lang's more immediate ancestors
had been townsmen of Selkirk for at least seven generations. Thus
in 1650 we find a John Lang mentioned as a freeman, and in 1656 as
an officer in the Guild of Tailors; and another appears as Deacon
in 1680 and in 1699. John Lang "the younger," probably his son,
was Deacon of the same craft in 1705, 1723 and 1742; and seems to
be so again in 1749, where he is referred to as "the elder," probably
in counterdistinction from another John Lang "the younger" who
was Deacon in 1753. One John Lang, probably the eldest of these,
was a town councillor of Selkirk in 1709, and it is recorded, either
of him or his son, that in 1711 a certain "Robert Thorbrand of the
Incorporation of Tailors, alleged a scandelous libel against Deacon
John Lang—which the Council deemed the Justices incompetent
to try."

A probable relation was also a certain Bessie Lang, accused by
the Kirk Sessions in 1714 of "invoking God's curse upon Bailie
Tudhope's family, hoping the Bailie's house would come to
desolation, and that the hare would kittle in his hearth"—a similar
expression to that used by Thomas the Rhymer a few centuries
earlier, in one of his most famous prophecies.

* According to Mrs. John Lang, whose husband was the son of
Andrew Lang's eldest brother, Patrick, there is no foundation
whatsoever for the legend of Gipsy blood in the Lang family.
Lady Fayrer, however, whose father was Andrew's favourite
brother, John (part author with him of *Highways and Byways on
the Border*), tells me that, if only a legend, it was at least " a
cherished one of my uncle's, and one which he and his brothers
loved to think might be true."

A son of the John Lang who was Deacon in 1753, was the Andrew Lang (born 1712) who was Town Clerk in 1743, and in successive years Procurator Fiscal and Clerk of Supplies. He was the first of five generations of Langs who held municipal office in Selkirk, and by the end of the eighteenth century the family was established as one of the most important in the town. This seems to have been a distinction of dubious merit in the early years of the new century when, besides having fallen upon evil times between lack of employment, bad seasons, and foreign wars, "the town was torn by opposing factions, Langs and Hendersons being its Montagues and Capulets"[6]. This state of affairs had begun to die out by about 1832 when the trade guilds ceased to have any political significance, and ended completely a little later when the great weaving industry was established independent of local influence.

Son of this first town clerk Andrew Lang, was another John, who was chief magistrate in the early years of the nineteenth century when Walter Scott first became Sheriff-Depute of the Shire.

It was a time of great unrest and alarm, as an invasion by the French under Napoleon, who lay at Boulogne with an immense army fully equipped, and waiting only a favourable opportunity to embark, was expected daily.

Of the most notable incident in the Border district at this time, Sir Walter Scott, who himself participated in it, tells us in a note to *The Antiquary*[7]: "Almost every individual was enrolled either in a military or civil capacity, for the purpose of contributing to resist the long suspended threats of invasion, which were echoed from every quarter. Beacons were erected along the coast, and all through the country, to give the signal for everyone to repair to the post where his peculiar duty called him, and men of every description fit to serve held themselves in readiness on the shortest summons. During this agitating period, and on the evening of February 2nd, 1804, the person who kept watch on the commanding station of Home Castle, being deceived by some accidental fire in the County of Northumberland, which he took for the corresponding signal light in that county with which his orders were to communicate, lighted up his own beacon . . . Through the Border counties the alarm spread with rapidity, and on no occasion when that country was the scene of perpetual and unceasing war was the summons to

B

arms more readily obeyed. . . . The Selkirkshire Yeomanry made a remarkable march, for although some of the individuals lived twenty or thirty miles distant from the place where they mustered, they were nevertheless embodied and in order in so short a period that they were in Dalkeith, which was their alarm post, at about one o'clock on the day succeeding the signal . . . though many of the troopers must have ridden forty or fifty miles without drawing bridle."

The family of John Lang, chief magistrate of Selkirk, was, so his great-grandson tells us, "aroused late one night by the sound of a carriage hurrying down the steep and narrow street. Lord Napier was bringing, probably from Hawick, the tidings that the beacons were ablaze. The town bell was instantly rung, the inhabitants met in the market-place, and the whole force . . armed and marched to Dalkeith."[8] John Lang's son, Andrew, was absent in Edinburgh on business at the time, and John himself was ill and unable to ride; but Mrs. Lang prepared and sent her son's arms, uniform and horse to Dalkeith, so that he could join his troop with the least possible delay. Meeting her the following year, after her husband's death, Scott complimented her on the readiness she had shown "in equipping her son with the means of meeting danger," and he records her answer: "None can know better than you that my son is the only prop by which, since his father's death, our family is supported. But I would rather see him dead on that hearth than hear that he had been a horse's length behind his companions in defence of his king and country."

This Andrew Lang (grandfather of the subject of this book), was Sheriff-Clerk during most of Sir Walter's term of office. As described officially in 1820, he was "a man fearing God, of the true Pro.estant religion now publicly professed and authorized by the laws of this realm, expert in common affairs of the burgh, and a burgess," and Scott was "never slow to admit that Lang was as well qualified as himself to be sheriff. Their relations were those of intimate personal friendship. . . . More than once or twice was the Shirra beholden to the Shirra-Clerk for assistance in emergencies of impecuniosity."[9]

In 1819, shortly after his re-election, Lang was called upon to receive Prince Leopold as a guest of the town, and to officiate at the ceremony of granting him the freedom of the burgh, on which occasion, Scott notes, "Lang made an excellent speech—sensible, and feeling, and well delivered. The Prince seemed much surprised at this great propriety of expression and behaviour in a magistrate whose people seemed such a rabble, and whose whole band of music consisted of a drum and a fife."[10] Finally, in 1832, Lang was elected representative elder to the General Assembly.

His son, John Lang, also became in time Sheriff-Clerk, and for a short time, his second son, Patrick, held that office before his departure to Australia in 1878.

In 1843 John Lang married Jane Plenderleath Sellar, daughter of Patrick Sellar (1780-1851) of Westfield, Morayshire, factor to the first Duke of Sutherland; and the eldest of their eight children, Andrew, was born on 31st March of the following year at Viewfield, their home in Selkirk.

The house, which stands in its own large garden well back from the main street and overlooking the valley, is a long, low building of grey stone, of one storey only, though with a basement that forms a lower floor on the valley side where the land falls away sharply.

In the house opposite lived a well-to-do family of manufacturers by the name of Roberts: their eldest son, Alexander, was of the same age as Andrew Lang, and was an early friend of his, while the other children of both families were on fairly intimate terms. The youngest of the Roberts's still remembers her early years at Selkirk, and her daughter, Miss Helen Harrison, has recorded for me some of these recollections.

"Viewfield was just across the road from Wellwood, and mother was there constantly . . . Andrew was twelve years older than her, but she used to play with his sister Nellie . . . She says that it was a beautiful house and a lovely nursery. I imagine that there was probably more comfort and culture at Viewfield than was usual in those days. The Lang's father was Town Clerk and a Solicitor, and therefore socially much superior to the manufacturers. . . . Mother says she regularly went for walks with Nellie and the governess."[11]

An early glimpse of Andrew at the age of eight is afforded by his aunt, Mrs. E. M. Sellar (wife of William Young Sellar, 1825-1890, the well-known Professor of Humanity at Edinburgh University, and authority on Latin literature), who records a visit to the

Border in June 1852. "At Selkirk we stayed with the Langs at Viewfield . . . and I made the acquaintance of my nephews: the eldest (Andrew), a handsome, dark-eyed boy, shy and somewhat *farouche*, evading his new aunt's affectionate advances, and fearing her kisses as much as the hero of the lyric feared those of the gentle maiden! I little thought then of the strong friendship that would exist between us in after years."[12]

Many of Andrew's childish activities may be gathered from his Border fairy-tale, *The Gold of Fairnilee*, which he once described as "only a lot of childish reminiscences." Fairnilee, the old ruined house on the grassy bank above the Tweed not far from Selkirk, was one of his favourite haunts as a boy; perhaps he came here on his fishing expeditions with Alexander Roberts, who afterwards built the great modern house close beside the remains of the original building. In the story we hear of Randal and Jean fishing in Caddon Burn and the Burn of Peel, exploring the hills and woods in the vale of Tweed, following the little streams up to their sources, hunting for golden nuggets in their waters, or damming the swift-flowing burns. In winter they track the rabbits and hares and foxes through the snow with the big sheep dog "Yarrow," slide upon the frozen boat-pond, or feed with their porridge the wild game, made tame by the cold. Thus must Andrew and his brothers and sister also have passed the time, more especially in the long winter evenings when, like Randal and Jean, "they sat by the nursery fire and those were almost the pleasantest hours, for the old nurse would tell them old Scotch stories of elves and fairies, and sing them old songs." There were stories of "The Red Etin, or some other awful bogle . . . of Whuppity Stoorie, the wicked old witch with the spinning-wheel," and stories of monsters in the lochs, and kelpies, and other strange creatures of local superstition. "She was a great woman for stories, and believed in fairies and bogles . . . Other stories the old nurse had about hidden treasures and buried gold. If you believed her, there was hardly an old stone on the hillside, but had gold under it."[13] Perhaps among these legendary hoards was "the Roman treasure still buried near Oakwood Tower, under an inscribed stone 'seen in the memory of living man' "[14], and certainly she told of the Gold of Fairnilee, hidden, so said the tale, near the prehistoric ruins of the Camp of Rink, where Andrew and Patrick Lang dug for it in vain.[15]

The old nurse in the story is called Nancy, and she seems to be an exact portrait of Andrew's own nurse whom E. M. Sellar mentions in her reminiscences: "This summer (1857) Mrs. Sellar had a visit from her daughter, Mrs. Lang, accompanied by her three handsome boys and their old and very Scotch nurse Nancy. Mrs. Lang had spent the winter before at Clifton, where Nancy was always taken for a foreigner . . . Nancy was a good, faithful soul, whose whole interest was in her master's family, and she lived and died in their service."[16]

One of Lang's earliest pastimes, and one to which he remained faithful until the end of his life, was angling: "The majority of dwellers on the Border," he says, "are born fishers . . . Like the rest of us in that country, I was born an angler, though . . . my labours have not been blessed, and are devoted to fishing rather than to the catching of fish . . . My first recollection of the sport must date from about the age of four." One sees how whole-hearted was the delight in fishing from the confession which follows: "In a moment of profane confidence my younger brother once asked me: ' What do you do in sermon time ? I,' said he in a whisper, ' — mind you don't tell—I tell stories to myself about catching trout! ' To which I added a similar confession, for even so I drove the sermon by."[17]

But it was something above and beyond the actual sport cf fishing, something deeper and more fundamental, that appealed to Lang then and throughout his life. "It was worth while to be a boy then in the south of Scotland, and to fish the waters haunted by old legends, musical with old songs . . . Memory that has lost so much and would gladly lose so much more, brings vividly back the golden summer evenings by Tweedside, when trout began to plash in the stillness—brings back the long, lounging solitary days beneath the woods of Ashiestiel—days so lovely that they sometimes in the end begat a superstitious eeriness. One seemed forsaken in an enchanted world; one might see the two white fairy deer flit by, bringing to us, as to Thomas the Rhymer, the tidings that we must back to Fairyland. . . ."[18]

Besides the romance of the Border and its associations, it was inevitable that the enchantment of books should very soon begin to influence Lang's mind. The early imaginings of a child, before the spell of his reading falls on him, may be the most wonderful and mysterious—and these Lang himself held to be the only true imagination that was worthy of note in a child—but they are mostly intangible and difficult to recapture, merging as they do into the second and more vivid stage of child-life, that of the more usual "imagination," when he enters into the golden world of fairy-tale and romance which is as real to him as the actual life of the nursery. Nor do we usually separate imagination from the child's completely absorbing ability to "play at things," as Lang seems to have done. Looking back to the mental state of his earliest recollected days, Lang maintains that "Of imagination, the power of ' playing at things ' and summoning ' invisible playmates '—I am sure I never had an ounce *after* I learnt to read. From that remote hour I let other authors do my imagining for me, while I saw less bookish children living in fantasy, in a world of dreams."[19] Yet he admits, without recognising any contradiction, that he possessed the power, which we would naturally call imagination, of translating the invisible, intangible world of the story-books into a living, moving pageant in which he had a part: "Not all of us," he says, "have been bookish children, but we who were bookish, acted the scenes which we read, and I remember, as a Roman engineer, taking part in the siege of Jerusalem with a battering ram which, to the eyes of adults, bore the aspect of a long, hard, round cushion."[20]

But such amusements as these came of necessity after Lang had learnt to read, which interesting initiation took place about the age of four by the simple process of picking out the letters and words that composed the elegy of Cock Robin, which he had previously learnt by heart. A nursery legend tells that after this it was Andrew's custom to arrange six open books on six chairs, and go from one to the other, perusing them by turns ! "The first books which vividly impressed me," he recalls, "were naturally fairy books and chap books about Robert Bruce, William Wallace and Rob Roy . . . They did not awaken a precocious patriotism; a boy of five is more at home in Fairyland than in his own country. The sudden appearance of the White Cat as a queen after her head was cut off, the fiendish malice of the Yellow Dwarf, the strange cake of crocodile eggs and millet seed which the mother of the Princess Frutilla made for the Fairy of the Desert—these things, all fresh and astonishing, but certainly to be credited, are my first memories of romance."[21]

"When I was a little boy," Lang remarks apologetically in the preface to a book of fairy stories [22], "it is to be supposed that I was a little muff; for I read every fairy-tale I could lay my hands on, and knew all the fairies in *A Midsummer Night's Dream*, and all the ghosts in Sir Walter Scott, and I hated machinery of every description. These tastes and distastes I have never overcome, but I am pretty sure that they are unusual in little boys."

Andrew's first introduction to Shakespeare came before he was six: "Memory holds a picture, more vivid than most, of a small boy reading the *Midsummer Night's Dream* by firelight in a room where candles were lit, and someone touched the piano, and a young man and a girl were playing chess . . . The fairies seemed to come out of Shakespeare's dream into the music and the firelight. At that moment I think that I was happy; it seemed an enchanted glimpse of eternity in Paradise; nothing resembling it remains with me out of all the years."

Following on this came a visit to England (probably to Clifton), where Andrew found more Shakespeare, and some odd volumes of the *Arabian Nights*.

Back again in Scotland a year later, a new and enduring delight in the opening world of literature awaited him: "We lived in Scott's country, within four miles of Abbotsford, and, so far, we had heard nothing of it. I remember going with one of the maids into the cottage of a kinsman of hers, a carpenter; a delightful place, where there was sawdust, where our first fishing rods were fashioned. Rummaging among the books, of course, I found some cheap periodical with verses in it. The lines began:

"The Baron of Smallholme rose with day,
        He spurred his courser on . . ."

A rustic tea table was spread for us, with scones and honey, not to be neglected. But they *were* neglected . . . Scott is not an author like another, but our earliest known friend in letters; for, of course, we did not ask who Shakespeare was, nor enquire about the private history of Madame D'Aulnoy. Scott peopled for us the rivers and burn ides with his reivers; the Fairy Queen came out of Eildon Hill and haunted Carterhaugh; at Newark Tower we saw "the embattled portal arch"—"Whose ponderous grate and massy bar had oft rolled back the tide of war,"—just as, on Foulshiels, on

Yarrow, we beheld the very roofless cottage whence Mungo Park went forth to trace the waters of the Niger, and at Oakwood the tower of the Wizard, Michael Scott."[23]

Another early literary experience was recalled by Lang many years later, and preserved in verses, which have never yet been published, though a few copies were privately printed by their recipient, Clement K. Shorter, in 1912. The poem is called "Ode on a Distant Memory of *Jane Eyre*" and runs:—

"My years were VIII when first I read ' Jane Eyre,'
    I was not shocked, but I was in a fright
Lest Mrs. Rochester were lurking there
    To set on fire my curtains in the night.

"As through the wondrous masterpiece I read,
    No blush upon my early forehead came;
But when I learned how ill the girls were fed
    At school, I said it was ' a beastly shame!'

"I did not bother with the love affair,
    I skipped the bits about a bore called John,
Poor Mr. Rochester I thought a bear,
    His sins I never dreamed of thinking on!

"The pictures that Jane Eyre was wont to draw,
    I thought, and justly thought, extremely quaint,
And sometimes tried to copy them, with awe
    And with an inexpensive box of paint.

"I could not guess how, later, Mr. Birrell
    Would prove what masterpieces these things be;
I left the book to chase an errant squirrel,
    Or munch the casual apple from the tree.

"Days of my childhood in the grey old garden,
    Books that engaged my green, unknowing mind,
Hours in the haunted cloisters of Pluscarden,
    How fair you seem, how faint, how far behind!

"Uncas and Chingachgook, and many a Prince
    Of Faery thronged the gracious garden plot,

But if you ask me, 'have I read it since,
  ' Jane Eyre ' ? ' I frankly own that I have not! "

.   .   .

The madwoman and the starvation of the children stuck in his memory, Lang tells us, "with a Red Indian's ghost, who carried a rusty ruined gun, and whose acquaintance was made at the same time."

On the whole, after the fairy-tales, Lang's favourite reading as a small boy seems to have been in books by Cooper and Mayne Reid, particularly any dealing with Red Indians, for whom he had a partiality shared in later years by the Zulus in Rider Haggard's romances. These stories of course inspired many of the games which Lang and his brothers played in early days at Viewfield— not always with the most fortunate results. On one occasion Andrew tells us that "as a very small boy I once made and consumed, with distasteful results, certain cigarettes. This I did, not that I liked smoking, but that Captain Mayne Reid's heroes made and smoked cigarettes. They also took scalps, fought grizzly bears, and associated with earless trappers. Circumstances made it impossible for me to imitate these feats; but I could and did roll cigarettes and make arrows with stone heads. This was an example of the inebriation of romance."[24] "I remember I bought a tomahawk, and, as we had also lots of spears and boomerangs, from Australia, the poultry used to have rather a rough time of it. I never could do very much with a boomerang, but I could throw a spear to a hair's breadth, as many a chicken had occasion to discover."[25]

The normal, healthy love of excitement and the joy in deeds of violence also endeared the romances of a writer like Kingsley to the Lang boys. Andrew records this predilection: "What a quantity of blood Amyas Leigh shed, to be sure, and what a slayer was Hereward the Wake! When that romance first came out in *Good Words*, we boys, on a Sunday, would reckon up Hereward's bag for the month. In one chapter he did not kill anybody, he only ' thought of killing ' an old woman! This was disappointing to his backers! "[26]

It should be emphasized, however, that even at the earliest date this interest in bloodthirsty fiction was a delight in heroism and in the doing of mighty deeds, and was accompanied by an almost morbid fear of inflicting or even witnessing pain. "Cruelty made me ill," Lang tells us, "and I skipped the passage where they roast the commendator of Crossagnel in *Tales of a Grandfather*. I could hardly persuade myself to kill a trout, and even now I would as lief restore him to the water. I saw cruelty practised by other children with horror . . ."[27]

It was perhaps this healthy, primitive spirit of adventure, and the continual society of his brothers and of other boys of the neighbourhood that prevented Lang from suffering any of the morbid terrors of the rather gloomy Calvinism of that age and country. Stevenson, "the child alone," has recorded many of his own early terrors, and dwelt upon the effect of the Shorter Catechism upon his mental development; of him Lang is probably thinking when he says that "unlike other Scots of the pen, I got no harm from the Shorter Catechism, of which I remember little, and neither then nor now was nor am able to understand a single sentence. . ."[28] "Beyond a strong opinion that I should be a ' goat ' at the Last Day, I can remember no religious speculations of my own . . . The idea of the Deity made little impression; the Shorter Catechism, which had to be learnt by heart, seemed meaningless, and did not even excite curiosity; . . . I do remember thinking that the Angels who made love to the daughters of men, were the gods— Apollo and Zeus and Hermes—under another name. One's infant reason was mythological, not theological in bias."[29]

And thus the first ten years of Andrew Lang's life passed peacefully enough in his pleasant Selkirk home, broken only by the one long visit to England.

Towards the end of this time he went to the town Grammar School as a day boy, but this does not seem to have interfered much with his own activities.

One sees him as a quiet, shy and very bookish boy, delighting in all things of the romantic past, and in the freer games and "plays" of his own countryside, happy in the association of his brothers and friends, but tending to grow more reserved and aloof, to seek for his truest solace in the world of books.

It is almost from this period that Mrs. Harrison's earliest recollection of him dates; she remembers him as "a boy buried in a book, and quite oblivious to his surroundings, and certainly with no use for little girls."

CHAPTER II

Edinburgh Academy

AT the age of ten Andrew Lang was sent to the Edinburgh Academy, where for the first two years he lived, "a rather lonely small boy, in the house of an aged relation." Even when he moved into a "master's house" at the age of twelve he was as far as possible from the usual atmosphere of the English boarding school.

This fortunate state of affairs prevented the normal "school-influence" from having much effect on Lang, and is probably a most important factor in the formation of his gifts, for the ordinary experiences of a full course of schooling seem usually to be inimical to the romantic and poetic tendencies possessed by so many children.

That Lang realized the effect a normal schooling has on the majority of children, is shown very clearly in some of his remarks on the early life of Robert Louis Stevenson: "I have often thought," he says, "that most children had a touch of genius which fades into the light of common day as they reach the age of eight or nine. Small boys are often unconscious poets, but one term of pre-paratory school brings them down to the flattest prose. Their sole desire is now to be exactly like all the other boys, and to obey every jot and tittle of the absurd, self-made code of schoolboys. It is lads who, like Shelley and R. L. Stevenson, decline to cease to be themselves, who resolutely retain their natural tastes and pursue the studies in which they are born to excel, that become men of genius, remaining child-like in many ways, even when in age mature."[30]

It must not be assumed, however, that Lang was at all conscious at the time of the unusual advantages of his schooldays, or of the effect that they were likely to have on one of his quiet and imaginative disposition. He came straight from the healthy, open-air life of the Border, from fishing and exploring and playing at reivers or covenanters with the other Selkirk boys; moreover, being devoted to cricket (even though football was ever more of a pain than a pleasure), he was not at all either unboyish or anything of a "molly-coddle."

But he must have been a quaint child at the age of eleven: rather serious, a trifle precocious, and already beginning to acquire the astonishing store of miscellaneous knowledge which was to characterize him in after-life.

One little glimpse of him at this period is given in a letter from George Dundas (afterwards Lord Manor), at that time Sheriff of Selkirkshire, to Andrew's father, who was then his Sheriff-Clerk: "I had the pleasure two or three Saturdays ago, of seeing your son, Master Andrew, here, and was exceedingly amused and entertained by him. He is a clever and very curious little fellow, with more general information than I ever remember having met with in one of his age. One of his most startling facts was brought out on the occasion of my showing him and the other boys of the party a collar of the Order of St. George, and explaining how St. George, the Cappadocian, after being an Archbishop, had become the Tutelar Saint of England. "Oh, if it's him," said Andrew, "he was a mean fellow; I know very well about him. He was a bacon-contractor for the Roman army." I was a good deal astonished at this information, and questioned the boy whence he had it. He only answered: ' Oh, I know very well; he was a mean fellow and a bacon-contractor.' On coming home, and referring to Gibbon, I found that it was so, though I had quite forgotten the fact in the history of the saint. The boy has many things in his character and manner that require to be corrected and watched—as all boys of any character have; but on the whole he is a remarkably nice little man, and I venture to prophesy that he will ' make a spoon or spoil a horn ' yet."[31]

What little it is possible to glean at this distance of Lang's days at Edinburgh comes mainly from one of his few autobiographical essays, "Adventures Among Books," and thus turns chiefly upon his literary pursuits of that time. "I was," he tells us, "rather an industrious little boy . . . I had minded my lessons, and satisfied my teachers—I know I was reading Pinnock's *History of Rome* for pleasure—till ' the wicked day of destiny ' came . . . *Pickwick* was brought into the house. From that hour it was all over, for five or six years, with anything like industry and lesson books. I read *Pickwick* in convulsions of mirth. I dropped Pinnock's *Rome* for good. I neglected everything printed in Latin, in fact, everything which one was understood to prepare for one's classes . . . A conscientious tutor dragged me through the Latin Grammar, and a constitutional dislike to being beaten on the hands with a leather strap urged me to acquire a certain amount of elementary erudition. But, for a year, I was a young hermit, living with Scott in the *Waverleys* and the *Border Minstrelsy*, with Pope and Prior, and a translation of Ariosto, with Lever and Dickens, David Copperfield and Charles O'Malley, Longfellow and Mayne Reid, Dumas, and in brief, with every kind of light literature that I could lay my hands upon."

Andrew's novel reading reached finally such a pitch that all works of prose fiction were forbidden him. However, as the result was merely that he read *Don Juan* instead, the edict was soon raised. The only writer that he found in those days whose influence at so early an age was at all to be regretted, was Edgar Allan Poe, whose stories caused Andrew, always sensitive and imaginative, many nights of terror and wakings of a morning in deadly fear lest he should find himself the premature occupant of a coffin!

After two years at the Academy, Andrew left his retreat with the "aged relation," and went into "the very different and very disagreeable world of a master's house." Being rather a delicate and timorous boy, Andrew suffered from a certain amount of bullying, and he probably speaks from personal experience when he describes an unpleasant amusement of the older boys in which "tall stools were piled up in a pyramid, and the victim was seated on the top, near the roof of the room. The other savages brought him down from this bad eminence by hurling other stools at those which supported him"; or again when he narrates how the elder boys were in the habit of practising knife-throwing between (and consequently often through) the fingers of a small boy who was made to stand with his hand outspread against a door.[32]

Lang did not, however, find his school life altogether unpleasant, and this was largely owing to the master, D'Arcy Wentworth Thompson, in whose house he was, first at Bellvue Crescent, and then in Brandon Street. "One can never say how much one owes to a schoolmaster who was a friend of literature, who kept a houseful of books, and who was himself a graceful scholar and an author," wrote Lang in "Adventures Among Books"; and in a private letter at Thompson's death he spoke of "his kindness, and as I think now, sagacity to a morbid, useless little boy."[33]

In May 1857, Andrew was in the "Thirds" under Trotter, whose class, Sir D'Arcy Thompson speaks of as "not a specially distinguished one, but it included some kindly and well-remembered names. There was John Chiene for one, beloved of generations of medical students; there was Francis Cadell, the physician, and there was Allan Menzies, afterwards professor in St. Andrews, a man of singular piety and great learning."

The following October, Patrick Lang, Andrew's next brother, came to the same house. "He was close-fisted, boy and man," Sir D'Arcy recalls, "while Andrew had ever the open hand. But Pat was singularly good-looking, even beautiful . . ."

School work was varied from time to time with visits to travelling menageries. "Roland's Assault-at-Arms" (the annual fencing display in the music-hall), and archery practice, besides much cricket. Andrew never could quite get into the first eleven, though he was captain of the second. "He was never much of a bat but it is told of him that his bowling was ever sound and dependable."

In reading, his most important finds at this time were Thackeray and Tennyson. Even earlier he had made surreptitious attempts to read *Vanity Fair*, when that book was still considered unsuitable for a boy of ten. A little later he found *Pendennis* and *The Newcomes*, but the most important find occurred in 1855, or early the following year, when *The Rose and the Ring* first appeared. "It was worth while to be twelve years old, when the Christmas books were written by Dickens and Thackeray. I got hold of *The Rose and the Ring* I know, and of the *Christmas Carol*, when they were damp from the press"; and the former of these remained ever Lang's favourite among literary fairy stories, the supreme example of its kind.

Although it was only the out-of-school reading in English literature that was of any service to Lang, he received a certain amount of official teaching in the subject, though he did not consider it of much value, holding that literature could not be taught: "When at school I must have been one of the most literary of my young companions; indeed, as Scott said when a boy, ' You

can't think how ignorant these boys were! ' Like the rest, I went to
an English class until I was fourteen, after which I was supposed
to know all about English literature, and turned to higher things.
Dismal hand-books about Gower and Lydgate were thrust into our
reluctant and grubby little fists. My memory is not soiled with the
recollection of the contents of any of these manuals . . ."[34] "My
revered master, Professor D'Arcy Thompson, not being an English
master, taught me most of what I ever learned about English
literature by leaving a truly desirable set of good books within
reach, and by showing me what struck him as being worth reading
in the contemporary literature of that distant age".[35]

At that time Lang does not seem to have been a great reader of
poetry, Scott being his dearest love among the poets; but during
his schooldays at least two more poets swam into his ken—Longfellow and Tennyson. Years later he wrote of the former that "To
read ' Voices of the Night ' . . . is to be back at school again, on a
Sunday, reading all alone on a summer's day, high in some tree,
with a wide prospect of gardens and fields."[36] Of Tennyson, whom
he always considered among the very greatest of poets, he said that
he could remember "no such fresh and poignant pleasure in books
as reading the first four Idylls as a boy."[37]

The only other event of importance to Lang's future at this time
is his first introduction to Homer. His classical learning had been
attained only with pain and grief: "Greek, for years seemed a mere
vacuous terror . . . Horace, to a lazy boy, appears in his odes to
have nothing to say, and to say it in the most frivolous and
vexatious manner," while Cæsar, Virgil, Xenephon and Euripides
presented no additional attractions, until he first began to read the
Odyssey in the original: "to myself," he says, "Homer was the real
beginning of study."[38] Only then did he begin to take any interest
in the classics, though the Homeric stories had been familiar
favourites for some time: "When, aged ten, I tried the *Iliad* in
Pope, I could not taste it; but in the artless prose of Bohn, the
Iliad gave me much pleasure . . . At the age of fifteen I found no
poetical merit in the *Phoenissae*, but then I knew the language very
ill . . . On the other hand, at the same age, and as ill-equipped,
I found much enjoyment in the *Cyclops* of Euripides, which we
read along with the *Odyssey*. I remember saying, in an essay, that
Tom Brown was the best book extant—after the *Odyssey* . . . Even

the dull boys in the fifth form revelled in Homer, and made themselves into bands who adopted the heroic names, and played at the
leaguer of Ilios . . . Of the *Georgics* I remember, especially as a
schoolboy, the charm of the story of Aristæus . . ."[39]

With the discovery of Homer and the first experience of "the
surge and thunder of the Odyssey," ended Lang's schoolboy
discoveries and explorations into the exciting jungle of literature
wherein each must find for himself his own choice paths and
glades and lingering places. Already it was into the mysterious,
fairy-haunted thickets of romance that he was most apt to wander
and where he was most readily at home. Scott, Malory and Homer
were already his, and of Thackeray his choice was for the fairy
realm of King Valoroso and for the literary London where
Pendennis dwelt—that same half-savage place where Dickens also
was to be found, spinning the greatest novels in our literature
between the woof and warp of romance and realism—blending the
opposing materials of life into a single living canvas as perhaps no
other author has ever quite succeeded in doing.

Still also the romance of everyday lingered with Andrew, though
he was drawing further and further from the golden age of make-
believe. Perhaps the last of these day-dreams was dreamt at
Edinburgh during the more dreary sermons in Broughton Church:
"Many a weary hour my boyhood passed therein," he says, "I
remember constructing a romance that the Elders had concealed
a treasure behind a panel in the wall which closed my schoolmaster's pew."[40]

But now, as might be expected, such stories and the more
poetic of his thoughts were beginning to struggle for a literary
form. Early poems were seldom written down, and none are extant
before those of his St. Andrews' period; but some existed, and
were tried on his mother, who was of the opinion that Andrew
would never be a poet: "a decision in which I straightway
acquiesced," says Lang, "for to rhyme is one thing, and to be a poet
quite another."

Nor do any of his schoolboy prose-romances survive, though of
the plot of one of them he was always ready to speak with great
relish. This was an historical romance of the reign of Mary Stuart,
written for a competition—in which it did not win a prize. Lang
thus describes his first work of fiction: "You must know that

Queen Elizabeth was singularly like Darnley in personal appearance. What so natural as that, disguised as a page, her Majesty should come spying about the Court of Holyrood ? Darnley sees her walking out of Queen Mary's room, he thinks her an hallucination, discovers that she is real, challenges her, and they fight at Faldonside, by the Tweed, Shakespeare holding Elizabeth's horse. Elizabeth is wounded, is carried to the kirk of Field, and laid in Darnley's chamber, while Darnley goes out and makes love to my rural heroine, the lady of Fairnilee, a Kerr. That night Bothwell blows up the kirk of Field, Elizabeth and all. Darnley has only one resource. Borrowing the riding habit of the rural heroine, the lady of Fairnilee, he flees across the Border, and, for the rest of his life, personates Queen Elizabeth. That is why Elizabeth, who was Darnley, hated Mary so bitterly (on account of the kirk of Field affair) and *that is why Queen Elizabeth never married!*"[41]

CHAPTER III

St. Andrews and Glasgow

IN November 1861 Lang matriculated at St. Andrews University, and entered into residence at the newly-constituted St. Leonard's Hall. This was, he tells us, "in effect something between an Oxford Hall and a master's house at a public school, rather more like the latter than the former. We were more free than schoolboys, not so free as undergraduates. There were about a dozen of us at first, either from the English public schools, or from the Edinburgh Academy. Fate, and certain views of the authorities about the impropriety of studying human nature at St. Andrews after dark, thinned our numbers very early in the first session. Then we settled down to work a little and play a great deal. . . ."[42] In this "joyous place of residence," Lang spent two winters and one summer, "the happiest time of my life, ever dear and sacred in memory."[43]

Of this period of his life, Lang tells us to a great extent in his essay "Old St. Leonard's Days" (recently made available by Mr. J. B. Salmond in his admirable centenary compilation, *Andrew Lang and St. Andrews*). As regards work, though Lang tells us that he did but little, that recollection seems to have been guided by modesty rather than by strict historical accuracy, for in the session of 1861-2 he took "Second Latin," "Second Greek," "First Mathematics," "Logic and Metaphysics"; and in 1862-3 "Third Latin," "Third Greek," and "Moral Philosophy." In Greek he did extremely well ("I was usually a bad second to my friend Mr. Wallace, now Professor of Moral Philosophy at Oxford"), and very creditably in all the rest, except in mathematics, in which alone he gained no honours.[44]

It was, however, here as at Edinburgh, in his individual reading that Lang did most: "Probably the greater part of the work one did was reading odd old books out of the library for oneself," he admits. "I remember studying Paracelsus and Petrus de Abano, and

Cornelius Agrippa, and a few alchemists, and the novels of Lord Lytton, and a good deal of English poetry."

J. M. Anderson gives an interesting list of the books which Lang took out of the University library: besides volumes of periodicals, he had Burton, Iamblichus, Michael Scot and Albertus Magnus during his first year; and in his second, Browning, Spenser, *The Ingoldsby Legends* and Aeschylus, Benvenuto Cellini and Raleigh's *History of the World*, Dasent, Grimm, the Mabinogion and many other books of folklore, and of the magicians Porta, *The Alchemistical Philosophers* and Cornelius Agrippa. On the Cornelius Agrippa he wrote: "Hoc opus diligenter perlexi, et dico ut in amplissimo verbi sensu Bosh vel Rot vel Bolly sit."

Of the magical books Lang says: "These are really but disappointing writers. It soon became evident enough that the devil was not to be raised by their prescriptions." Legend tells us that this conclusion was the result of personal experiment, and that Lang was in the habit of practising necromancy and alchemy in the haunted tower in the cathedral precincts at St. Andrews.

During the second session of the existence of St. Leonard's Hall, the discipline, which had at first been rather too strict, was relaxed to a certain extent—owing probably to the unfortunate necessity of expelling a number of the students the previous year for being out after hours. This enabled Lang and several others to join the University Literary Society. His association with this reached its termination shortly after the reading of a paper which is thus described in the minute book: "January 10th, 1863. Mr. Cox, for Mr. M'Gregor, read an essay on 'Sir William Wallace.' The essay was ably written, but the conclusions were startling and even untrue. While Edward I. was represented as a mild and merciful ruler, the essayist could find for Wallace no parallel in modern history except the notorious Nana Sahib. Even the efforts of the Scots to maintain their independence were represented more as a rising against lawful authority than as international war. The Society manifested its non-acceptance of these and sundry other conclusions by refusing, and that by a large majority, the customary vote of thanks."[45]

Many years later Lang, as honorary member of the Society, told the tale of this early indiscretion, and explained that his attack proceeded from no unpatriotic motive, or from any lack of appreciation for Wallace (one of his favourite heroes as a boy) but simply from a desire "to enliven in some degree the Society's proceedings, which were too apt to lapse into dullness and monotony."[46]—"After this performance," says Lang, "I conceived that my personal safety and dignity would be best consulted by withdrawing from the somewhat stormy debates of the Society."[47]

Most interesting among the activities of Lang at St. Andrews is his association with the undergraduate magazines. Of these there were, in his day, two: *The St. Andrews University Magazine*, a printed monthly periodical which appeared from February 1863 to January 1864, and the more interesting *St. Leonard's Magazine*, a manuscript production prepared once a week, under the editorship of (and usually nearly all from the pen of) Lang himself—the only magazine which he ever edited.

Allan Menzies, afterwards professor of Biblical Criticism at the University, who was Lang's contemporary at St. Leonard's, as he had been at Edinburgh Academy, describes Lang's association with the *St. Leonard's Magazine:* "I think Lang wrote most of every number of this magazine himself, and often illustrated his articles in an arresting way. When Friday night arrived, and no contributions had come in, we feared we should have no magazine that week. But it was there, nevertheless; the editor shut himself up on Friday night and had the twelve pages ready for us in the morning."[48]

This account is supplemented by Lang himself: "It was only a manuscript affair, and was profusely illustrated. For the only time in my life I was now an editor, under a sub-editor, who kept me up to my work, and cut out my fine passages. The editor's duty was to write most of the magazine—to write essays, reviews (of books by the professors, very severe), novels, short stories, poems, translations, also to illustrate these, and to 'fag' his friends for 'copy' and drawings. A deplorable flippancy seems, as far as one remembers, to have been the chief characteristic of the periodical—flippancy and an abundant use of the supernatural."[49]

In 1863 a selection from this magazine was printed at St. Andrews in a blue-paper-covered pamphlet of fifty pages, all the contents being by Lang except for three stories and two poems. Of Lang's contributions the poem *Nugae Catullinae* is the only one readily available (it was included in the *Poetical Works* of 1923—

Volume II, page 198); this is a pleasant little poem, apparently from the Latin. Two other sets of verses are preserved in transcript in the library at Dundee, but are of no interest or literary value, being topical, and not even amusing. Four of Lang's drawings from a later number of the manuscript magazine are reproduced by Mr. Salmond, and exhibit quite a considerable talent for amusing illustrations, rather in the style of Thackeray or Doyle. Throughout his life Lang was accustomed to illustrate his private letters with amusing pen-and-ink sketches, though he never seems to have attempted to develop his gifts in this medium.

In the *St. Andrews University Magazine* appeared Lang's very first poems and essays ever to be printed. The earliest of these is a long poem, written very much under the influence of William Morris, and called "Sir Launcelot." This poem had already been refused by at least one London editor, Edmund Yates: "When I was a lad at St. Andrews, I made my first literary endeavour by sending a piece of verse to *Temple Bar*. Of course, it was about Sir Launcelot, and his adventure in the chapel in the waste, where a wounded knight was borne and laid beside the altar . . . The rhymes rode on the quest in vain . . ."[50] The poem appeared in due course at St. Andrews (March 1863), and is reprinted by Mr. Salmond in *Andrew Lang and St. Andrews*. Lang's further contributions, none of which have been reprinted, consist of three essays ("Flos Regum," *March* 1863; "Scottish Nursery Tales," *April* 1863; and "Spiritualism Medieval and Modern," *November* 1863) and one other poem (November 1863), "Dei Otiosi." This must be the poem which Lang mentions nearly forty years later in a letter to the *Academy* (26th January 1901) when refuting the critic's claim that William Watson was the first poet to write rhymed elegiacs in English: after mentioning Tennyson, Lang adds: "At the age of seventeen I also published a piece in rhymed elegiacs—when Mr. Watson, I dare say, was unborn!" As one of the earliest extant examples of Lang's poetry "Dei Otiosi" is worth reprinting:

"Why should we care for the gods, who care so little for us?
    Far from the ways of men, sitting apart at their ease,
Little they reck of our joys, and few they cause of our sorrows,
    There on the still blue peaks where never cometh the breeze.

"Never they mingle with men, nor heed their earthly doings,
   Silent they sit far off, slumbrous and happy and still;
Never they trouble us now, with their wiles and weary wooings—
   Still as the still grey rocks on the Olympian hill.

"Never rewarding the just, they never punish the unjust;
   Down on their own fair fanes, reckless the thunderbolts fall;
And the wintry rains, and the long bright shafts of the sun just
Fall on the good or the bad, painful or pleasant to all."

Very little else can be gleaned of Andrew Lang's life at St.
Leonard's: the only one of his contemporaries to write of these
days, Allan Menzies, says that "Lang was then, as he remained to
the end, a graceful figure, full of interests, ready to enter on discussion on any subject, never pushing or intruding on anyone, yet
a warm friend to the men he cared for, never pressed or in a hurry,
not given to work at unattractive subjects, but spending time and
effort freely on many a subject the student is not called to take up."
   Lang shared a room with A. G. Henderson (afterwards Sheriff),
but his dearest friend was Henry Brown, the rather fragile-looking
youth on whose shoulder his hand is resting in the College Group
of 1861-62. Before the group was taken the following year, Henry
Brown had died—and his death made a most profound impression
on Lang, to whom ever after, for his sake, St. Andrews was a
"haunted town." The poem *Clevedon Church, In Memoriam H.B.*
is dedicated to Brown, and Lang compares his loss with Tennyson's
bereavement, from which his thoughts fly

"Back to the winter rose of northern skies,
   Back to the northern seas.
And lo, the long waves of the ocean beat
   Below the minster gray,
Caverns and chapels worn of saintly feet,
   And knees of them that pray;
And I remember how we twain were one
   Beside that ocean dim,
I count the years passed over since the sun
   That lights me looked on him . . ."[51]

In prose as well as in verse Lang refers to the loss of Henry Brown—again comparing his death with Hallam's in his short Life of Tennyson, where he says: "There was a young reader to whom ' All Along the Valley ' (1864) came as a new poem in a time of recent sorrow: ' The two and thirty years were a mist that rolled away,' said the singer of *In Memoriam*, and in that hour it seemed as if none could bear for two and thirty years the companionship of loss."[52]

But the most notable poem associated with Henry Brown, and one of the best-known poems that Lang ever wrote, is "Almae Matres."

This is professedly a poem of place—("*St. Andrews* 1862. *Oxford*, 1865") it is headed—but the sentiment for the place is mingled inextricably with that for the person, with whose memory it is most closely associated.

> "O, ruined chapel, long ago
>   We loitered idly where the tall
> Fresh budded mountain ashes blow
>   Within the desecrated wall:
> The tough roots broke the tomb below,
>   The April birds sang clamorous,
> We did not dream, we could not know
>   How soon the Fates would sunder us!
>
> "O! broken minster looking forth
>   Beyond the bay, above the town,
> O, winter of the kindly North,
>   O, college of the scarlet gown,
> And shining sands beside the sea,
>   And stretch of links beyond the sand,
> Once more I watch you, and to me
>   It is as if I touched his hand!
>
> "And therefore art thou yet more dear,
>   O, little city grey and sere,
> Though shrunken from thine ancient pride
>   And lonely by the lonely sea,
> Than these fair halls on Isis side,
>   Where Youth an hour came back to me! "

The poem first appeared in *Ballades and Verses Vain* 1884 (pages 79 to 81) published only in America. But on its first publication in England the following year (in *Rhymes à la Mode*), besides a few minor alterations, the last line of the first verse quoted above was altered to

"How hardly Fate would deal with us,"

thus making the application to a specific sundering of two friends unapparent until the last line of the next verse. The original line seems to have been restored in the four-page print of the poem issued in 1887 for a bazaar for the Students' Union, but the revised version is that of all the published texts except the American first edition.

The date at which the poem was written is very doubtful (many years after it appeared, Lang told the students in St. Andrews that it was composed in a hansom cab, but he did not say when). Edmund Gosse, giving no authority, says "written (I think at Oxford) in 1865," but this seems rather early, as it did not appear until so many years later. On the other hand, the date at the head— "Oxford, 1865"—seems to be inexplicable—for he came up to Oxford in 1864. The year of the St. Andrews' date might refer to that in which he knew Brown (actually Lang was at St. Andrews from 1861 to 1863), but the most obvious interpretation is that the two dates are those at which the poem was actually written. Professor Blyth Webster, however, in his excellent lecture on "Andrew Lang's Poetry" (Oxford, 1937, p. 28) dates its composition tentatively, at about 1883.

Early in the summer of 1863, Andrew Lang left St. Andrews to spend a session at Glasgow University with the object of qualifying for a Snell Exhibition to Balliol. Of his time at Glasgow, which he described as "undesirable exile," very little can be recovered. He disliked the place, and hardly ever mentions it anywhere in his writings. One poem only deals with it—the Scots "Waitin' on the Glesca Train" which was set to music in 1898 by R. T. Boothby (*Poetical Works*, 1923, Vol. iii, page 75)—but this is not complimentary, and makes no reference to the University.

When Lang was there, the red gowns were still worn, but only at the Blackstone examination—"The Glasgow gowns appeared very skimped, in contrast with the flowing academic dress of St. Andrews. The College . . . was the black old quadrangle, guarded by an effigy of some heraldic animal, probably the Scottish lion, in whose mouth it was thought unbecoming to thrust a bun. Blackness, dirt, smoke, a selection of the countless smells of Glasgow, small, airless, crowded rooms . . . these things make up a picture of the Old College of Glasgow. Now there is a new and magnificent building in a part of the town which enjoys, for Glasgow, a respectable atmosphere."[53]

The feeling of exile is accentuated by the fact that Lang does not seem to have taken any part in the less academic activities at Glasgow, but turned back to St. Andrews in every way possible. Thus, though no longer its editor, Lang continued to contribute to the *St. Leonard's Magazine*, sending reviews, drawings, and sets of verses—the latter of no very outstanding qualities, as the following example shows:

> "I am about as jolly as
>   If I were down a well,
> And not a spark could pierce the dark
>   And lighten up my cell.
> My days are dim, and grey and grim,
>   With the shadow of the Snell."[54]

While working for the scholarship, Lang seems to have competed, unsuccessfully, for the Blackstone prizes. These are awarded for an oral examination in selected books in Greek and Latin respectively: "The professor is the examiner, and decides the prize. The competitors take their seats in turn, in a curious antique chair, with an hour-glass in the back, and with a stone seat." The prize-winners in Lang's year were Thomas Shute Robertson and Henry Craik (both later of Balliol), and Lang remembered that neither of them made a single mistake in the examination. Two other incidents remained in his memory from this occasion, which he relates as follows: "In the Latin Blackstone, a student (*not* the winner) translated a phrase in Juvenal ' the screaming fathers.' ' What is the Latin for screaming, Mr. — ? ' asked Professor Ramsay. "*Squalentes*, Sir, *Squalentes patres*, the squalling fathers.' In the Greek Blackstone, Professor Lushington handed his own Aeschylus to a spectator, and examined without book, calling the competitor's attention to such grammatical expressions and turns of phrase as he thought desirable, a singular proof of his great memory."[55]

In April, 1864, Lang won his Snell Exhibition to Balliol, thus following his uncle, Professor W. Y. Sellar. This scholarship was of some standing, and supplied a sum of about £105 per annum each for two students, who then proceeded to Balliol—where, however, they were not entitled to wear a scholar's gown.

On leaving Glasgow, Lang spent the summer term at Loretto School, Musselburgh, near Edinburgh, of which he tells us: "In the summer before I went up to Balliol, I had nothing to do, and was nearly dead after a winter at Glasgow University. The Head (Dr. H. H. Almond) very kindly allowed me to come to Loretto for the summer term to read Greek with Mr. Beilby, fresh from Cambridge . . . In the Long, the Head, with a little boy called Campbell, and I went on a fishing tour. We went to a cottage in Laggan, where I mainly lived on cherry-gum and oat cakes . . . There were three hundred lochs in the parish, all good then, but I was so ill from overwork at Glasgow that I scarcely fished, and was, in my opinion, most disagreeable company."[56]

CHAPTER IV

Balliol and Merton

IN the Michaelmas term of 1864 Andrew Lang came up to Oxford to matriculate at Balliol: "How fair Oxford seemed after the black quadrangle and heavy air of Glasgow," he says. "In one of October's crystal days with the elms not yet stripped of their gold, and with the crimson pall of red leaves swathing the tower of Magdalen, Oxford looks almost as beautiful as in the pomp of spring. To the freshman care is unknown, and the shadow of the schools does not overcast his new liberty."[57]

Lang was at Balliol in the days before the rebuilding of the college: only the chapel was new ("this resembles in hue the best streaky bacon," to quote his own description); but "the outer quad had a charming gate-tower and wore an air of great antiquity, due to the blackened and crumbling stone. I am very averse to knocking down old edifices and raising new, but Balliol was actually dangerous, falling about our ears." The new hall was also unbuilt, the present library being still used for that purpose. "Here," Lang tells us, "we tried to eat the worst, and in practice, the most expensive dinners in Oxford."

Lang had rooms in the inner quadrangle: "After ' Fisher's Buildings,' at right angles to it is a set of buildings which makes no architectural parade: here my own lot was cast, in a one-windowed room under the pediment."[58] Later he moved out to rooms in the Turl, which in those days sported a row of small trees.[59]

Very little indeed is recorded of Lang's life at Balliol, but a roughly adequate picture is given by A. G. C. Liddell, who came up at the same time as Lang, and who published many years later an account of his own experiences. Of the oral examination preceding matriculation he tells us: "I was introduced into the hall at Balliol where all the dons were assembled. Some six or seven youths besides myself presented themselves to the examiners. The paper work I got through pretty well, but was a good deal disturbed when called up to construe before the terrible Jowett, though surprised at the mild benevolence of his appearance."

Of even more interest is Liddell's picture of the college life as he knew it: "I do not think that I have ever lived in a pleasanter society than was to be found at Balliol in 1865. It was in those days a small college, about eighty in number, made up chiefly by batches of boys from all the leading public schools, with a contingent of Scotchmen. The Balliol scholarships were eagerly competed for, and, with the exhibitions, attracted many of the best scholars in the country . . . All the public school men, with some of the politer Scotchmen, lived together in intimate fellowship, so that the college consisted of a large circle of friends and acquaintances, outside which was a small band of reputed barbarians . . . The main difference between Balliol and the other colleges at that time was that at Balliol it was the fashion to read, even if (which was rare) a man hunted two days a week as well. All members of the college were supposed to go in for honours in at least one school, and were liable to be dismissed if they showed signs of slackness."

The "politer Scotchmen" would have included the Snell Exhibitioners, who, being men who could seldom afford to be idle, constituted the nucleus of the reading set.

"My first introduction to my future comrades," continues Liddell, "was achieved by a breakfast at Farwell's, who lived in a small garret in the front quad. The Oxford breakfast of those days was a fearful meal. It began with fried soles and eggs and bacon, and continued with chops and steak of the most solid character. These were followed by apricot jam, and finally by a large tankard of spiced beer, in winter, or cider cup in summer. Of course this *Epularum lascivia* was confined to banquets, the ordinary breakfast being of more usual dimensions. After the first start at Farwell's, I had to go through a great many breakfasts and wines, as it was considered the correct thing to entertain the freshmen in this way."[60]

When Lang came up, Scott (part author of the Greek Lexicon) was Master of Balliol, and Jowett, who became Master soon afterwards, was senior tutor. "The staff of tutors was far the best

in Oxford," and included Edwin Palmer, T. H. Green and
Newman. For Jowett Lang had always the highest regard and
veneration, both as his pupil, and in later years as his friend. He
had been a contemporary and friend of Lang's uncle, William
Young Sellar, and of Matthew Arnold, who was Professor of
Poetry during Lang's undergraduate days. Jowett seems to have
been a most stimulating teacher, and to have possessed in particular the art of "fitting his pupils to make the most of their
capacities, and not only to be but to appear all that they were
worth."[61]

"I knew him first," Lang recalls, "when I was fourteen (we met
on the Table of Lorne). He was the tutor of two of my uncles, and
my own. I have frequently walked and talked with that best
and most loyal of friends: in town, in the country, at Oxford, as a
boy, an undergraduate, a fellow of my College, and after leaving
Merton for good, I saw much of the Master. . ."[62]

Of one of these walks during his Balliol days Lang tells us,
recalling that Jowett, "after a long walk with a hungry undergraduate, remarked ' We'll send round to Cripps for a cold pigeon
pie and a greengage tart, and have a jollification.' Now the man had
meant to ' do himself very well ' at the Mitre. So simple and
ascetic were the manners of the Master while still a tutor."[63]

The work at Balliol was more concentrated than at other
colleges, as besides the usual lectures and tutorials, a weekly essay,
in Latin and English alternately, had to be prepared and read before
the Master every Saturday. "This," says Lang, "might have been
good literary training, but I fear the essays were not taken very
seriously. The chief object was to make the late learned Dr. Scott
bound on his chair by paradoxes. But nobody ever succeeded.
He was experienced in trash." Lang's own tutor, Thomas Hill
Green, told him once that he wrote essays as if for a penny paper,
but this must have been on a particular occasion, as Lang's essays
as an undergraduate seem to have been very much the envy of his
contemporaries. "Like others of our set," writes Liddell, "I
occasionally had recourse to Andrew Lang, whose good nature and
extraordinary power of disquisition made him willing and able to
knock off an essay on any subject in half an hour."

Outside these strictly academic qualifications, Lang also shone
as a writer, as another of his contemporaries, Lord Kilbracken,

records: "He was brilliant in conversation, took a great interest in games (though he played them badly), and, as a writer, was already nearly, if not quite, as admirable as he was in later life, which is saying a good deal. I shall never forget listening to an essay of his on Rabelais, which he read to an audience of two or three at the meeting of a small Essay Club to which he and I as undergraduates belonged: it filled me with amazement, and from that moment I always anticipated for him real greatness as a writer. . . He was, moreover, in the true sense of the word, a poet . . ."[64]

Whether he wrote much as an undergraduate, Lang does not record, but there is no sign that he engaged in literary ventures on anything like the scale of his St. Andrews' activities. "The gods had not made *us* poetical," he says in *Adventures Among Books*, lamenting the dearth of undergraduate literature at the period between *The Oxford and Cambridge Magazine* of the William Morris set, and *Love in Idleness* of a later generation. "There existed a periodical entirely devoted to verse but nobody knew anybody who wrote in it." This was *College Rhymes*, edited for some time by "Lewis Carroll." "A comic journal was started," continues Lang; "I remember the pride with which, when a freshman, I received an invitation to join its councils as an artist. I was to do the caricatures, of all things . . . But the whole thing died early and not lamented." It has, unfortunately, proved impossible to discover even the name of this one among the multitudinous ephemeral undergraduate magazines, scarcely any of which managed to survive for more than a few numbers.

The only humorous paper of the period seems to be *The Harlequin*, which blossomed and died in 1867. If this was the paper referred to by Lang, he was far from being a freshman at the time of its brief career. It does contain cartoons faintly in the Thackeray style, but if Lang had a hand in these, it was with a collaborator, each being signed with a monograph of the letters A.L.I.R. In the literary contents, which are of a very low standard, there is no trace of Lang's style.

The only regular university paper at this time was *The Oxford Undergraduates' Journal*, and to this Lang contributed three parodies of popular poets, which appeared anonymously on 6th March 1867, headed "Why they don't stand for the Poetry chair." The poets parodied are Swinburne, Browning and Shairp, the first of which is probably the most entertaining:

> "Oh frantic and festive Dolores,
>   Shall I leave thee, ferocious and fair,
> For the sterile old Common Room stories,
>   For the chapels, the chaff and the chair;
> For the dwellings of dons and of doctors;
>   For the maids of the *Turl* and the *High*;
> For the wrath on the lips of the Proctors!
>   Our Lady, not I!
>
> "They poisoned the flower of the Maytime,
>   They walked in the ways of the *Broad*;
> The night was as light to them; daytime
>   Was dark where the feet of them trod:
> They were prompt to pursue and discover,
>   Demanding one's ' college and name.'
> Thou shalt keep me, thy languidest lover,
>   Our Lady of shame! "

Swinburne had been among his latest discoveries in literature since the day on which, in the Union reading-room, he had chanced to pick up a pretty white quarto called *Atalanta in Calydon*, and fallen straightway captive to the unique charm of one of the few poems that set Swinburne among the immortals. "*Atalanta* was a revelation; there was a new and original poet here, and a Balliol man, too."[65] As his own earliest poems bear witness, Lang's admiration for Swinburne was profound: on one occasion he quoted him in a Latin essay as "poeta ille noster." "Who is he—Milton ? " asked Mr. T. H. Green. "Not Milton, sir, Mr. Swinburne," was the answer, and Mr. Green only sniffed . . . Colleges know little of their greatest men, and know that little wrong."[66]

The devotion to Swinburne extended even as far as submitting poems in his style for the Newdigate prize. The subject set in 1867 was "Marie Antoinette," and "the examiners did not rise to" Lang's attempt, of which only one line survives (imitated subconsciously from a line in *Chastelard*) wherein somebody's hands are described as being

> "Made of a red rose swooning into white."[67]

It is also recorded that he wrote another prize poem on
"Mexico"—"in the manner of Captain Mayne Reid, but did not
send it in."[68]

Of other poets, Tennyson still was among the most admired, as
indeed he remained when maturer judgment set many of his early
favourites lower on the slopes of Parnassus: Morris had already
ceased to be for Lang the poet *par excellence*—*Jason* seeming dull
after the astonishing morning beauty of *Guinevere*. Morris's early
prose stories in *The Oxford and Cambridge Magazine*, however,
seemed to Lang ever among the great things of romantic literature,
and he set *The Hollow Land* very far above the later prose romances,
admitting to that class only, perhaps, a true literary successor
of Morris's stories, that strange, nearly forgotten little tale of
Swinburne's, "Dead Love," which Lang found and delighted over
in *Once a Week*.

But a newly-discovered poet of his latest undergraduate days
was Matthew Arnold: his verses, says Lang, "I fell in love with one
long vacation, and never fell out of love. He is not, and cannot be,
the poet of the wide world, but his charm is all the more powerful
over those whom he attracts and subdues. He is the one Oxford
poet of Oxford, and his 'Scholar Gipsy' is our 'Lycidas'—."
At this time Arnold was Professor of Poetry, but Lang never
attended his lectures, which were not compulsory, and which,
moreover, were delivered of an afternoon when "Cricket and
the river, and a hundred amusements are calling to us, and who
can be deaf to their voices ? "[69]

Lang had taken a First Class in Classical Moderations in 1866,
and in 1868 he followed this with a First in "Greats." Thus
there was little time for any very concentrated labours in other
directions.

He was, however, writing a certain amount of poetry, most
of which appeared a few years later in *Ballads and Lyrics*. Of these
early poems he wrote, in a copy of the book belonging to Clement
K. Shorter:

> "They were scribbled in sketchbooks and flybooks,
>   In lectures, on lochs, by the seas:
> And wherefore do people who buy books
>   Go purchasing *these* ?

"A scholar was I, in the way to
  Be idle with pencil and pen,
And I rhymed—while the Master read Plato—
  Of Phæacian men.

"When Ettrick was sullenly frozen
  With snows on the hills and the plain,
The tune for my singing was chosen
  Of ' The Sirens Again.' "[70]

.   .   .

The poem mentioned here, "The Sirens' Music Heard Again,"
was the first thing by Lang that was ever published in the "professional" press: it appeared in *Once a Week* on 28th January 1868,
and Lang records that he received a guinea for it, which he
invested in a volume of Lingard's *History of England*.[71]

Having secured his First in "Greats," Lang entered for the Open
Fellowship at Merton, with most gratifying results: "The most
comforting words that the present writer ever heard in his life were
merely his own name. ' Who has got the (Merton) Fellowship ? '
' Mr. Lang.' A foreigner would have embraced the College
messenger, but I did manage to refrain."[72]

On 23rd December 1868, it is recorded in the Register of
Merton College, that "the following gentlemen were elected to be
probationers of the College: Mr. Andrew Lang of Balliol College
for the Open Fellowship, and Mr. E. Arbuthnott Knox of Corpus
Christi College for the Clerical Fellowship. On the same day Mr.
Andrew Lang was admitted by the Warden to be a probationer of
the College"; and the Fellowship was ratified on the same date a
year later.

How soon Lang entered into residence at Merton cannot be
determined exactly, but he was certainly living in College during
the whole of the Trinity term 1869, as the Buttery account books
testify. But it was not until the following year, when he was a full
Fellow, that his residence can be traced with any accuracy. At first
he seems to have lived in the rooms on the second floor at
the north-west corner of the Fellows' Quadrangle, overlooking the
Meadows (Fellows, 4, 6), rooms afterwards occupied by F. H.
Bradley, who was elected in December 1870. But for most of his

D

time at Merton, Lang had the rooms above Lecture Room "A," on the first floor of staircase five in the Fellows' Quadrangle. These he decorated with an ornate door frame, imported by him from the south of France, and some simple carving on the mantelpiece, which he is said to have executed himself.

Nowhere does Lang make more than the most passing reference to his seven years at Merton, and none of his contemporaries have written of him at this time, so that only the most superficial picture of his life during this period can be recaptured.

The hero of Lang's novel *The Mark of Cain*, is represented as being "Fellow of St. Gatien's College, Oxford," and while the character is only superficially Lang himself, the college described is almost certainly Merton. Lang, like Maitland, "had been in the Oxford Movement just when æstheticism was fading out, like a lovely sun-stricken lily, while philanthropy and political economy and Mr. Henry George were coming in like roaring lions. Thus in Maitland there survived a little of the old leaven of the student of the Renaissance, a touch of the amateur of "impressions" and of antiquated furniture."[73]; but while Maitland was always struggling against this "side" of his "culture," Lang seems to have cultivated it in himself, albeit with the quiet humour of one who can smile at his own enthusiasms. Mrs. E. M. Sellar recalls that Lang, who was staying with them in Mull in 1871, "being then under the influence of Rossetti and Morris, . . . declared that Clough's poems were poetry about the Thirty-Nine Articles. ' Then what subjects would *you* select as suitable for poetry ? ' was his uncle's somewhat indignant question . . . his nephew's ambiguous reply was ' Apple-blossom,' which made us all laugh and realize . . . that each generation has its own prophets and heroes."[74]

Lang's taste being "still in the Blue Closet of Gothic fancy," the description of Maitland's rooms applies to his own in decoration as well as from the point of view of architectural accuracy. "Maitland left the queer bare slit of a place called his bedroom (formed, like so many Oxford bedrooms, by a partition added to the large single room of old times), and moved into the weirdly æsthetic study, decorated in the Early William Morris manner," which "ghastly room . . . looked cosy and even homelike when the lamp was lit, when the dusky blue curtains were drawn . . ." Mandell

Creighton, who was a contemporary of Lang's at Merton, also came under the same influence: "Æstheticism" his biographer, tells us, "was strong in Oxford (in 1867) owing to the presence of Walter Pater, one of its most gifted exponents . . ." When Creighton settled in his Merton rooms in 1868, "he had space to gratify his taste for beautiful things. He began to frequent old curiosity shops and to buy blue china and old oak . . ."[75]

Of Lang's more official activities only a general picture can be gained. During 1870 and 1871 he was regular in his attendance at college meetings: these were originally held only about twice a year, but Creighton had been mainly instrumental in instituting a far larger number, usually about four each term, at least by 1870. These debates, says Arbuthnott Knox, "were often long and sharp, for we all of us had equal rights, equal concern in the welfare of the College, and fairly equal conceit of our own infallibility. To these common-room debates, in which such men as Creighton, Wallace, Bradley and Sidgwick took part, I look back as of supreme educational value. Hollow arguments, inconclusive reasonings, baseless prejudices, met with short shrift. No one who had been through that school could, after it, become a satisfactory purveyor of platitudes or unfounded generalizations."[76] Lang's duties at Merton do not seem to have been very much more than nominal, and he never held any office in the College. From time to time he, with others of the Fellows, was asked to act as Examiner in Fellowship elections; he was on the committee appointed to report on a memorial to Bishop Patteson, who had been a Fellow of the College; and is said to have been instrumental in having removed from the hall a marble tablet recording that in 1815 the Czar Alexander slept in Merton, which was passed at a meeting of the Senior Common Room on 21st May 1872. He used to lecture occasionally, and his habit of sinking his voice whenever making a humorous remark became a custom with lecturers that still endures.[77]

While living in Merton, Lang made use of the library, the books taken out ranging from Grote and Freeman to Tylor's *Primitive Culture* and Cornelius Agrippa. He also "made a great effort to have the works of George Eliot put in the Merton Library, esteeming her the peer of Shakespeare; but . . . Bradley managed to defeat this proposal."[78]

During these years Lang spent most of his long vacations in various parts of Scotland with the Sellars, and in 1870 went to France and the Black Forest with them. His cousin Florence Sellar (Mrs. F. A. MacCunn), some ten or fifteen years his junior, recollected how he used to write humorous plays in verse for the family to act, and even recalled one of them which presented, in modern setting and diction, the return of Agamemnon and "Mrs. Menelaus" from Troy—to find Clytemnestra and the other Grecian wives enjoying a quiet game of whist at Mycenæ![79]

But the even tenor of life at Oxford was rudely broken for Lang in the autumn of 1872, when he suddenly developed lung trouble, and was ordered to a warmer climate for the winter. For some time it was uncertain whether the disease would prove fatal, but a second winter abroad, this time at Mentone on the Riviera, effected more or less of a cure.

During the later sojourn abroad, Lang first made the acquaintance of Sidney Colvin, who, on 31st January 1874 introduced him to Robert Louis Stevenson, then also seeking for health under an even more imperative threat from consumption. "It was not without some trepidation," writes Colvin, "that I first brought them together in those Mentone days, for I suppose no two young Scots, especially no two sharing so many literary tastes, were ever more unlike by temperament and training. On the one hand the young Oxford don, a successful and typical scholar on the regular academic lines, picturesque by the gift of nature, but fastidiously correct and reserved, purely English in speech, with a recurring falsetto note in the voice—that kind of falsetto that bespeaks langour rather than vehemence; full of literature and pleasantry, but on his guard, even to affectation, against any show of emotion, and consistently dissembling the *perfervidum ingenium* of his race, if he had it, under a cloak of indifference and light banter. On the other hand, the brilliant, irregularly educated lad from Edinburgh, to the conventional eye an eccentrically ill-clad and long-haired nondescript, with the rich Lallan accent on his tongue, the obvious innate virility and spirit of adventure in him ever in mutiny against the invalid habits imposed by ill-health, the vivid, demonstrative ways, every impulse of his heart and mind flashing out in the play of eye, feature and gesture, no less than in the humorous riot and poetical abundance of his talk."[80]

First impressions on either side were certainly inclined to be unfavourable:—Stevenson wrote to his father next day, in a deprecating vein: "Yesterday we had a visit from one of whom I had often heard from Mrs. Sellar—Andrew Lang. He is good-looking, delicate, Oxfordish, etc."[81] Lang, on the other hand, was inclined to condemn Stevenson as a poseur and would-be æsthete—but was more than converted on reading his earlier essays. Within a very short time a warm friendship sprang up between these two, and during the next ten years they saw much of each other, particularly in London in the late 'seventies. In the summer of 1874 Stevenson came to Oxford and stayed with Lang in Merton, while in the spring of 1876 Lang was in Edinburgh, and Stevenson went with him and Florence Sellar (Mrs. MacCunn) to a performance of *Macbeth*, with Salvini in the title rôle, of which Stevenson wrote a review for the *Academy*.[82]

Lang seems to have spent the first part of the winter of 1874-75 abroad, but was back at Oxford in January 1875, when he was present at a college meeting held on the 15th, at which it was passed "That a year of grace be granted to Mr. Lang in view of his approaching marriage, such year to begin with the 10th April."

When Lang first became a Fellow of Merton, the Statutes had laid down that "if any Fellow shall marry . . . his Fellowship shall thereby become vacant, provided that in all such cases it shall be lawful for the College to grant him a year of grace from the time at which he shall so have become disqualified, if it shall think fit." But in 1871, after considerable discussion, the Statutes were amended, and passed by Privy Council (Merton being the first college to take such a step) with the clause appended that "a Fellow may nevertheless, if he shall at the time of his marriage . . . be an Officer of the College, and if in the opinion of the Warden and Fellows it shall appear to be desirable in the interest of the College, be retained in his Fellowship . . .Not more than four officers in all shall be capable of being so retained in their Fellowships at the same time." Creighton, who was the leader in this reform, was the first to take advantage of it, and three other Fellows immediately followed his example, while a fifth was anxious to do so: as he wrote at the time: "Merton always has been regarded as the most advanced and maddest college in Oxford; but the spectacle of all its Fellows rushing headlong into matrimony at once, will make everyone in Oxford die with laughter."[83]

Lang had held no office at Merton, and so was, strictly, not eligible as a married Fellow; but it seems most likely that his departure from Oxford was not caused only by this, as a number of the married Fellows had already left, leaving places that he might well have filled. In 1874 he had begun writing almost weekly reviews for the *Academy*, and was well embarked on his journalistic career; moreover, he never considered himself to be a scholar of the strictest academic type, and may well have felt himself somewhat restricted by his position at Oxford. It is possible also that other things tended to make Oxford a place of too poignant memories and regrets—though of this there is no proof beyond the most nebulous hints supplied by chance words in one or two places among his writings.

But his love of Oxford was deep and sincere, even if allowed only to be second to that which he felt for St. Andrews. The impossibility of dating "Almae Matres" prevents any definite inference being drawn from it—moreover the Oxford date (1865) prefixed, even if not that of its composition, definitely proves that he is referring only to his undergraduate days. But the quiet charm of the place was assuredly on him when he describes Oxford here as:

"A land of waters green and clear,
    Of willows and of poplars tall,
And, in the spring-time of the year,
    The white may breaking over all,
And Pleasure quick to come at call,
    And summer rides by marsh and wold,
And autumn with her crimson pall
    About the towers of Magdalen rolled;
And strange enchantments from the past,
    And memories of the friends of old,
And strong Tradition, binding fast
    The ' flying terms ' with bands of gold."

But later he wrote: "I always think of the landscape in that low light which the French painters prefer: when the melancholy wind, and the grey, wandering waters round Godstow seem to repeat and remember the story of the place, and not to have forgotten Rosamund . . ."[84]

The only reference of a more definite nature occurs in the literary essay "Adventures Among Books," where he says: "Unfortunately, life at Oxford is not all beauty and pleasure. Things go wrong somehow. Life drops her happy mask. But this has nothing to do with books."

But to read his first prose book, *Oxford* (1879) is to see how much his second Alma Mater meant to Lang, and to realize, perhaps, at least part of the reason why after ten years and more spent there, he chose to leave it while it was still fresh and beautiful to him.[85]

Whatever may have happened to sadden him in his earlier years at Merton, a new and happier era was opening for Lang by 1874, when he became engaged to Leonora Blanche Alleyne (youngest daughter of C. T. Alleyne of Clifton and Barbadoes), whom he may have met through their mutual friends, Mandell Creighton and his wife. That summer Lang brought his fiancée to visit the Sellars at Kenbank, near Dalry, and Mrs. E. M. Sellar says that "we were all greatly taken with her, and she has remained the constant friend of every member of the family ever since."[86]

They were married at Christ Church, Clifton, on 17th April 1875, and soon after settled at 1 Marloes Road, Kensington, whence they never moved, except in later years to spend the winter at St. Andrews.

CHAPTER V

The Lost Poet

ALTHOUGH Andrew Lang published almost no poetry during his undergraduate days at Oxford, it is probable that he was writing a considerable amount, and he was certainly doing so during the first few years of his Merton Fellowship. For on 1st January 1872 there appeared his earliest book: *Ballads and Lyrics of Old France, with Other Poems.*

His last undergraduate literary discoveries, he tells us, had been of France and the Renaissance, and he had at once begun to translate poems from Villion, Ronsard and Du Bellay, besides the later romantics, Alfred de Musset, Gerard de Nerval, and Theophile Gautier.

These made up the first portion of his book, together with a few ballads and folk songs, mainly from the modern Greek; but practically half the volume consisted of the "Other Poems."

The translations are the work of a master in that difficult art, and have the notable excellence of avoiding any marked mannerism or style typical of the translator rather than the original—a failing from which neither Rossetti nor Swinburne could escape. Swinburne, indeed, was a great admirer of Lang's translations, and is said to have preferred many of them to the originals.

With the earlier French poets, Lang was exploring new fields, soon to become popular. "In the 'sixties," he recalls, "I think I can remember hearing Mr. Ruskin ask ' Who is Villon ? ' and I certainly lent him the works of that poet with whom he had been unacquainted."[87]

Here also the formal old French verse forms, Ballade, Rondeau and Villanelle made one of their earliest appearances in English since the Middle Ages, as gracious, unforced forms of poetry.

But it is with the "Other Poems" that the greatest interest lies. Here was Lang's first advent as a serious poet, and he made a beginning of as fine a promise as any of the greatest poets could have desired. "Those of its friends who have known it all their lives," writes Professor Blyth Webster, "find few first books of verse this side of *The Defence of Guinevere* to wear as well."[88]

A certain number of the poems, particularly those of his undergraduate period, are strongly imitative, mainly those in the section "Hesperothen" (which contains his first published poem "The Siren's Music"). Of these he must have been thinking when he wrote in his verses to Clement K. Shorter already quoted:

> "It was evil example that brought me
> To rhyme, and to run to the Row,
> And Swinburne and Tennyson taught me
> Whatever I know."

But these form only a small minority, limited almost entirely to the one section.

The most notable division of the original poems is that headed "Ave"; and here the keynote is struck of the truest and deepest poetry, and the intensest feeling, both in verse and prose, throughout all Lang's work.

"My mind is gay, but my soul is melancholy," Lang is reported to have said; and it is from the melancholy soul that the true poetic feeling shines through his best writings; very seldom is it strongly apparent, the habitual shyness and reserve of the man hiding it from almost any conscious manifestation, but occasionally the mask slips aside, exhibiting for a startling moment the great and sincere poet who was lost to us in Andrew Lang.

There are a number of forms in which Lang's deepest, most soul-compelling feelings become evident. In his love of the Border country and of St. Andrews, but still more powerfully in the associations which they have for him; in the stirring heroism of some noble deed, some glorious death of fact or fiction—General Gordon or Colonel Burnaby, Socrates, Joan of Arc, or Nada the Lily; or in the romantic, idealistic beauty of the dream-perfection in literature, Helen, Rosalind or Di Vernon.

More strongly again, does the welling over of poetry come in the sorrow over his lost friend of St. Andrews' days, Henry Brown; in "Almae Matres" and "Clevedon Church."

But, most powerful of all, there is another inspiration shining behind the best poems of all Lang's career, these poems in the section "Ave," and others, growing fewer and further apart in later volumes; also by more vague and distant flashes in *The World's Desire.*

One interpretation of this underlying inspiration was suggested by Mr. Desmond MacCarthy, writing on the appearance of Professor Blyth Webster's lecture on Andrew Lang's poetry in 1937: "It appeared to me," he wrote, "that Lang's authentic original note as a serious poet had really been a poetic platonism of a fay-like kind. He appeared to me then as one whose deeper love, out of which he had so seldom written, was for the lips that never could be kissed; as a poet who, all his life, had been homesick for he knew not what . . ."[89]

Now as nearly all Lang's truest and sincerest poetry proceeds from the basic idea of lost or disappointed love, there is, naturally, a strong temptation to assume that he is speaking out of his own experience. This is perhaps the one point in Lang's life where the complete absence of the ordinary facilities of biography—letters, diaries and the like—is felt as a serious loss. It is, also, the very point over which he would most have resented any attempt to raise even a corner of the veil. It is not easy to comprehend fully the extent of Lang's excessive shyness and reserve; it is to be felt, rather than described, and must be respected, while we may regret it.

There is no evidence, beyond that of the poems, that Lang ever suffered from such a loss as is reflected in "Ave" and such poems as "Good-bye," "Another Way" and "The Singing Rose," but it is a possibility to be borne in mind when considering his approach to romantic literature, and his supersensitiveness towards the unnecessarily tragic in fiction.

Were it susceptible of proof, it would explain his apparent attitude to Oxford, the association with melancholy and tears that it seems to have had for him, and the disjointed paragraph from *Adventures Among Books* already quoted: "Unfortunately, life at Oxford is not all beauty and pleasure. Things go wrong somehow. Life drops her happy mask."

If it were to the Oxford years that we must turn for this incident, the most probable period seems to be about 1868 to 1870, during Lang's early years at Merton. It is of the grey walls up which the roses climb towards his window, of the green, shadowy lawn

beneath the ancient lime trees, and of the long terrace leading to
the leafy-framed vista of Madgalen Tower, that he is surely
thinking in his poem "The Singing Rose," which appeared so long
afterwards in *Grass of Parnassus* (1888):

> *"White rose on the gray garden wall,*
> *   Where now no night-wind whispereth,*
> *Call to the far-off flowers, and call*
> *   With murmured breath and musical,*
> *Till all the roses hear, and all*
> *   Sing to my love what the White Rose saith* . . .

       .   .   .   .   .   .

"Once more I hear the sister towers
    Each unto each reply,
The bloom is on those limes of ours,
The weak wind shakes the bloom in showers,
    Snow from a cloudless sky;
There is no change this happy day
Within the College gardens gray!

"St. Mary's, Merton, Magdalen—still
    Their sweet bells chime and swing,
The old years answer them, and thrill
A wintry heart against its will
    With memories of the spring—
That spring we sought the gardens through
For flowers which ne'er in gardens grew.

       .   .   .   .   .   .

"In vain we sought the Singing Rose
    Whereof old legends tell,
Alas! we found it not 'mid those
Within the gray old College close,
    That budded, flowered, and fell—
We found that herb called ' Wandering,'
And meet no more, no more in Spring."

       .   .   .   .   .

The first poem in the "Ave" section of *Ballads and Lyrics* is "Twilight on Tweed" (written 1870), a poem of place, with the association of loss only apparent in the last verse:

> "Twilight, and Tweed, and Eildon Hill,
>   Fair and thrice fair you be;
> You tell me that the voice is still
>   That should have welcomed me."

It has often been assumed that this refers to Henry Brown; but it seems almost certain that all the poems in the section have a common inspiration, and what that is can be seen beyond a doubt in some of the others, such as "Lost in Hades," which is among his best sonnets:

> "I dreamed that somewhere in the shadowy place,
>   Grief of farewell unspoken was forgot
>   In welcome, and regret remembered not;
> And hopeless prayer accomplished turned to praise
> On lips that had been songless many days;
>   Hope had no more to hope for, and desire
>   And dread were overpast, in white attire
> New born we walked among the new world's ways.
>
> "Then from the press of shades a spirit threw
>   Towards me such apples as these gardens bear;
>   And turning, I was 'ware of her, and knew
>   And followed her fleet voice and flying hair—
> Followed, and found her not, and seeking you
>   I found you never, dearest, anywhere."

As the first poem had reached a double excellence by combining the inspiration of person as well as place, so does the last in this section, "A Sunset on Yarrow," again linking the lost one with the Border country.

Of the other poems in *Ballads and Lyrics*, the most notable are to be found in the section "Songs and Sonnets," where the suppressed agony of "Good-bye" is matched only with the gentle

wistfulness of "Fairyland," which was revised and re-issued from
time to time in Lang's career. Also the earliest of his poems to
Helen, the World's Desire, are noteworthy: "The Shade of Helen"
in particular, where he makes exquisite use of the Stesichorian
legend that only the *eidolon* of Helen went with Paris to Ilion.
To her he was to return ten years later in his next serious verse
volume, *Helen of Troy*. Between the two books he had issued in
verse only the *Ballades in Blue China* in their two earliest editions.
Even here the serious note is not quite absent, for besides Lang's
constant habit of mingling grave with gay, there are the sonnets,
"In Ithaca," "Homer," "The Odyssey" and "Natural Theology,"
besides one or two ballades that belong to the higher order of
poetry. As the ballade is generally associated with light verse, and
as moreover Lang shared with Henley and Dobson the honour of
being supreme master in this delicate, whimsical medium, it is
worth quoting one of his serious ballades to show to what poetic
use this form could be put by one who was so at home in it as Lang.
The "Ballade of Autumn" belongs to the "lost love" poems as
surely as any in the early volume, and again goes to prove where
Lang's surest inspiration lay:

> "We built a castle in the air,
>   In summer weather, you and I,
> The wind and sun were in your hair—
>   Gold hair against a sapphire sky:
> When Autumn came, with leaves that fly
>   Before the storm, across the plain,
> You fled from me with scarce a sigh—
>   My Love returns no more again!

> "The windy lights of Autumn flare:
>   I watch the moonlit sails go by;
> I marvel how men toil and fare,
>   The weary business that they ply!
> Their voyaging is vanity,
>   And fairy gold is all their gain,
> And all the winds of winter cry,
>   ' My Love returns no more again! '

"Here, in my castle of Despair,
  I sit alone with memory;
The wind-fed wolf has left his lair
  To keep the outcast company.
The brooding owl he hoots hard by,
  The hare shall kindle on thy hearth-stane,
The Rhymer's soothest prophecy—
  My Love returns no more again!

"Lady, my home until I die
  Is there, where youth and hope were slain:
They flit, the ghosts of our July,
  My Love returns no more again! "

Concerning *Helen of Troy* it is hard to speak with any finality. Here Lang comes into direct comparison with the leading poets of his time, with Morris in *Jason* and *The Earthly Paradise*, with Swinburne in *Tristram*, and with Tennyson in many things from the *Idylls* to *Oenone*. It was the period of long narrative poems, or rather that period had reached its peak and was in decline. The majority of readers could cope only with a few of such works, the writing of the acknowledged poets, and *Helen of Troy* met with no very enthusiastic welcome.

Yet the merits of the poem are many, and though passages show the influence of the Pre-Raphaelite poets, much is fresh and new, escaping from "the close of heavy flowers" into the "large air" and clear sunshine of Homeric Greece. Great though was Lang's love and understanding of Homer, his nearest alliance with the classical world is with those poets of the Alexandrian school with whom abode the last clear, wistful echo of the golden age of Greek literature.

In *Helen of Troy* it is not of Homer that we think, but of such a writer as Apollonius of Rhodes:—and still more nearly of that almost forgotten poet Quintus of Smyrna, who caught the last true notes of the Homeric music, and in an artificial age wedded artifice to the large utterance of an elder world in his poem of the Fall of Troy, the swan song of the old heroic tradition. Quintus was ever a favourite with Lang; not only did he supply the *mythos* for much of *Helen*, and the basis of the later *Tales of Troy and Greece,* but at one time Lang toyed with the idea of translating him, publishing in the *Illustrated London News* (3rd and 10th September 1892) specimens and an appreciation, lamenting that no one seemed anxious to commission the work. Even then no publisher rose to the bait, and Quintus was reserved for another fate—to make his first appearance in English in the laborious mediocrity of A. S. Way's well-intentioned blank verse.

In Lang's poem we see the ancient legendary world as through a haze of soft misty colours, the verse falling with gentle, rather languorous music, lulling us as with that Nepenthean draught which Helen pours for her guests in the *Odyssey*. "Of all my little books the sleepiest" wrote Lang in a copy of the poem many years later, and it is this dream quality that is most apparent in *Helen of Troy.*

Thus it cannot be judged with the highest examples of poetry, for it never draws near enough to the true regions of the soul to excite any of the deeper and more universal emotions. There is over the whole of it a touch of wistful melancholy, a flavour of sadness and regret which adds poignancy to its sweetness and beauty; but the whole is rather a delicately wrought tapestry, spun in the misty blues and greens wherein Morris delighted, than any window opening on to a living world of men and women of like sorrows as ourselves.

Lang failed in *Helen of Troy* largely through having mistaken his true medium, narrative poetry being the fashion of the day. For in no long-sustained work does he ever come near to the heart of his mystery, and only in Heaven-sent moments could the veil be dropped from the disinherited dreamer that was the true Andrew Lang.

The reception of *Helen* discouraged Lang—and no writer was ever more easily discouraged than he. Henceforth he wrote less and less serious poetry, speaking of himself as a cicala on the lowest slopes of the hill of the Muses, and of his poems as the "Grass of Parnassus," the pretty little autumn flower that grows only among the foothills.

Ballades and Verses Vain (1884) and its English counterpart, *Rhymes à la Mode* the following year, combine grave and gay in almost equal quantities, the serious poems including "Almae Matres" and "The Last Maying" and the gentle melancholy of

«Νήνεμος Aἰών» with its longing for the quiet repose of a
dreamed-of past, far from the hurry and vulgarity of the contemporary world, with which Lang felt so little in harmony.

"I would my days had been in other times,
  A moment in the long unnumbered years
  That knew the sway of Horus and of hawk,
  In peaceful lands that border on the Nile.

"I would my days had been in other times,
  Lulled by the sacrifice and mumbled hymn
  Between the Five great Rivers, or in shade
  And shelter of the cool Himalayan hills.

"I would my days had been in other times,
  That I in some old abbey of Touraine
  Had watched the rounding grapes, and lived my life,
  Ere ever Luther came, or Rabelais!

"I would my days had been in other times,
  When quiet life to death not terrible
  Drifted, as ashes of the Santhal dead
  Drift down the Sacred Rivers to the Sea! "

In 1888 came *Grass of Parnassus*, a collection of serious poems
more than half of which were reprinted (often in revised form)
from the earlier volumes. Among new pieces are "The Singing
Rose" and "Clevedon Church," "A Dream" and "Another Way,"
the last two being among the best of the "lost love" poems,
enshrining such verses as:

"Last night, last night, in dreams we met,
  And how, today, shall I forget,
  Or how, remembering, restrain
  Mine incommunicable pain ?

"Nay, where thy land and people are,
  Dwell thou remote, apart, afar,
  Nor mingle with the shapes that sweep
  The melancholy ways of sleep.

"But if, perchance, the shadows break,
    If dreams depart, and men awake,
    If face to face at length we see,
    Be thine the voice to welcome me."

Here also occur some of Lang's earliest utterances of that other inspiration, the reverence which he felt for noble deeds and heroic actions. For Lang, in common with so many imaginative men who are doomed by reason of their fragile health to a life of inaction, had an almost passionate admiration for the doers of deeds. We do not know whether, like Stevenson, his greatest regret was that he could not have been a soldier, but like him he was prepared to hero-worship the great leaders and martyrs of the period. Stevenson at one time was preparing to write a life of Wellington for the series of English Worthies which Lang edited for Longmans; Lang himself, with his changeless aversion for politics, contented himself with writing poems on the death of Gordon or Colonel Burnaby, or on Melville and Coghill at Isandlhwana. Later he sought for his heroes in the Past, writing "Loyal Lyrics" to Prince Charlie and Joan of Arc, though in the Jacobite poems, treating the White Rose but as a symbol of old loyalties to the spirit of romance which towards the end of his life became more and more his refuge from an uncongenial world.

Grass of Parnassus marks practically the end of Lang's career as a serious poet, and indeed only the songs in *The World's Desire*, and a few snatches made up in dreams catch the deep sincerity of the early poems. The translations from the *Greek Anthology* which began to appear in this volume, and were considerably increased in a later issue, reflect the melancholy of his soul: his affinity with these poets, Rufinus and Antipater and Meleager, is very marked, and he is at home with them in middle life as he had been twenty years earlier with the romantic poets of old France. But already he is dwelling in the past, and the poetry that will live has been written.

To consider Lang as a poet "the world does not yet know how good and true," he must be judged on but a slender selection out of the considerable bulk of his verse writings. (There were some 400 poems collected in the *Poetical Works* of 1923, and over 200 more are not included, often for no apparent reason.) Perhaps

E

some fifty poems, together with nearly that number of translations from the Greek and French, represent the poetry of Andrew Lang. To read these, and to re-read them again and again is to realize how excellent a poet he could be, and how poorer is our literature for the taste of the intermediate generations that have gone so far towards forgetting him.

Lang can never be the poet of the wide world, and perhaps his poetry, as his essays and stories, appeals most nearly to those among his readers who are by inclination bookish, who do not shame to steal away at times from the glare and hurry of today into the tranquillity and peace of the remembrance of things past. To read Lang's poetry (as also his romantic prose writings) is to wander among the fallen rose petals and beneath the old grey lime trees of our vanished youth, to dream once more as when we first trod those ways when all was bright and dew-spangled in an early morning of spring, and to come forth once more into the dust and glare, chastened and strengthened, with at heart that tranquillity which sees, beyond the stress and turmoil of the noonday, evening waiting for us in the cool, green places of the spirit.

CHAPTER VI

The Divine Amateur

THE account in the last chapter of Lang as a serious poet overstepped the bounds of chronology in order to treat his poetry as a whole. But the years of his poetic flowering saw him also extending his range in other directions, so varied and versatile as to reduce the function of poet merely to the position of one amongst many others.

Although the most professional of writers, both from the point of view of earning his living solely by his art, and as regards his high ideals of the brotherhood of the pen, Lang can most aptly be described in Henley's phrase "The Divine Amateur," taking the word in its original sense of one who loves what he does. Much of Lang's secret lay in this fact, and practically none of his voluminous writings could ever be considered hack-work: from the first he was given his own way by editors, who would strive to secure and retain him at any cost; and, moreover, the multifarious nature of his interests and the number of subjects in which he was an expert made it difficult to find a subject that was other than a labour of love.

He began his literary and journalistic career peculiarly well qualified to follow the bent of his genius, and George Saintsbury writing some years after Lang's death, doubted "whether anybody, undergraduate or don, Oxonian or Cantab., about the year 1869 possessed knowledge of ancient and modern literature, coupled with power to make use of it in a literary way, to a greater extent than Lang . . . For a compound of scholarship and light-handedness, of multilegence and complete freedom from pedantry, of what may be called literary good manners, infinite wit and a peculiar humour he had, I think, in his own generation no equal—certainly no superior."[90]

In spite of its many excellencies and its high promise, *Ballads and Lyrics* made no stir on its appearance at the beginning of 1872,

and it was nearly fifteen years before the first edition of 500 copies
was exhausted. As Lang himself wrote once in a copy of the book:

> "This first æsthetic lily
>   Broke through the sandy plain,
> In seasons late and chilly
>   It bore the wind and rain.
>   The Critics came not nigh it,
>   The Public did not buy it;
>   Indeed I can't deny it
> Bloomed hopelessly in vain."

Apart from this, the only work which his Merton years produced
was a series of essays prefixed to an edition of Aristotle's *Politics*
prepared for University students by the Rev. W. E. Bolland, a
Past Master of Merton (later Vicar of Embleton and Headmaster
of Worcester Cathedral Grammar School). This, Lang records,
was among the classical works which had made most impression on
him as an undergraduate, and the melancholy wisdom of it had
effectually disenchanted him with contemporary politics. The
essays (which were reprinted in a separate volume in 1886) are
chiefly noteworthy as one of the earliest examples in Lang's work
of his habit of drawing parallels between the survivals of civilized
Greek life and the customs of the lowest savages—a practice
which, however well sanctioned by authority at the present, was
looked upon in the 'seventies and 'eighties as little short of
sacrilegious, when it was introduced by Lang, who was a pioneer in
the field of comparative anthropology.

Another scheme that was born at Merton was the prose translation of the *Odyssey* with which the name of Andrew Lang is most
generally associated to most people. For the book was to have been
his own unaided work, and only later did S. H. Butcher join him
in this famous collaboration. "Among the early memories which
I possess," wrote W. L. Courtney, "is a companionship with
Andrew Lang when we were both Fellows of Merton, and when,
in the beautiful garden of Merton, the translation of the *Odyssey*
was first attacked."[91]

Of Lang's individual translation, a specimen copy of Book Six
was printed privately, with no title page or author's name, in 1877.

This blue paper bound pamphlet of fifteen pages is among the rarest of Lang's works.

Meanwhile, in 1874, Lang had begun in earnest upon his journalistic career, publishing on 10th January of that year his first review of "current novels" in *The Academy*, to which he was a fairly constant contributor for at least the next ten years. And when, in 1875, he was settled in London, he began writing numerous "leaders" for the *Daily News*, besides reviews and other contributions to *The Saturday Review*.

The least noticed literary venture of the time—and perhaps the most famous in after days—was that mysterious weekly paper called *London*, which flourished inconspicuously from 3rd February 1877 to 5th April 1879. The original editor was a certain Caldwell (or Glasgow) Brown, notorious from Stevenson's essay "A College Magazine," who was financed in his undertaking by the Tory party leaders. At first the paper paid its contributors well, but presently Brown disappeared from the scene (he is said to have gone to Mentone and died there), leaving William Ernest Henley in charge. This fiery titan of journalism, but newly out of the Edinburgh Infirmary, gathered about him, with the uncanny power that attended every one of his editorial ventures, a small group of the best young writers of the day—Stevenson, Lang and George Saintsbury making, with himself, the main body of contributors during 1878, the year of Henley's reign. Stevenson's important contribution was *The New Arabian Nights*, while Henley, besides political "leaders," published many of his best poems. Saintsbury's share is uncertain, but Lang, besides a certain amount of unimportant prose, was responsible for a number of humorous ballades, such as "The Ballade of the Summer Term" (11th May 1878) and "The Ballade of the Three Graces" (25th May 1878), besides a few serious poems, including "Love's Easter" (18th May 1878) and "The Last Maying" (27th July 1878). About this time Henley's brother Joseph recollected seeing Lang call at the *London* Office one day, sit down in a chair, take up pen and paper, and begin writing, "pausing now and then as if feeling for a word. By and by he rose and handed the paper to Henley, who read it through almost at a glance, and said: ' Most excellent; thank you; greatly obliged.' With an exquisite smile the caller then took his leave . . . he had

just knocked off a ballade, which was duly published in the
following week's *London*."[92]

The career of this paper, though brilliant, was brief, and within
the year both Lang and Saintsbury were free to devote as much
time as they cared to the steady work for the *Daily News* and
Saturday Review. The first of these only employed Saintsbury for
a short while, though Lang remained faithful to it until the
'nineties, when press of work (mainly on his *History of Scotland*)
forced him to give up leader writing: Saintsbury, on leaving the
Daily News, became sub-editor of the *Saturday Review* (edited by
Lang's friend, Walter Herries Pollock), so that he and Lang
continued to see almost as much of each other for many years;
indeed, Saintsbury was probably Lang's most intimate friend
between about 1875 and 1885, when they were accustomed to walk
home together from the City to Kensington three or four days a
week—a walk of more than an hour and a half, to Lang's home at
1 Marloes Road: "Walk up the Cromwell Road until you drop—
and then turn right," as he used to describe the way. Working for
the *Daily News*, Lang early showed the astonishing power of
writing brilliant articles, packed with learning and humour, under
any conditions, and at amazing speed. Sir Henry Lucy, in those
days a colleague of Lang's, describes a scene that must have been
of almost daily occurrence: "It was the habit of the editor (Frank
Hill) to meet his staff at four o'clock in the afternoon in his office
in Bouverie Street. The purpose of the gathering was to select
topics for leaders to appear on the following morning, and allot the
subjects to various writers. It was no infrequent thing to find
Lang sitting at the table with an open book at his left hand, in his
right a pen. The editor, who rather plumed himself on his conversational gifts, was accustomed to discuss a variety of current
topics, members of the staff here and there getting in a word. All
the while Lang, quickly turning over the leaves of the book he was
reviewing, went on writing, occasionally contributing a pointed
sentence to the conversation. He had usually finished his work
by the time the conference closed, and sauntered off to his club."[93]
"I have known him get his subject from Hill," writes another
colleague, Richard Whiteing, "and there and then sit down at
the corner of the table to turn out his leader well within
the hour. When it was done, he gathered up his slips from the

floor, and without a glance of revision sent them upstairs to the printer."[94]

"No other such combination of poet, scholar and journalist has been known in Fleet Street," wrote Richard Le Gallienne, who describes Lang as "wearing his panoply of learning as though it were a garment of iridescent gossamer, turning the dryest subject to favour and to prettiness, particularly the prettiness of an elfish, incalculable wit . . . His 'leaders' in the *Daily News* read like fairy tales written by an erudite Puck."[95]

Largely on the strength of these "leaders," and also for much of his acknowledged work, Lang the essayist became almost a cult in the early 'eighties.

A group of young writers including the novelist, W. Pett Ridge and Mr. Bernard Shaw, "counted the day empty unless an article by Lang appeared," and the individuality of his style made the absence of a signature immaterial to the enthusiast. It is sad that the prodigality of Lang's genius has left so many of these early essays in the oblivion of lost daily papers. He himself never thought them worth collecting, and would not even make a selection from the monthly article of later years "At the Sign of the Ship" in *Longmans' Magazine*, though his imitators re-issued their *causeries* in many instances: Quiller-Couch's *From a Cornish Window* being a case in point.

But a number of the *Daily News* articles do survive, thanks to the enthusiasm of Pett Ridge, who suggested to Kegan Paul the publisher that a selection of them would make an excellent volume. Paul directed him to undertake the job: "The newspaper office did not wish its file to be inspected, because the sum paid to each contributor was entered there, and I went day after day, in my luncheon hour, to the British Museum, and made a selection. When, at the finish, Andrew Lang reviewed the list, it was discovered that I had, in choosing the unsigned articles, made two errors: an early one I had credited to him was by William Black, and a later one by Richard Whiteing."[96]

The book appeared in 1889 as *Lost Leaders*, and still remains among the most charming and enjoyable of Lang's literary essays, and a very pleasant guide to some of his numerous minor devotions: such as the origins of various games and Thackeray as an illustrator.

But earlier than this, Lang had become to some extent the idol of the "cultured" set, at the time when the Morris movement was passing through the phase of brilliantly brittle culture, the "Æsthetic" movement of the young Oscar Wilde, from which, in certain limited circles, it degenerated about 1890 into the Decadent, or *Fin-de-siècle* movement of the *Yellow Book* writers and artists.

Lang was never a blind or whole-hearted follower of any "cult" in letters, but the half-humorous observer who could play at most things with a skill that was the envy of the devotees. From the decadent movement he turned away in disapproval—being too old, perhaps, by the 'nineties to find any amusement in a pose. Moreover, among the writers of the new movement were those who would exalt the realistic and the sordid in art and life to the place of the highest literary ideal—and from such tendencies Lang shrank more and more intolerantly towards the end of his life.

But in the early 'eighties he was as much the prophet of the newest "craze" as any serious writer of the day: "I have lived with the earliest Apostles of Culture," he writes, in humorous apology for his later delinquencies, "in the days when Chippendale was first a name to conjure with, and Japanese art came in like a raging lion, and Ronsard was the favourite poet, and Mr. William Morris was a poet too, and blue and green were the only wear, and the name of Paradise was Camelot. To be sure, I cannot say that I took all this quite seriously, we too ' have played at it,' and know all about it. Generally speaking I have kept up with Culture. I can talk (if desired) about Saint-Beuve and Mérimee and Félicien Rops; I could rhyme 'ballades' when they were ' in,' and knew what a ' *pantoum* ' was . . ."[97]

His second prose book (apart from the translations) appeared in 1881 in a series called "Art in the Home": *The Library*, dealing in a light and charming way with book-hunting, rare editions, Elzevirs, famous bibliophiles, old bindings, and book collecting in general; an additional chapter, on "Modern English Book Illustration" was supplied by Austin Dobson, and a frontispiece and decorations by Walter Crane, while besides the cheap edition, a limited number of copies appeared in a sumptuous form on large, hand-made paper—a format in which the majority of Lang's books before about 1895 were issued, in limited editions ranging from about fifty to two hundred and fifty copies.

Much in the same style, but with a more general and enduring appeal was the volume of essays, collected from such papers as the *Magazine of Art* (Henley's second brilliant editorial venture) and the *Contemporary Review*, and issued in 1886 as *Books and Bookmen*. These essays range from "Literary Forgeries" and "Curiosities of Parish Registers" to "Japanese Bogie Books" and "Elzevirs" with a pleasant simplicity and charm veiling the deep learning that informs the whole in a way that must have delighted, and should still delight, the general reader.

Letters to Dead Authors of the same year does a similar service to a selection of the greatest writers of the past, whom Lang addresses in their own particular style (using verse in the cases of Pope, Byron and Omar Khayyam) in a shrewd blend of appreciation and criticism, inviting a re-reading of their works rather than stating any "last word" about their failings or achievements—and, by the very manner of writing, conveying both his own enthusiasm and his own well-tempered criticism. In the Epistle to Mr. Pope (which W. P. Ker called "a true poem in the glorious old couplets, noble in argument . . . and faultless in style"), for example, he ends:

"Thus Time with sordid Alchemy and dread,
  Turns half the Glory of your Gold to Lead;
  Thus Time,—at Ronsard's Wreath that vainly bit—
  Has marred the Poet to preserve the Wit,
  Whose Knife cut cleanest with a poisoned Pain—
  Who almost left on Addison a Stain:
  Yet thou (strange Fate that clings to all of thine!)
  When most a Wit doth most a Poet shine;
  In Poetry thy *Dunciad* expires,
  When Wit has shot ' her momentary Fires.'
  'Tis Tragedy that watches by the Bed
  ' Where tawdry Yellow strove with dirty Red; '
  And Men, remembering all, can scarce deny
  To lay the Laurel where thine Ashes lie! "[98]

And the majority of the prose letters catch and suggest the style and manner of the author addresssd just as delightfully.

This is perhaps the most successful of Lang's lighter volumes of literary conversation. His *Letters on Literature* of 1889 do not keep so high a level of excellence, though the ones on "Aucassin and Nicolete," and "Books about Redmen" are a never-ending delight.

In a more formal and accepted manner are the *Essays in Little* of 1891, mainly reprints from journals and magazines. The papers on Stevenson, Kipling, Kingsley and "The Buccaneers" stand out most particularly—that on Kipling being the first appreciation of his work to be published in this country.

The *Letters to Dead Authors* had nearly all appeared between July and December 1885 in *The St. James's Gazette*, the evening daily paper edited in the 'eighties by Frederick Greenwood, and still remembered as the first medium by which Barrie became known to London readers.

At this time, and until the early 'nineties, Lang was one of the most constant contributors. Sidney Low (who succeeded Greenwood in 1889) writes of this paper that: "The *St. James's* had a position of its own in those days. Its circulation was what would now be called contemptibly small, but its influence was out of all proportion to the number of copies sold. It was distinctly the organ of the 'governing classes,' and it was read by them with a reverential attention which always surprised, and sometimes amused me. As its news service was never really good, it depended almost entirely on the strength and quality of its writing . . . Our staff at this period might be called remarkable. J. M. Barrie, Rudyard Kipling, Andrew Lang, Edmund Gosse, George Saintsbury, Gilbert Parker, Anthony Hope Hawkins, H. D. Traill, David Hannay, Mrs. Lynn Linton were among the more regular contributors" [99], while occasional writers included Lewis Carroll, Kenneth Grahame and Richard Jeffries.

Much of Lang's lighter verse appeared in the *St. James's*, besides his few serious political poems such as those on Gordon. Of the humorous verse, a great deal remains uncollected, and even C. M. Falconer, who made a manuscript transcript of all the Lang poems unreprinted in 1904, has overlooked a few—signed as well as unsigned. One of the most amusing is the parody "Mariana in Kensington," an anonymous poem omitted by Falconer; while of those included by him (and the transcript was revised by Lang, so the ascriptions may be taken as authoritative) the most unusual and least characteristic is the sonnet "Love's Ritual" (11th August 1892. Unsigned), which runs as follows.

"A soulless pleasure—that I ever spurned,
　'Tis but to take love's sacrament in vain;
But now the converse lesson have I learned,
　That formless love is unavailing pain.
False love, and soulless is unreal seeming,
　That to an idle ceremony turns;
True love fulfilled not is but painful dreaming,
　And all in vain for want of fuel burns.
Love, like religion, hath its perfect rite,
　When outward worship clothes the deep desire,
When joy is robed in garments of delight,
　And light and heat reveal the hidden fire.
If with maimed ritual I must adore,
Were it not best to go to church no more ? "

An astonishing glimpse of Andrew Lang the poet among the second-rate satires, and excellent but light-hearted ballades and verses vain which make up the majority of his contributions— "Ballade of Aesthetic Adjectives," "The Garden of Bric-a-Brac," "Doris's Books," "The Old Cricketer's Lament," and many more.

In the kingdom of light verse, Lang in the early 'eighties knew no master, and his peers were Henley and Dobson alone. The introduction of old French forms into English poems had begun with the Villon translations of Swinburne and Rossetti, and flourished after Lang's *Ballads and Lyrics of Old France* and the essays of Dobson and Saintsbury, besides Lang himself.

One facet of the earlier æsthetic movement had been the craze for collecting Oriental vases—"blue china"—which seems to have originated with Rossetti and spread swiftly among his friends and their followers. By the end of the 'seventies the collecting of Oriental china had become almost the symbol of the new game of æsthetics and culture—the "Blue China movement," as we may perhaps be permitted to call it.

"There's a joy without canker or cark,
　There's a pleasure eternally new,
'Tis to gloat on the glaze and the mark
　Of china that's ancient and blue;

> Unchipped all the centuries through
> It has pass'd, since the chime of it rang,
> And they fashioned it, figure and hue,
> In the reign of the Emperor Hwang! "[100]

Thus Andrew Lang celebrated it in 1880 in his *XXII Ballades in Blue China* (increased to "XXXII" the following year, and revised and enlarged from time to time—the large paper edition of 1888 containing a drawing by Sybil Longman of "The Blue Closet" that combines Pre-Raphaelitism and "Blue China" more deliciously than any conscious parody could do). Ballades, Triolets, Rondels and Villanelles became the rage: "Mr. Dobson, an old offender, debauched my green, unknowing middle age," says Lang, "and I began actually to *think* in ballades! "[101]

While these airy trifles were usually in the lightest vein, the underlying melancholy in Lang's nature often imparts to them a touch of wistfulness and tender regret that seems almost to give a soul to these unsubstantial ghosts; and lines and snatches linger in the memory whence the shadows of vain things pass, leaving no trace:

> "We wandered out of yesterday,
> Went maying through that ancient May,
> Whose fallen flowers are fragrant yet—"

> "Like the shifting shade that lies
> On the moonlight-silvered stream,
> So you rise when dreams arise,
> *Following darkness like a dream!* "

> "I'd leave all the hurry, the noise and the fray,
> For a house full of books, and a garden of flowers!"

The charm is rarely absent from Lang's verse, even when he "plays at" the culture of the moment, even when he seems to dwell contentedly with Dobson and Gosse and Graham Thomson in the Palace of Bric-a-Brac—

> "Here, where old Nankin glitters,
> Here, where men's tumult seems

As faint as feeble twitters
  Of sparrows heard in dreams,
    We watch Limoges enamel,
    An old chased silver camel,
    A shawl, the gift of Schamyl,
  And manuscripts in reams.

.   .   .   .   .

"The foolish people raging
  O'er Bradlaugh and o'er Bright,
They know not the assuaging
  Of what is ' good ' and ' right ':
    Of coins that 'scaped the Vandals,
    Of daggers with jade handles,
    Of broidered Syrian sandals,
  Of bowls of Malachite.

.   .   .   .   .

"Can kings or clergies alter
  The crackle on one plate ?
Can creeds or systems palter
  With what is truly great ?
    With Corots and with Millets,
    With April daffodillies,
    Or make the maiden lilies
  Bloom early or bloom late ? "[102]

.   .   .   .   .

But in that Palace, which has many chambers curiously
fashioned, Lang wandered often in the early 'eighties, and he
lingered in few that he did not adorn.

In the art of the theatre Lang took little interest, and confessed
that he was "conscious of an entire ignorance of the stage, and a
lack of enthusiasm for the drama"[103], and that he "would almost as
lief go to a meeting of the British Association as to a theatre."[104]
Yet in spite of this, he used the dramatic form occasionally—in
such poems as "The New Pygmalion" (a little humorous lyric
drama still buried in *Longmans' Magazine* for January 1883), and

"The Mystery of Queen Persephone," and in the parody "A New Shakespeare." One full-length play intended for acting rather than for reading, he does seem to have written: *The Black Thief, a New and Original Drama (adapted from the Irish), in Four Acts. Privately Printed.* 1882. This, the rarest of all Lang's works, is to be found in no public library, and has so far proved completely "introuvable." "Very rare indeed, the author's only dramatic work" ran Lang's own description of it in the copy from his library sold at Sotheby's on 5th December 1912—and the present writer can, alas, supply no more information about it, save to hazard a guess that the play was based on one of the Irish folk-tales, perhaps "The Black Thief and the Knight of the Glen," which is retold in *The Red Fairy Book*.

One of the early versions of *Parson Kelly* seems to have been in the form of a play, and Lang assisted Mr. A. E. W. Mason in this experiment with the material, but it was soon abandoned in favour of the novel as finally published.

Only once does Lang seem to have been responsible for the review of an actual play in performance, and that was the classical pageant *The Tale of Troy*, which he dealt with in *The Academy* on 9th June 1883, treating almost entirely of the play and of the archæological accuracy of set and costumes.

An early experiment in the dramatic form is the trifling "skit" "The Press View" in the *Pall Mall Gazette* for 11th January 1882, and this leads to the consideration of Lang's attitude to the visual arts. The promise of the humorous drawings of his undergraduate days was not followed up, and Lang never seems to have attempted to draw in after years, except in occasional letters to more intimate friends. The series to Rider Haggard, preserved at Ditchingham House, contains one or two of such drawings, slight in themselves, but always interesting and forceful.

But as an art critic Lang attained to a certain ephemeral reputation in his early London years—writing, apparently, for *The Pall Mall Gazette* in particular, though the unsigned notices are impossible now to identify, being as much in the nature of "hack-work" as Lang ever descended to. For the Millais exhibition organized by the Fine Arts Society in 1881 he prepared a catalogue prefaced with a careful criticism of Millais' work which still makes good and agreeable reading, and from which a long quotation appears in the standard biography of the painter. As late as 1888 he is writing his humorous "Dialogues of the Galleries" in collaboration with Henley—*Pictures at Play. By Two Art Critics*, with amusing illustrations by Harry Furniss.

Lang had already shown his skill in parody by the delightful perversion of "Hugh Conway's" Christmas thriller, *Dark Days*, which appeared in a paper-bound, shilling edition, in 1884, as *Much Darker Days*, by "A. Huge Longway."

Lang's authorship was early suspected, and Walter Pollock, the editor of the *Saturday Review*, trapped him into admitting it by giving him a copy to review; and he describes Lang's comical discomfort until he finally flung the book down, exclaiming with laughter: "What's the use, you know I wrote it! "[105]

On one occasion Lang did review a work of his own—the volume of the *Encyclopædia Britannica* containing his article on Molière, in which he had detected a fault too late to be corrected. "I reviewed the volume," he says, "and I pitched into Mr. Lang for airing his habitual inaccuracy in these solemn pages."[106]

Following the exceedingly clever and amusing parody of *Dark Days*, Lang was concerned in another anonymous satire of rather a different type: *That Very Mab* (1885), in which he collaborated with May Kendall, who is probably responsible for most of it, though Lang certainly had a share in it (as May Kendall admits in dedicating her novel *From a Garret* to him a couple of years later), in spite of the fact that he habitually speaks of her as the author. The book is a satire on contemporary civilization—science, politics, the social state, and so on, very much in the manner of all May Kendall's prose writings: indeed, before long she gave up literature entirely, to devote herself to social reform and work among the poor. Only the account of the missionaries who frighten Queen Mab away from Samoa at the beginning of the book, and the chapter called "The Origin of Religion," with the child who recognizes Queen Mab as her "invisible playmate," and begins praying to her (though brought up a strict atheist), suggest Lang's authorship. Even the poems in the book, for the most part of a satirical nature, are in the style of May Kendall's acknowledged verses—though these themselves seem to be inspired by Lang, whose influence shows strongly in a number of minor poets of the period, including Graham Rosamund Thomson and the earlier work of Richard Le Gallienne.

As a whole *That Very Mab* is a dull and disappointing book, the better sparks of humour very occasional, and the topical allusions tedious and unilluminating, even to the student of the period.

Setting aside *He*, the parody of Rider Haggard's *She*, which will be dealt with at a later stage, Lang's most successful volume of parodies is *Old Friends* (1890), a series of letters written between the characters in various works of fiction narrating how they chanced to meet personages out of the works of other authors— characters whose paths must surely have crossed, if we consider the world of fiction as a real, three-dimensional place.

"*Pendennis* and *David Copperfield* came out simultaneously in numbers, yet Pen never encountered Steerforth at the University, nor did Warrington in his life of Journalism, jostle against a reporter named David Copperfield . . . Assuredly Dugald Dalgetty in his wanderings in search of fights and fortune may have crushed a cup or rattled a dice box with four gallant gentlemen of the King's Mousquetaires. It is agreeable to wonder what all these very real people would have thought of their companions in the region of Romance, and to guess how their natures would have acted and reacted on each other."[107]

This was the idea which suggested to Lang his volume of "Essays in Epistolary Parody," and the result is one of the most entertaining of his books. Characters from past and contemporary fiction meet and have adventures together—and the letters telling of these super-mundane encounters are presented each in the style of the character who is supposedly writing, recapturing the manner and trick of the author, and in many cases parodying the more salient features of his work with the gentle irony of one who loves, and yet is not blind to the faults in the beloved—faults that have become a dear and necessary part, a cause of yet deeper affection.

Only in the case of the correspondence between Piscator and Christian is a more serious note sounded—and to these letters George Saintsbury turned on the day in July 1912 when the mortal remains of Andrew Lang were being laid to rest in the kirk-yard of St. Andrews, and reading them felt that he was brought near to the faith and spirit of his lost friend.

But as a whole the book sparkles with humour: Allan Quatermain writes to Curtis of adventures more startling than ever Haggard chronicled; Catherine Morland visits the home of Mr. Rochester,

and finds her love of the "Gothick" fully satisfied; M. Lecoq
arrests a suspicious character named Pickwick, and writes to his
English confrère Mr. Bucket for instructions—This is the Paradise
of Romance as Lang imagined it, and dreamed that it might be:

> "For mansions we know not nor number,
> There is room in the realms of the air,
> Our heroes may sleep not, nor slumber,
> And Porthos may welcome us there! "[108]

CHAPTER VII

Mythologist and Classical Scholar

WHILE Andrew Lang, the "Divine Amateur" of letters, was delighting and entertaining the world with poetry and essays, as later with fairy-tales and romance, Andrew Lang the scholar, the "late Fellow of Merton College," was producing work of the highest academic worth in the most varied fields of Anthropology, and in the study and interpretation of Homer.

It would be possible only for an expert to go deeply into the extent and value of Lang's work in these branches of study, and the most that can be attempted here is a brief, surface account of his Anthropological and Homeric labours, with the fundamental criticisms and appreciations drawn from the writings of those more qualified to utter them than the present writer.

The interest in folk-lore came of a very early root, and dates back to the days of Lang's childhood at Selkirk. In the large old barn at Viewfield, its walls still decorated with fading frescoes painted by the French prisoners of the Napoleonic wars, Andrew and the other Selkirk children used to meet of a summer's evening, when twilight put an end to cricket, and there tell to each other the ancient folk-tales of the country which they had heard from their parents and nurses; and on other occasions he and his brothers and their friends visited two old ladies in the district who would recite to them the old stories learnt in their own youth, such as that of "Nicht, Nought, Nothing," which Lang published later in *Custom and Myth*[109]. Lang's interest in Popular Tales being thus awakened, he began to read all the collections that he could lay hands on, the chief being Sir George Dasent's *Tales from the Norse*, which first appeared in 1859 when Lang was about fifteen. Continuing these studies at St. Andrews, where the books borrowed by him from the University library include Dasent's *Norse Tales* and *Burnt Njal*, Grimm, *The Mabinogen*, and many more, he published as the second of his essays ever to appear in print, "Scottish Nursery Tales" in the *St. Andrews' Magazine* for

April 1863. At Oxford Lang began to study the origin and defusion of popular tales more thoroughly, being specially influenced by the works of J. F. M'Lennan and J. B. Tylor.

The whole study of Anthropology had a strong romantic appeal for Lang, who felt that: "The natural people, the folk, has supplied us, in its unconscious way, with the stuff of all our poetry, law, ritual: and genius has selected from the mass, has turned customs into codes, nursery tales into romance, myth into science, ballad into epic . . . The student of this lore can look back and see the long-trodden way behind him, the winding tracks through marsh and forest and over burning sands. He sees the caves, the camps, the villages, the towns where the race has tarried, for shorter times or longer, strange places many of them, and strangely haunted, desolate dwellings and inhospitable. But the scarce visible tracks converge at last on the beaten ways, the ways to that city whither mankind is wandering, and which it may never win. We have a foreboding of a purpose which we know not, a sense as of will, working, as we would not have worked, to a hidden end. This is the lesson, I think, of what we call folk-lore or anthropology."[110] Feeling this romantic attraction to the subject, Lang did not approach it solely from the scientific standpoint, but, as was usual with him, related it to the many other branches of knowledge and literary interests that were his—thus coming to the study from a new and original angle whence he could consider it fairly in relation to general human culture, without any of the narrowing influences of so many exact scholars of the time.

Reading, in the early 'seventies, from the mythology of the most primitive races, and from the literature of the highest civilizations, from the historians and thinkers of Greece and Rome as freely as from the field-anthropologists and the historians of more recent peoples—(the books taken out by him from Merton library in March 1872, for example, include Tylor's *Primitive Culture*, Prescott's *Conquest of Mexico*, and Dennis' *Etruria*)—Lang was struck more and more by the fact that the most divergent races— Aryans, Aztecs and Australians—often delighted in the very same tales, with almost identical incidents, but with characters bearing completely different names.

Now at that date the accepted explanation—so firmly accepted that it was actually taught in schools—accounted for all myths by "a disease of language," and traced the races who told these tales back to a common origin in an early civilization among the Aryans who dwelt in the Himalayas. The great prophet of this creed was Professor Max Müller (a German by birth, but holding a chair in Philology at Oxford)—and naturally Germany produced the most devoted and painstaking adherents to this system of mythology.

It was from Tylor that Lang had received the Anthropological method, as opposed to the Philological then in vogue, but it was Lang who first applied this method to the subject of the diffusion of myths and popular tales, using the wild legends of primitive man to explain the obscure survivals of grim savagery in Greek literature. His earliest writing on this new approach was the essay "Mythology and Fairy Tales," in *The Fortnightly Review* for May 1873, which Professor Soloman Reinach describes as "the first full refutation of Max Müller's mythological system based on the Veda, and the first full statement of the anthropological method applied to the comparative study of myths."[111]

It is needless to follow Lang through all the intricacies of his verbal warfare with Müller and the Philologists, almost needless to dwell for more than a passing word on even the most readable of his own mythological works. *Custom and Myth* (1884), a collection of papers dating some from the early 'seventies, is pleasant reading still, and better yet is *Myth, Ritual and Religion* (1887), probably his most enduring work of this kind, which examines the primitive and savage survivals in the "civilized" mythology of Egypt, Greece, Scandinavia, Mexico and so on, comparing them with the beliefs and practices reported of Maori and Zulu and Algonquin almost our contemporaries in time.

But much even of these books tends to be polemical, and the later works are even more obviously so,—and are consequently of interest now almost solely as records of a stage in the history of anthropological studies.

Probably Lang's most enduring contribution to the study of folk tales, besides chapters in *Myth, Ritual and Religion*, is to be found in his introductions to Grimm (1884), *Cupid and Psyche* (1887), Perrault (1888), and Kirk's *Secret Commonwealth of Elves, Fauns and Fairies* (1893), and this was the most important service that he rendered to anthropology proper.

But his labours did not end with the demolition of Max Müller, and in his next step another early influence came into play—his devotion to ghost stories and to the magical writings of the old Mages, Cornelius Agrippa, Petrus di Abano, and the like. Although never a spiritualist in the usual sense, the undoubted phenomena of seances, the interpretation of dreams, and the proven seeing of ghosts and wraiths, were all of absorbing interest to Lang, and besides being a founder and early president of the Folk-lore Society, he did like services to the Society for Psychical Research.

Himself, he was never quite sure whether or not he had seen a ghost, but one or two wraiths were certain in his experience. "I have beheld only a brace of apparitions," he writes regretfully. "The first was the wraith of a scholar, at the moment either dead or dying, far from Oriel Lane in Oxford, where I encountered his appearance. The second, fortunately, appeared without any such cause, and for no motive whatever . . . I have passed nights in a haunted castle, with the whole haunted wing to myself, and that when I was young, ill, and overworked: I have occupied the ghostly chamber where the original of Dickens's Miss Haversham lived and died in her mouldy bridal raiment; but in spite of expecting with fear and trembling all sorts of horrors, I never saw or heard anything to establish the existence of a bogey."[112]

The ghost was that of Professor Conington, which Lang encountered standing beneath the lamp-post opposite the main entrance to Oriel College, early in October 1869. He told the story to a number of people, amongst them his contemporary at Balliol, Lord Kilbracken, who relates it circumstantially in his *Reminiscences* (1931).

The wraith is described by Lang in 1894: "My own experience was simply seeing, and speaking to, a relation who was crossing a large and brilliantly lighted hall. The figure, that of a girl, was dressed in dark blue serge. She did not answer. I entered the room she had that moment left, and there she was, dressed for dinner, in white. By no conceivable possibility could there be a mistake in identity."[113]

In 1901 he saw another wraith, an experience which is minutely described in the *Monthly Review* of March 1903; and a few months before his death in 1912 he saw the death omen of his family—a spectral cat.

Lang's attitude to psychical phenomena, while quite devoid of superstition, was not incredulous: "I do firmly believe," he wrote, "that there are human faculties, as yet unexplained, as yet in-consistent with popular scientific 'materialism.' But when Mr. Myers goes further, and expresses belief that messages from the dead are uttered by Mrs. Piper, or given by table-tilting, or auto-matic writing, I cannot march with him."[114]

Lang's interest covered the whole field of such phenomena, from the mediums and crystal-gazers of his own day, to the ghost stories of Apuleius and Pliny the Younger, to the Wesley ghosts and the Drummer of Tedworth, and also to superstitions of savages, to the doings of Zulu witch-doctors as well as of alchemistical philosophers.

"The interest, to minds not superstitiously inclined, of all such stories, lies in their *uniformity*, *wide diffusion* and *ancient circulation*. Thus the tales of haunted houses, whether as attesting a real force, or merely the uniformity of human error, become part of the domain of anthropology. The science which investigates the common and universally distributed customs, myths and rites of mankind, savage or civilized, is also concerned in observing these superstitions."[115]

By this means Lang linked psychical research with his anthro-pological studies, and produced a volume of essays mainly focussed on the former subject, under the title of *Cock Lane and Common Sense*, in 1894, and in 1897 the more popular volume, *The Book of Dreams and Ghosts*, which set out mainly to tell in strictly historical form, all the best attested psychical stories, from classical times to contemporary savage parallels imparted to Lang by his cousin James Jasper Atkinson who had emigrated to the South Seas.

Lang's psychical studies were linked, after his usual manner, with such other pursuits as his historical work, and as early as 1895 he had produced a privately printed pamphlet on *The Voices of Jeanne d'Arc*, to which he returned some dozen years later in the biography, *The Maid of France*.

But in the region of anthropology, side by side with the con-sideration of psychical phenomena, which he adduced as the origin of such savage practices as fetishism, or of the powers of medicine men and witch-doctors, a new theory was developing which had found expression in *The Making of Religion* (1898), based on the Gifford lectures delivered in the previous year at St. Andrews. Professor Tylor had used "Animism," or the ghost theory, as the origin of religion, but Lang, after a careful study of Australian creeds and legends, ventured upon a new suggestion; that the earliest and most natural belief of primitive man was in a single God the Creator, the righteous Maker and Judge of men, and that degradation rather than evolution had followed in the wake of the earliest stages of civilization.

"Lang's reasoning about the savage notion of a God All-Father and Judge of men, is, as it stands, quite acceptable," writes Professor Reinach, but the weak point in the thesis is the lack of completely reliable evidence, and the danger that even the earliest Australian savages sounded on the subject may have received the indirect influence of missionaries.

The propounding of Lang's theory raised a storm of controversy, and as a whole produced no such satisfactory a result as his earlier laying of Max Müller and the Vedic Bogey. The monotheistic theory seems to have become a trifle of an obsession with him, though never sufficiently to obscure his acute critical and historical faculties. In 1899 he re-wrote *Myth, Ritual and Religion* to bring it into line with his newly-developed theories, with which he again dealt in *Magic and Religion* 1901. Following this with an increased interest in the development of human institutions, he produced *Social Origins* in 1903, under the same cover as a posthumous treatise by Atkinson called *Primal Law*, and thereby came into conflict with James Frazer over the question of Totemism, a subject in which the clear views of Lang's earlier years seem to have become rather obscured, and the determination of finding the primitive belief in religious purity to have prevented him from realizing the deeper implications of Totemism itself. In consequence of this, neither *The Secret of the Totem* (1905) nor *Method in the Study of Totemism* (1911) can be placed on the high level of his earlier books.

Considered as a whole, Lang's work in all sections of anthropology was of greatest and most permanent value in the region of popular tales and folk-lore, and his greatest feat the overthrow of the philological interpretation of myths. His books are, for the student of the subject, practically obsolete now—though the earlier ones make delightful reading for the amateur.

"It is difficult to believe that his fundamental ideas," wrote Solomon Reinach, "can ever become obsolete and be discarded. Lang has taught us that folk-lore is not, what it still was for Grimm's school, the debased residue of higher mythology, but that higher or literary mythology rests on the foundation of folk-lore. He who demonstrated that and made it a key to the darkest recesses of classical mythology has conferred a benefit on the world of learning, and was a genius."

Of Lang's own personal attitude to his anthropological studies, ample evidence has been preserved. Of all the many sides of his literary labours, this was the favourite, the subject in which he would most rather have chosen to excel. The late Professor Marett records that on one memorable occasion in the early years of this century he walked back to Merton with Lang after a dinner party, and as they neared the College, Lang remarked to him: "If I could have made a living out of it, I might have been a great anthropologist !" "So speaking in a most solemn way," continues Marett, "and before I could protest that his services to anthropology had been immense, he disappeared into the lodge door that the porter had just opened for him; and I fancied that I had been offered a glimpse of the real man, beneath an exterior for the most part singularly guarded and ironic."[116]

It was some time before anthropology as a subject in itself was recognized at Oxford, though Tylor was for long curator of the museum. On 3rd October 1891 Lang, then president of the Folk-lore Society, headed a visit of the International Folk-lore Congress to Oxford, made a speech of thanks to Tylor for conducting the party round the Pitts Rivers Collection, and then entertained many of the members to lunch in Merton. By the end of the century the subject was becoming a more recognized academic study, and being more and more considered in relation to archæology and to the classics. By 1908 Marett, who shortly afterwards was made Reader in Anthropology, was arranging for a course of lectures (published as *Anthropology and the Classics* 1908) by such authorities as Sir Arthur Evans, Lang, Gilbert Murray and J. L. Myres. Lang's lecture was on "Homer and Anthropology," and points to another field of knowledge in which he was a first-class authority.

In his earliest studies of folk-lore it was the similarity of primitive legend and classical myth that had attracted and fascinated Lang;

while Homer had at once appealed to the poet and the romantic in his nature.

Lang, it must be remembered, was a considerable classical scholar, and his knowledge of Greek was profound and very exact. Almost his earliest work was the translation of the *Odyssey*, originally undertaken alone, but produced finally in collaboration with S. H. Butcher in 1879. The merits of this and of the companion version of the *Iliad* with Walter Leaf and Ernest Myers in 1883, are strikingly high, and it is by these translations that the name of Andrew Lang is probably best remembered at the present day.

When these books appeared they were hailed straightway as classics in the narrow field of translations that survive their own period. "There seems no reason why the work should not be accepted as great, even final work, as a real and abiding acquisition to English literature," wrote the critic of *London* (15th February 1879)—Henley or Saintsbury perhaps—and for many years but few dissenting voices were raised. It was not until the late 'nineties that Samuel Butler arose in the full bloom of far-fetched originality, declaring that Nausicaa was the author of the *Odyssey*, and translating both epics into conversational prose that often approaches bathos and occasionally slang. "The difference between the Andrew Lang manner of translating the *Odyssey* and mine," wrote Butler, "is that between making a mummy and a baby. He tries to preserve a corpse (for the *Odyssey* is a corpse to all who read Lang's translation), whereas I try to originate a new life, and one that is instinct (as far as I can effect this) with the spirit though not the form of the original."[117]

The general complaint against Lang's translations was the archaic flavour which it was always his habit to impart to the diction. Lang does this consciously, and justifies the practice in his Homeric versions: "I would humbly plead that we were translating Greek which is itself archaic and composite, which never was a spoken language, and that we used no words so nearly obsolete that they are not familiar to readers of the English Bible."[118]

Professor Gilbert Murray, the greatest of all English translators from the classical Greek, describes the Butcher and Lang *Odyssey* as "a beautiful book," and points out that although in prose, and a very literal translation, it is yet a poem, and one with an exquisite style of its own—even if not quite the style of Homer as that wonderful form appears to the Greek scholar.[119] That these versions are still the most popular and widely-read of any, goes far to disprove the claim sometimes put forward that they are hopelessly "dated."

Turning aside from Homer for a while, Lang produced his unaided translation of *Theocritus, Bion and Moschus* in 1880 (preceded by "Specimens" privately printed the previous year), which is widely considered his most successful work as a translator. Here the style suits even better than in the Homeric versions, and the artificiality of the Hellenistic age found a more certain echo in Lang's own genius.

This affinity with the late Greek world is marked very clearly in the verse translations which he made in the following decade from the *Anthology*, most of which appear in the revised edition of *Grass of Parnassus* (1892) in a section called "The Little Garland." As an example may be quoted the lament from Meleager, "Heliodore Dead," which was first published as a song in Rider Haggard's *Cleopatra* :

> "Tears for my lady dead,
>   Heliodore!
> Salt tears and ill to shed,
>   Over and o'er,
> Tears for my lady dead,
>   Sighs do we send,
> Long love rememberèd,
>   Mistress and friend.
> Sad are the songs we sing,
>   Tears that we shed,
> Empty the gifts we bring,
>   Gifts to the dead.
> Go tears, and go lament!
>   Fare from her tomb,
> Wend where my lady went,
>   Down through the gloom.
> Ah, for my flower, my love,
>   Hades hath taken!
> Ah for the dust above,
>   Scattered and shaken!

> Mother of all things born,
> Earth, in thy breast,
> Lull her that all men mourn
> Gently to rest!

For the wistful tenderness of the music, and the closeness of word and spirit to the original, such renderings as this have never been surpassed—and equalled only perhaps by Cory in his version of the Callimachus lament for Heraclitus, and by Beeching in the lines from Alcman that Lang quotes in the preface to *Aucassin and Nicolete*.

And the humorous poet in Lang found also an echo in occasional corners of Greek literature, as the Cloud Chorus from Aristophanes shows, or this unreprinted piece from the *Greek Anthology* (which appeared in the *Illustrated London News* for 2nd March 1907):

> "A deaf man with a deaf man had a plea;
> The judge was much the deafest of the three:
> The plaintiff asked for three months' rent, his right;
> Defendant said: ' *I* grind my corn *at night* ! '
> The judge looked down: ' Why thus implead each other ?
> You're *both* her sons, must *both* support your mother! ' "

The number of verse translations from the Greek is, however, sadly meagre, and Lang seldom practised this art after the *Grass of Parnassus* collection; nor did he attempt a version in prose except in the case of the *Homeric Hymns*, which appeared in 1899, though he had published the "Hymn to Dionysus" as early as July 1886 in the *Magazine of Art*: and, as has been said, he was at one time anxious to translate Quintus of Smyrna into prose.

But from the time of the *Odyssey*, Lang had been interested in another side of Homeric scholarship. At first, he used his anthropological lore merely to elucidate obscure points in ritualistic or mythological survival; but, fortified thereto by a careful study of the world's epic and ballad literature—*Beowulf*, *The Kalevala* (on which he wrote an essay in 1872), *The Vedas*, the *Song of Roland*, besides the folk-ballads of Scotland and of Europe, and the Sagas—he turned his attention to the problem of the origin and authorship of the Homeric poems, publishing his first book on the subject, *Homer and the Epic*, in 1893.

The book, "a brilliant book," as Professor Shewan admits it to
be, was mainly polemical, and "shows up" the many and manifold
absurdities of "separatist" critics, who would dissect the *Iliad* and
Odyssey into a patchwork of many hands and times. Illustrating
from his cyclopædic knowledge of ballads, epics, fairy-tales and
civilized literature of all races, using his great and varied knowledge
of primitive culture and survivals, and illuminating the whole with
his humorous common sense and his gifts of literary appreciation,
Lang makes very satisfactory play with most of his opponents. And
if he does not prove any new theory, yet his book is, as Professor
Gilbert Murray, his most notable adversary in Homeric controversy, admits, "a contribution of real value. He shook a current
orthodoxy of criticism, and compelled it to reconsider its methods,
and to restate its problems."

From first to last Lang believed almost passionately in the unity
of Homer: as a poet and critic he could not conceive that two of the
world's greatest poems were other than the work of a single great
poet—the theory of a plurality of authors, of a compilation or
redaction in the early classical period, seemed to him unthinkable.
Interpolations there might be—the Lay of Demodocus, the last
book of the *Odyssey*, a few passages in the Catalogue of Ships,
perhaps—but these could not be more than trifling additions, and
the poems themselves were in essentials the work of one supreme
poet, Homer.

In his second book, *Homer and His Age* (1908), Lang set himself
to the problem from a different angle, trying to show that the
culture and the society described by Homer belong to one moment
of time, and could never be either the conscious archaising of later
poets, or the haphazard mingling of many centuries.

Lang placed the Homeric Age at the end of the second millen-
ium before Christ, a period long considered among the darkest in
history or pre-history, but just then, as a result of the excavations
of Sir Arthur Evans, and others, at Knossos and Mycenæ, emerg-
ing into brilliant sunshine as an age of peace and culture.

His last work, *The World of Homer* (1910) which is perhaps the
most enduring of the three, expands this theory, besides answering
and discussing the new "Separatist" views put forward by Professor Murray in *The Rise of the Greek Epic*.

The whole subject, though fascinating to the student of such things, is far too intricate and detailed to elaborate here. Only it may be said that Lang's beliefs as to the unity of Homer, as to the historical accuracy of his age, seem on the way to a glorious and triumphant ratification. Archæology supports the unity of the Homeric world more and more definitely, the excavation of Troy (interrupted by the war of 1939-45) is revealing even the poet's apparent knowledge of the place itself; the most recent discoveries in Crete and Greece tend towards it. All things point to the fact that, as Professor Shewan puts it in his lecture on *Andrew Lang's Work for Homer*, "Lang was right in his view of Homer and his age . . . Those who agree with Lang can await further developments without misgiving, indeed, with confidence that, in Pindar's words, the days to come will prove the wisest witnesses."

Such things, both of Homeric and Anthropological scholarship, are for the specialist; but we may read what Lang, the great interpreter, wrote of all these matters in his straightforward, lucid, fascinating style, and delight in them for their own interest and for the sake of the strange genius who loved them and wrote out of his love as surely as in his poems and his romantic tales.

We may follow him through the bewildering "witch wood" of *Myth, Ritual and Religion*, as through the more homely parkland of the *Homeric Hymns* and the essays on them, which Professor Murray ranked most highly of Lang's Homeric writings. But inevitably we shall return most often to the translations: to wistful lyrics of Meleager and Antipater and Asclepiades, but most surely of all to sunny plains of Sicily where Theocritus shepherded his flocks, and to the mysterious world of early Greece on whose shore breaks "The surge and thunder of the *Odyssey*"—that *Odyssey* to read which is, as Henley, poet and critic, knew and described, "to have a breath of the clear and serene airs that blew through the antique Hellas; to catch a glimpse of the large, new morning light that bathes the seas and highlands of the young heroic world. In a space of shining and fragrant clarity you have a vision of marble columns and stately cities, of men august in simple-heartedness and strength, and women comely and simple and superb as goddesses; and with a music of leaves and winds and waters, of plunging ships and clanging armour, of girls at song and kindly gods discoursing, the sunny-eyed heroic age is revealed in all its nobleness, in all its majesty, its candour and its charm."[120]

CHAPTER VIII

The Master of Fairyland

THE Border boy, dwelling in a land of old enchantments, among hills and rivers haunted by the legends and ballads of the early days, amidst woods fragrant with old songs and old beliefs, must almost of necessity have believed in fairies. Remembering how the Selkirk boys met together of an evening to "swap" fairy-tales, how Lang delighted to wander away up the wild and silent valleys with his fishing rod; how he would sit on the green slope between the old ruin of Fairnilee and the murmuring Tweed half seen amid the green leaves; and how he would hasten back to Viewfield in the twilight, half scared of the ghosts and bogles of which he had been reading and whose ancient haunts were among the places nearby and most familiar to him: remembering all these early influences, it seems only right that the name of Andrew Lang should still be linked most naturally and universally with fairy books.

In his boyhood the old fairy beliefs and legends, the real folklore, were still alive in the Border country: old Nancy, the Langs' nurse, would more than half have believed the stories of ghosts and fairies, of Whuppity Stoorie and the Red Etin, which she told to her little charges in the long winter evenings by the nursery fire.

And as Andrew grew older, he read for himself all the fairy-tales that he could possibly lay hands on. Madame d'Aulnoy came earliest, and Grimm's *Household Stories*; the fairies of literature in *A Midsummer Night's Dream*, and of humour in *The Rose and the Ring*, but most of all, the old traditional tales, told to him orally at first, accessible only in Grimm, and in the sophisticated versions of Perrault, and the collections derived from the *Cabinet des Fees*, but increasing year by year as he grew older—growing as the basic fairy-tale collections were issued: *The Heroes* (1856), *Heroes of Asgard* (1857), Planché's *French Fairy Tales* (1858), Dasent's *Tales from the Norse* (1859).

Folk-lore and ballad literature were thus the deepest and most potent influences on Lang as a boy, and their influence was increased and broadened into an intellectual as well as a sentimental interest as he became more and more engrossed in the study of anthropology.

Thus it was as an anthropologist that Lang came first to the serious consideration of fairy stories, and the result was that for long he felt almost a distaste for the more literary tales. "The folklorist is not unnaturally jealous," he wrote, "of what, in some degree, looks like folk-lore. He apprehends that purely literary stories may win their way, pruned of their excrescences, to the fabulous, and may confuse the speculations of later mythologists . . . There was a time when I regarded all *contes*, except *contes populaires*, as frivolous and vexatious."[121]

But even by the time that his first collection of traditional fairy-tales, *The Blue Fairy Book* (1889) appeared, Lang had fallen away from his earlier and rather fanatical intolerance, and had already written three literary fairy stories of his own.

The "Fairy Book Series," however, contained little besides traditional tales, although these were adapted and re-written so as to make them suitable for children. It is actually only the first of the series that contains much besides folk-tales—and Lang departs further than he ever does in later volumes from any settled scheme. Thus, besides five stories from Madame d'Aulnoy, one from Madame Le Prince de Beaumont and one adaption from Madame de Villeneuve, there are two from *The Arabian Nights*, and—strangest choice of all—a condensed version of the first part of *Gulliver's Travels* made by May Kendall. How Lang came to allow this last to be included is inexplicable, for it is quite alien to anything in any of the fairy books, which never again depart from the traditional tales further than Madame d'Aulnoy, Hans Andersen and "The Three Bears."

But the book was an experiment, and of a kind that must have caused a certain amount of anxiety to Longman, the publisher, even with the great "draw" of Lang's name. For at that time the fairy-tale had almost ceased to be read in British nurseries, and the novel of child life, the stories of Mrs. Ewing, Mrs. Molesworth, and L. T. Meade, were the only fare. Writing early in 1889 in her history of children's books, Mrs. E. M. Field says: "At the present moment the fairy-tale seems to have given way entirely in popularity to the child's story of real life, the novel of childhood, in which no effort is spared to make children appear as they are." But just before the publication of the book early in 1891, she added a note: "Since the above was written eighteen months ago, the tide of popularity seems to have set strongly in the direction of the old fairy stories."[122]

It would probably be no exaggeration to say that Lang was entirely responsible for this change in the public taste; for *The Blue Fairy Book* (1889) and *The Red Fairy Book* (1890), were both enormously popular from the very start, and the later volumes in the series were sure always of a wide and appreciative welcome.

The earlier fairy books were issued also in limited editions on large paper, and for the first two of these Lang wrote Introductions of some interest which do not appear in the ordinary editions. Otherwise, his own share in any of the fairy books is limited almost exclusively to the Preface—and, of course, the actual selection and choice of the stories included. These are drawn from nearly every race and nation of the ancient or modern world, and are the finest and most enduring monument to Andrew Lang the folklorist.

The tales themselves were retold, translated or adapted mainly by Mrs. Lang, though in the earlier volumes she had the assistance of many people, including May Kendall, Florence Sellar and Sir W. A. Craigie. The *True Story Book* and its sequel boast a greater variety of authors, including Rider Haggard, Florence Sellar and Lang himself, who told the story of Joan of Arc at some length.

Only in the first two fairy books proper does Lang re-tell any of the stories, and there his work is of considerable interest. In *The Blue Fairy Book* he takes the story of Perseus, drawing his material from Pindar, Simonides and Apollodoros, but he recasts it in the form of an ordinary folk-tale by the suppression of all personal and local names; Perseus is simply "The Prince," while even the Herperides appear as "The Western Fairies," singing a song as non-committal as their name:

"Round and round the apples of gold,
Round and round dance we;
Thus do we dance from the days of old
About the enchanted tree:

> Round and round and round we go,
> While the Spring is green or the stream shall flow,
>   Or the wind shall stir the sea."

The similar song which Danæ sings is, however, an actual translation from the lyric contained in a fragment by Simonides.

The absence of names is not, of course, essential to the ordinary folk-tale; but in the case of such a story as this, it is only by such a suppression that it can be regarded with any ease as a fairy-tale of the type best exemplified in the Grimm collection, and not merely as a fragment of the grand legendary history of Homeric Greece.

In *The Red Fairy Book* (1890), Lang re-tells "The Story of Sigurd" from Morris's version of the Volsunga saga, and treats it rather as he had done "The Terrible Head," though without suppressing the names. This gives us the impression that Lang considered a northern setting still to be suitable for a fairy-tale, but that the Greek scene, by literary association, was no longer sufficiently simple and wild. Lang supports this in an interesting essay on "Literary Fairy Tales" which he prefixed as an Introduction to a story by the Dutch writer, F. van Eeden, which appeared in English as *Little Johannes* in 1895. After discussing the usual ingredients of "The Märchen, or child's story," he goes on to say that "The civilized peoples have elaborated their child-like tales into the chief romantic myths, as of the Ship Argo, and the sagas of Heracles and Odysseus . . . European peasants keep them in shapes far more akin to the savage than to the Greek form."

It could, however, be argued that the Greek myths present versions of the traditional tales containing far purer traces of their savage origin than the oral tales handed down by peasants, vitiated and adulterated from generation to generation, until recorded by the folklorists of the nineteenth century.

However this may be, Lang's aim is obvious, and in none of the other fairy books does he include any but savage or folk-tales, the *French Cabinet des Fées* and Hans Andersen being the only sophisticated stories admitted. And he does not again attempt to adapt any stories from the "higher mythology" of Greece, Egypt or Scandinavia, though, of course, the northern folk-tales are included.

G

When, later, he came to re-tell the Greek myths for children, he presented his *Tales of Troy and Greece* (1907) in the tradition of Kingsley's *Heroes*; and we feel that it is Lang the classical scholar rather than Lang the folklorist who is telling of "Odysseus the Sacker of Cities" or "The Story of the Golden Fleece."

Now although Lang never wavered from his devotion to the old traditional fairy-tales, he did soften in his early austerity towards the literary, sophisticated and burlesque fairy story. Writing in *The Academy* of 16th May, 1874, he solemnly rebukes Charles Deulin for not presenting his *Contes du Roi Gambrinus* in their primitive Märchen form: but in 1886 Lang himself re-tells the story of *Johnny Nut and the Golden Goose* from Deulin's book, and in so doing sophisticates his original still more. Again, in *The Academy* of 15th July, 1875, in reviewing Mrs. Ewing's *Jan of the Windmill*, Lang's highest praise for her method is that she "never burlesques things old" as do other writers for children—yet among these other condemned story-tellers Thackeray stands supreme, and twenty years later Lang is praising him for his treatment of the traditional fairy-tale in *The Rose and the Ring*, where he "burlesques it with a kindly mockery."[123]

But it was out of his profound knowledge of folk-tales and his intimate acquaintance with all the formulæ of the traditional stories that Lang drew the inspiration for his own original tales. Only in *The Gold of Fairnilee* does he stay away from what had become the recognized method of writing a modern fairy-tale; but in the Pantouflia stories, and also in the little *Princess Nobody*, he is following in the steps of a respectable literary tradition, taking Thackeray as his most immediate model.

In its earliest form the literary fairy-story grew directly out of the folk-tale, and was indeed little more than a sophisticated version of the popular original. Charles Perrault seems to have laid the foundation stone of the fairy edifice with his *Contes de Ma Mere Oye* in 1697, for although he is telling the old folk-tales such as "Cinderella" and "Toads and Diamonds," he is inclined to polish his original and to make it as polite and genteel as may be; and, most important innovation of all, wherever his basic tale introduces a ghost, daimon or wonder-working beast, he substitutes a fairy.

Now the true fairy represents, on the whole, a distinct tradition, which may best be dealt with when considering such a work as *The Gold of Fairnilee*; but Perrault took the literary product of the old stark folk superstition, which had already been refined and made a creature of beauty and imagination by Shakespeare and the poets, and grafted it on to the Märchen stem, where of old it grew not. For the "fairy-tales" of the brothers Grimm boast few fairies, and they are rare indeed among the traditional tales of other nations.

A year after Perrault's famous little book, Madame la Contesse de Murat laid even more stress on the identity of the characters in her *Contes des Fées:* but the greatest name in the annals of fairyland is that of Madame d'Aulnoy, who began to produce her fairy-tales during the first years of the eighteenth century.

"Madame d'Aulnoy is the true mother of the modern fairy story," says Lang. "She invented the modern Court of Fairyland, with its manners, its fairies . . . its queens, its amorous, its cruel, its good, its evil, its odious and its friendly fées; illustrious beings, the councillors of kings, who are now treated with religious respect, and now are propitiated with ribbons, scissors and sweetmeats. The fairies are as old as the Hathors of Egypt . . . but Madame d'Aulnoy first developed them into our familiar fées of fairy-tale . . . It is from Madame d'Aulnoy that *The Rose and the Ring* of Thackeray derives its illustrious lineage. The banter is only an exaggerated form of her charming manner."[124]

The country of the literary fairies is a most accommodating clime, and absorbs to itself every possible characteristic that it can encompass. Madame d'Aulnoy's fées were human-sized beings who dwelt in courts closely resembling that of Louis XIV; but the genuine fairy of old belief was of dwarfish ancestry, and had been drastically reduced in stature by Shakespeare, and such crude followers of his delicate suggestion as William King and the anonymous author of "Queen Mab's Invitation," thus paving the way for the usual type of tiny fairy common in Victorian stories. And it needed but to graft on to them the wings that grew between the minute shoulders of the Rosicrucian sylphs of the Count de Gabalis and "The Rape of the Lock," to complete the picture.

At the dawn of the Victorian period came the folk-tales of Grimm to complicate the issue; and so strong was their influence that German very soon became the language of fairyland—of Märchenland, we would fain say, borrowing the title from F. Anstey's delicious fantasy of the fairy world, *In Brief Authority*.

The year of Lang's birth, 1844, saw perhaps the earliest fusion of Grimm and the French Fairy Court, in a forgotten tale, *The Hope of the Katzekopfs* by the Reverend Francis Edward Paget, where the new tradition is exemplified very clearly.

And when Thackeray came in 1855 to construct the greatest of this kind of fairy-story, *The Rose and the Ring*, it remained only for him to introduce the hearty burlesque element from Fielding's extravaganza, *Tom Thumb the Great* (1730), which is best echoed in the heroic blank verse of his kings and princes, in their deliciously exaggerated characters, and in the names of many of his personages.

This type of story remained fairly static after Thackeray's book appeared, and little progress was made in its development until Lang came to it in the early 'nineties, and E. Nesbit produced her *Unlikely Tales* in and after 1900.

A few experiments were made after Thackeray to lead the fairy-story away in other directions. *Alice in Wonderland* appeared ten years later, and produced many worthless imitations, some of which, such as *Wanted—A King*, by "Maggie Browne" (Margaret Hamer) sought, without much success, to link up the new wonder tale with the older traditions.

Lewis Carroll himself also experimented in this direction, as the children's portions of *Sylvie and Bruno* show; but the general tendency was towards the tale of wonder in a real life setting, of which George MacDonald seems to have been the inventor, and which Mrs. Molesworth explored further in such of her early books as *The Cuckoo Clock* (1877), before joining the ranks of undiluted realism beside Juliana Ewing and L. T. Meade.

But Lang, before he came to write his more serious fairy-stories, and before *The Blue Fairy Book* had made him king undisputed of the nursery shelf, had tossed off, in the midst of his anthropological labours, a little *jeu d'esprit* that is now quite forgotten, *The Princess Nobody, A Tale of Fairyland* (1884).

This book seems to have been suggested to him by his friend and publisher, Charles Longman. For the firm had published in 1869 a tall, slim, green volume called *In Fairyland: Pictures from the Elf*

World, wherein "Dicky" Doyle (designer of the cover of *Punch* and illustrator of *The King of the Golden River*, and *The Cricket on the Hearth*) pictured in a series of forty paintings a vast and various number of elves and fairies, both winged and wingless, disporting themselves among flowers and trees, with birds and insects as playfellows. To accompany—but hardly to explain—these pictures, William Allingham had supplied a number of fairy poems.

It made a very attractive volume, and the pictures have a fascination and a charm that is all their maker's own—but it was hardly a children's book.

Lang, however, took most of the pictures and wrote a little fairy-tale to fit them. Some five illustrations are omitted, most of the rest are cut down, while the double-page "Plate IV" of the earlier volume is divided into nine sections which appear, uncoloured, throughout *The Princess Nobody*. Lang weaves his story round the pictures with considerable ingenuity, and very seldom do we feel that anything is brought in to account for an illustration; one or two that play no particular part in the story have little verses under them, but this is a rare concession.

Another difficulty, that of making the same person recognizable in a number of pictures—for there was little or no continuity in the original volume—is cunningly explained by the number of transformations that befall the hero, Prince Comical. Only one point seems to have baffled Lang, and that is why Princess Niente has wings in some pictures but not in others—and on this, wisely, he makes no comment!

The story itself is very slight, and consists mainly of a regrouping of certain elements traditional in many nursery tales and folk-legends, both savage and civilized.

It opens with the familiar childless King, promised a child on condition that he gives "Nobody" to the dwarfish prophet; in blithe ignorance the King promises—and finds on his return to court that a child has been born to him in his absence, a princess who, until he has chosen a name for her, has been called Niente or Nobody. When she grows up, the dwarf comes to claim her, and the King is forced to submit; but he offers Niente's hand in marriage to any prince who will restore her, and a whole host sets out, including Prince Comical, who is so ugly that all the rest make a mock of him. But he has a kind heart, and on the way he protects a Daddy-long-legs who is being tormented by some wicked fairies, and the grateful creature warns his deliverer not to sleep under the magic mushrooms. Prince Comical tells his companions, but they deride his warning, and are cast into an enchanted sleep. Guided by a friendly Black Beetle, Prince Comical steals the egg from the Blue Bird, who is thus persuaded to tell him where to find Niente. He then visits the Queen of Mushroomland, who transforms him from plain Prince Comical into handsome Prince Charming, and gives Niente to him on the one condition that he shall never know her real name. He, of course, discovers the name, speaks it—and the Princess "softly and suddenly vanished away." However, in the end, the Water Fairy, who was the godmother of the Princess, brings back Niente (or Gwendoline) to him. They journey home together, the other princes come out of their magic sleep, Prince Comical regains the form of Prince Charming (which he had lost when he spoke the forbidden name), and he and Gwendoline live happily ever afterwards.

The attraction of the story is very simple, and is of course inseparable from Doyle's delightful pictures. There is gentle, almost wistful, charm in the echoes of so many nursery tales, and Lang's rondeau at the end enshrines this sentiment:

> *Au temps jadis*! As Perrault says,
> In half-forgotten fairy days!—
> "There lived a king once and a queen,
> As few there are, as more have been,"—
> Ah, still we love the well-worn phrase,
> Still love to tread the ancient ways,
> To break the fence, to thread the maze,
> To see the beauty we have seen,
> > *Au temps jadis* !
> Here's luck to every child that strays
> In Fairyland among the Fays:
> That follows through the forest green
> Prince Comical and Gwendoline;
> That reads the tales we used to praise
> > *Au temps jadis* !

In 1888 Lang turned aside from the high road of the literary fairy story to seek his inspiration for *The Gold of Fairnilee* among the dark shadows of the genuine old fairy beliefs. But a year later he returned to the Fairy Court tradition, and wrote *Prince Prigio*, the first of his *Chronicles of Pantouflia*.

In this series, even more than in *The Princess Nobody*, Lang employs the methods which he assigns to the old folk-tales; "a certain number of incidents are shaken into many varying combinations, like the fragments of coloured glass in the kaleidoscope."[125] "Nobody can write a *new* fairy-tale; you can only mix up and dress up the old, old stories, and put the characters into new dresses."[126] "The old, old fairy-tales *are* the best: it is a very difficult thing indeed to write a good fairy story nowadays, but if I know a really good one, it is *The Rose and the Ring*."[127]

It is admittedly Thackeray that Lang follows, though just as Thackeray had added to the store laid up by Madame d'Aulnoy, so Lang goes still further than he, drawing incidents and citing authorities very far removed from the simple traditional tales. It is story-land rather than fairyland in which Lang's tales are set, and in *Prince Prigio* he acknowledges his "several obligations to the Learned," which include Allan Quatermain, Cyrano de Bergèrac and M. Paul Sébillot (an anthropologist); while in *Prince Ricardo* his most obvious debts are to Madame d'Aulnoy, Cornelius Agrippa, Ariosto, *The Arabian Nights*, and the history of Scotland.

But the guiding spirit is Thackeray's: King Grognio is own cousin to Valoroso, and Captain McDougal, who "maintained a stern military reserve" when the whole court was in tears, is nearly allied to Captain Kuttazoff Hedzoff. Indeed, Grognio claims descent, in the story, from Cinderella and Prince Giglio—by which means Lang "places" his stories in the history of Märchenland.

In the collected edition (*My Own Fairy Book*, 1896) of his fairy tales, Lang groups *Prigio* and *Ricardo* together as *Chronicles of Pantouflia* (under which title they were later reprinted as a separate volume) and he gives, in a Preface, a delightful account of the founding of the royal family of this "central European" kingdom, which was descended, he tells us, from the "Hypnotidœ" of Greece, and whose crest "is a dormouse, dormant, proper, on a field vert, and the motto, when translated out of the original Greek, means *Anything for a Quiet Life*."

Lang's own, slightly quizzical, account of his fairy stories describes them excellently: "In truth I never did write any fairy books in my life, except *Prince Prigio*, *Prince Ricardo*, and *Tales of a Fairy Court*, that of the aforesaid Prigio. . . . They are rich in romantic adventure, and the Princes always marry the right Princesses and live happy ever afterwards, while the wicked witches, step-mothers, tutors and governesses are *never* cruelly punished, but retire to the country on ample pensions. I hate cruelty: and I never put a wicked step-mother in a barrel and send her tobogganing down a hill. It is true that Prince Ricardo *did* kill the Yellow Dwarf; but that was in fair fight, sword in hand, and the dwarf, peace to his ashes, died in harness! "[128] As he wrote this in 1910, *The Princess Nobody* would have been long out of print; while he obviously considers that *The Gold of Fairnilee* belongs to quite a different class of story.

The first of the Pantouflia series, *Prince Prigio*, appeared in 1889, a little square green book, printed in green type (and also in a limited edition on large paper, printed in black) with illustrations by Gordon Browne (the son of "Phiz") who ranks with Walter Crane and H. R. Millar, the most popular and successful illustrators of children's books in the later Victorian and Edwardian periods.

The story begins in the usual way with the King and Queen who have everything to make them happy except children. At last, however, Prigio is born. Then comes the question of whom to ask to the christening: King Grognio is anxious to invite all the fairies, but the Queen does not believe in them, and refuses to encourage his foolish superstition. But the guests all refuse to come, and the fairies turn up uninvited, and leave Prigio a collection of magic presents such as the Sword of Sharpness, Seven-League Boots and the like; but the cross old fairy wishes that he shall be "too clever." When the party is over, the Queen clears away all the gifts (which she regards as "pantomime properties") into a disused attic, where they are soon forgotten. Prigio grows up "too clever by half," and earns everyone's dislike by being always right: "He showed the fencing master how to fence, and the professional cricketer how to bowl . . . He set sums to the Chancellor of the Exchequer . . . He found out all his tutors and masters in the same horrid way; correcting the accent of his French teacher, and trying to get his German tutor not to eat peas with his knife. He also endeavoured to teach the Queen-dowager, his grandmother, an art with which she had long been perfectly familiar! "

When Prigio and his two younger brothers, Alphonso and Enrico, are growing up, a Fire-drake appears in the neighbourhood and causes a drought in the country. King Grognio, who hated Prigio even more than other people did, "was not ill pleased, for," thought he, "of course my three sons must go after the brute, the eldest first, and as usual it will kill the first two and be beaten by the youngest. It is a little hard on Enrico, poor boy, but anything to get rid of that Prigio! " This fairy-tale reasoning did not, however, appeal to that Prince (who, by the way, was lying on a sofa "doing sums in compound division for fun"), and he pointed out that if the King were right, the youngest brother, Alphonso, was the correct person to send. Prigio, it should be stated, treated the matter so lightly because he had been brought up by his excellent mother not to believe in Fire-drakes, or anything else supernatural. The two younger Princes set forth in turn, but neither of them came back; and when Grognio called upon Prigio to follow their example, the Prince produced such excellent and conclusive reasons for not doing so, that the King "withdrew into a solitary place where he could express himself with freedom." When he returned from this "solitary place where he had been speaking his mind," he ordered all the court to pack up and depart from the palace, leaving Prigio there alone.

The Prince, deprived by the mischievous courtiers of cloak, boots and money, stumbles by chance on the fairy gifts, uses them, and is most puzzled when their properties begin to be apparent— until he meets the lady Rosalind, and falling in love with her, suddenly finds himself able to believe in fairy things. At length he sets out to slay the Fire-drake, having promised to give the horns and tail of it to his lady, and accomplishes its destruction by setting it to fight the Remora, or Ice-Beast of whose existence his vast reading makes him aware in the pages of Cyrano de Bergerac. A number of complications follow, including the incident of Benson, the butler (who obtains possession of the relics of the Fire-drake and straightway claims to have killed it). And finally Prigio is set the task of restoring to life Enrico and Alphonso, which he accomplishes with the aid of the "water from the Fountain of Lions"; and at the same time he restores a whole host of knights of "every

age and every clime" who had been frozen by the Remora—each
of whom "lifted his sword and shouted ' Long live Prince Prigio! '
in Greek, Latin, Egyptian, French, German and Spanish—all of
which the Prince perfectly understood and spoke like a native."
So all ends happily with the marriage of Prigio and Rosalind, and
he wishes, with the aid of the Wishing Cap, that he may "seem no
cleverer than other people," after which "he became the most
popular Prince, and finally the best beloved King who had ever
sat on the throne of Pantouflia."

Even this bald outline serves to show in what ways Lang
departed from the Thackeray model, and how he made this well-
explored region so much his own by means of the feeling for the
world of fiction as a real place, and by the whimsical use of
quotation and literary reference. It is, in fact, only a simplified
form of the method with which he had experimented in *The Mark
of Cain* and was to use again with increased effect in *The Disentanglers*. And it bears a certain relation also to the epistolary
parodies which he must have been writing at about the same time,
and which appeared the following year as *Old Friends*.

Such a method was admirably suited to the creation of Prigio
himself, who is most cleverly conceived; for he still remains
interesting and attractive even when living up to his name in the
most aggravating fashion. Another character whom Lang was well
able to portray was the Queen, who does not believe in fairies and
magic, even against the evidence of her own senses. Is there
perhaps a trace here of Lang's attitude of amused petulance
towards the "realist" young lady novelist of the period, whom he
describes in his anonymous satire "The Log-Rolliad":

> "While female Sceptics scream with acrid scoff
> Their Faith that *Miracles do not come off*!
> And then refute the story which they tell
> By this weird Portent, that *their* Stories sell! "[129]

Certainly she is a delightfully trying person, and her stubborn-
ness creates many opportunities for most amusing touches. When,
for example, she has, unintentionally, been transported from the
court to a distant castle by magic carpet, she refuses to return by
the same means, which she still considers "childish and im-

possible," and accordingly sets out by carriage. "The King, Benson and the Prince were not so particular, and they simply flew back to Falkenstein in the usual way, arriving at 11.35—a week before Her Majesty"—who arrives, very bored and quite convinced that nothing unusual has been happening, right at the end of the book!

Another amusing character is Benson, the English Ambassador's butler. A note in the Preface that "the return of Benson (Chapter XII) is the fruit of the research of the late Mr. Allan Quatermain," suggests that Rider Haggard had invented the incident; and the similarity between the speech of Benson and of Haggard's comic servants (such as Job in *She* or the butler in *The Ancient Allan*) may even mean that Haggard lent more practical help: otherwise, Lang has caught his friend's manner very delightfully. Haggard certainly advised Lang during the writing of the story, for Lang writes such questions as "Doesn't my fairy tale need a more vivacious beginning, and what about Alphonso and Enrico ? " in his letters of the period.[130]

And yet another debt, which Lang acknowledges in the Preface, is to "the lady" whose "invention of erudition" suggested Prigio's final wish which rounds off the story so satisfyingly: Mrs. Lang says that "the lady" was a little girl—her niece, Miss Thrya Alleyne.

The second in the series, *Prince Ricardo of Pantouflia: Being the Adventures of Prince Prigio's Son*, which appeared in 1893, is a pendant to the original book.

While Prigio had been kept from a belief in fairies and the use of magical properties, Ricardo goes to the other extreme, and spends his time dashing about the world on the Shoes of Swiftness, killing monsters with the Sword of Sharpness, much to the detriment of his education and his party manners. Prigio, in an attempt to teach him a lesson, substitutes shams for most of the fairy accessories, with the result that Ricardo fails in an attempt to restore Prince Charlie to the English throne, and is only rescued from a difficult situation by the resourcefulness of the magically-endowed Princess Jacqueline who is in love with him. Ricardo, profiting by his discomfiture, mends his ways, and (his education having in the meantime, we presume, embraced the works of Madame d'Aulnoy) sets out to slay in fair fight the Yellow Dwarf—

who is perhaps the only example of a villain left triumphant at the end of a fairy-tale.

Ricardo's next adventure is with the "Giant-who-does-not-know-when-he-has-had-enough," which ends in disaster, as Jacqueline is captured and shut up in the mountain under which dwells the Earthquaker. Prigio comes to her aid with his superior knowledge, and destroys the monster by dropping on to him a lump of the heaviest substance in existence, namely, Stupidity, which he fetches from its storehouse on the Moon. This also saves Manoa, the City of the Sun, which the Earthquaker was about to destroy, and which turns out to be ruled by Jacqueline's father. So all ends happily with her marriage to Ricardo, and Prigio remains King of Pantouflia—"No need such kings should ever die! "

Prince Ricardo is not altogether as successful as *Prince Prigio*, largely on account of its lack of plot, and the episodic nature of its incidents, which occasionally seem a trifle forced and unwieldy—while *Prigio* goes all with a swing and an inevitability that is irresistible.

The adventure with Prince Charlie bears no relation to the plot of the book, and is so alien as to seem a disfigurement, nor is the Giant quite as satisfactory a monster as either Fire-drake in *Prigio*, or even the Yellow Dwarf in *Ricardo*. This is the more to be regretted, as there are scenes in the book of exquisite humour, and touches also of poetic feeling that is absent from *Prigio*. The adventure on the Moon is one of these scenes, and the chapter describing how Princess Jacqueline "Drank the Moon" to learn King Prigio's secret is an even more charming example, and contains a very attractive magic spell, versified from Cornelius Agrippa's *Fourth Book of Occult Philosophy*:—

> "Oh Lady Moon, on the waters riding,
>   On shining waters, in silver sheen,
> Show me the secret the heart is hiding,
>   Show me the truth of the thought, oh Queen!

> "Oh waters white, where the Moon is riding,
>   That knows what shall be, and what has been,
> Tell me the secret the heart is hiding,
>   Wash me the truth of it, clear and clean! "

Prince Ricardo differs from its predecessor in being assigned to a definite period in history, for a reference to Beatrix Esmond, and the introduction of Prince Charlie at the age of fifteen would date it as 1735; from which we would assume that the events described in the main portion of *Prince Prigio* happened in 1718; but the cheque which King Grognio makes out to Prigio is dated 1768— a sad slip in chronology on the part of that monarch—or of the meticulous historian Andrew Lang!

Actually, *Prince Prigio* has no very definite period, and Gordon Browne's illustrations suggest the late middle ages or the early sixteenth century. But in *Ricardo* he observes the eighteenth century setting with care; as does A. A. Dixon, also, in *Tales of a Fairy Court*, even though in other respects he does not seem to have read his original with much attention.

As regards this, the last work in the series, very little need be said. It was published in 1907, and is very much an attempt to recapture the atmosphere of the earlier volumes. It is more a collection of short stories than a complete whole, and is built, not very carefully, round *Prince Prigio*, much of which has in consequence to be retold in a shortened form which departs from the original in a number of ways, such as the marriage of one of Prigio's brothers to the Giant's daughter—though in the former story we are told quite clearly that both brothers "were in love with their two cousins," Molinda and Kathleena, whom in the end they married. Though of little importance, such inconsistencies as this suggest that Lang's power of imagining the world of fiction and fairy-tale as a real world was of a spasmodic and unthinking kind, and not the result of any orderly and preconceived plan. Lang seems to have been a trifle untidy and vague in his habits— constantly losing important letters and manuscripts—and this lack of method is reflected in all his fiction, though it is surprisingly absent from his more serious work.

Tales of a Fairy Court is the most scrappy of the fairy stories, and the book as a whole is inferior to *Prince Ricardo*. Here, again, the introduction of an adventure in a Scottish historical setting detracts greatly from the verisimilitude. But in other respects the use of the traditional fairy machinery is as clever and as amusingly worked out as in the earlier books; though here, too, the lack of plot makes itself felt again and again.

This was the last of Lang's adventures into the realm of Fairy-land, and is itself isolated from the earlier period when he was exploring that dim region in so many directions.

Only in the editing of the old, old tales did he persist until the end of his life, and to cull these he was obliged to go ever further afield. And the unusual nature of the later "Fairy Books" helped still more to perpetuate the belief that Lang was actually the author of the whole series. As late as 1910, when *The Lilac Fairy Book* appeared, he is still denying this imputation: "My part has been that of Adam, according to Mark Twain, in the Garden of Eden. Eve worked, Adam superintended. I also superintend. I find out where the stories are . . . *I do not write the stories out of my own head.* The reputation of having written all the Fairy Books (a European reputation in Nurseries and in the United States of America) is . . . slowly killing me! "

CHAPTER IX

Fairnilee and Pantouflia

As a writer of original fairy stories, Andrew Lang was very much the literary man at play, and was usually content to let his light and Puckish fancy dance gaily among the scenes and situations of a generally accepted and somewhat artificial Fairyland.

But on one occasion he seems to have thrown off his habitual "cloak of indifference and light banter," and, seeking for a new and deeper well of magical and romantic inspiration, to have found it in the legends and memories of his much-loved Border home.

"For us," he writes, "the true poetry is the poetry that wakes again the true self; the wistful soul slumbering undisturbed in the tumult of the world, and only aroused, like the Sleeping Princess in the Scottish fairy-tale, by the magic song".[131] And in his case the magic song was the music of the Tweed and of the waters of the north wandering among the hills where dwelt yet the echoes of old story and old belief.

> "A mist of memory broods and floats,
>   · The Border waters flow;
> The air is full of ballad notes
>   Borne out of long ago.
>
> "Old songs that sung themselves to me,
>   Sweet through a boy's day-dream,
> While Trout below the blossom'd tree
>   Plashed in the golden stream."[132]

"The spirit of Faery," he said, "is a Northern spirit"[133], and it was this spirit that he invoked when he wrote *The Gold of Fairnilee* in 1888.

In deserting all the literary traditions of Fairyland and going for his inspiration to the Border ballads and to the ancient folk beliefs and superstitions, Lang was not acting unreasonably or from any spirit of forced innovation: for the fairies of the north are indeed the true fairies, and they were the products of the popular and literary creed of many centuries.

These fairies are of a confused origin—members, perhaps, of an early, persecuted race, dwarfish and earth-dwelling, or perhaps in origin the ghosts of men long dead. Certainly they are of a malignant disposition, and, beneath the frown of the Christian churchmen, came to be regarded as tributaries of the Devil, paying a "tiend to Hell" once every seven years, of an unbaptized babe or of some human willing to become subject to their reign. By night these evil visitants came to the homesteads of mortal folk to steal away children and leave hideous changelings in their place—a superstition still prevalent in Ireland about fifty years ago when a young woman was burnt by her husband on the charge of being a changeling. Such ancient beliefs die slowly, and only the modern age, science, industry and the annihilation of distance has succeeded in destroying them.

Among more literary classes the popular fairy-lore in the Middle Ages became diluted and changed by the addition of classical and romantic elements. Perhaps the best example of this is the Middle English poem of "Sir Orfeo," which tells the story of Orpheus and Eurydice in a setting of British fairy belief, making Persephone queen of that fairyland under the ground to which, in the ballad, the Fairy Queen leads Thomas the Rhymer.

Another confusion with the fairies was that of the elves of a more Teutonic origin, those elves who took charge of the infant Arthur in Layaman's *Brut*, endowing him with moral and physical virtues, and making him a present of fairy swords and armour.

Chaucer, in the *Canterbury Tales*, still speaks of

> "Pluto, that is the king of fayerye . . .
> Folwinge his wyf, the quene Proserpyne,"

but to him they have begun to seem beneficent spirits, and they perform a moral purpose in the story of Januarie and his false wife.

It was on such a substratum as this that Shakespeare built when, in Charles Lamb's phrase, he "invented the fairies." His transcendent imagination welded together all the earlier floating beliefs:

Oberon, the "fairy knight" of Huon of Bordeau; Titania, another name for Artemis, and so by a confusion with Hekate, none other than the "quene Proserpyne"; and Puck, the more English popular fairy, descended from the Teutonic elves, and became the Brownie, the earliest mention of whom, according to Lang, is in 1518, where John Major or Muir, in his *Dissertation on the Gospel of St. Matthew*, "speaks of Brownies as jocular spirits who do odd jobs about a house, throw stones and other objects, and are apt to provoke curiosity rather than alarm."[134]

But it was from the pre-Shakespearean conception of the fairy world that Lang drew his inspiration and his materials, nor does there seem to be more than one fairy story of a later date that has any very close relation to the lines on which Lang worked.

This isolated example is called *Alice Learmont*, and was written by Dinah Maria Mulock, the author of *John Halifax, Gentleman*, at a very early stage in her career. It appeared anonymously in 1852, and was re-issued as hers in 1884. It is quite possible that Lang may have known this story, though he makes no mention of it; but any similarity between it and *The Gold of Fairnilee* lies simply in the fact that the sources for the central theme in each story were the Border ballads of "Thomas the Rhymer" and "Young Tamlane." Dinah Mulock does not keep very near to the tradition, and shows the influence of the later literary conventions; her fairies, for example, have wings—a very late addition, dating probably from the Sylphs of Pope; but in other respects they claim to be pre-Shakespeare:—"he paints me," says the Fairy Queen in the story, "so little after received tradition, and so much out of his own fancy, that I hardly know my own likeness!"

Lang, however, does not allow any later tradition to influence *The Gold of Fairnilee*; indeed, one might almost hesitate to call it a "fairy story" in the ordinary sense—as Lang himself seems to have felt when he excludes it from the list of his original fairy-tales given in the Preface to *The Lilac Fairy Book*.

The plot is very simple, and concerns little Randal Ker of Fairnilee, whose father is killed at the Battle of Flodden (1513) in the first chapter of the story. Randal lives with his widowed mother at Fairnilee, with Jean, a little English girl captured in a Border raid, for companion. One Midsummer Day, Randal decides to visit a fairy well on the hills beyond Tweed; he reaches it about

H

nightfall, and when he has wished to see the Fairy Queen, she
spirits him away to Fairyland. Jean, Lady Ker and Nancy, the old
nurse, pass seven miserable years not knowing what has become of
Randal; but at the end of that time, Jean, who is now grown up,
visits the wishing well on Midsummer Eve, plucks the magic rose,
and wins back Randal by the Sign of the Cross. From Fairyland
Randal brings with him only a phial of magic water, a little of
which, when he had chanced to rub it on his eyes, showed him the
false and empty hollowness of the Fairy Queen and her realm.
The old nurse, hearing the story, takes the bottle, and by anointing
her eyes with it sees where the ancient treasure, the Gold of
Fairnilee, lies beneath the soil of the Camp o'Rink; Randal and
Jean dig it up, and with it buy food for the people in a time of
famine. And the story ends happily with the marriage of Jean
and Randal.

The description of Randal's abduction by the Fairy Queen is
taken, in one place almost verbatim, from "Thomas the Rhymer,"
and Jean at the well recalls Janet in "Young Tamlane":—

> "She had na' pu'd a red, red rose,
> A rose but barely three:
> Till up and starts a wee, wee man
> At lady Janet's knee."

And besides this legendary lore there is also a spice of history
behind the story: Lang writes, in a humorous apology for family
legends introduced into fiction: "Will the Kers of Faldonside be
down on this humble head because I have told a tale in which one
of them was carried off to Fairyland ? Fairyland was tributary to
the Evil One, and the clan *may* take offence! "[135]

But perhaps the chief inspiration for the story lay in the place,
Fairnilee itself, and in the associations that, from his boyhood, had
made it dear to Lang. Of the book he wrote to Rider Haggard at
some time in 1888, probably in answer to some criticism of the
plot: "I dare say you would have made more of the Scotch treasure,
much to Arrowsmith's (the publisher) advantage, but I can't do
fiction. It's only a lot of childish reminiscences of old times in a
better place than 1 Marloes Road."[136]

The amusements of Randal and Jean are clearly modelled on
those of the Lang children, just as the old nurse, Nancy, is the very

same as the Langs' nurse whom Mrs. Sellar describes in her
Recollections and Impressions. And the ruined house of Fairnilee
was a favourite haunt of Andrew and his brothers in their childhood; here he and Patrick Lang dug for treasure, and here he came
to fish, perhaps with his friend, Alexander Roberts, who built the
new house about 1905. When Lang was a boy, Fairnilee belonged
to the Pringles of Haining, and later to their descendants, the
Pringle-Pattersons. Lang describes the place very lovingly, "The
house of Fairnilee, hidden by its woods, on the right hand of
the road which runs by Tweed, exactly opposite the house of Yair.
Here the Fairy Queen trysted with Thomas the Rhymer. Here the
philosopher who now prattles passed many an hour in his boyhood,
'thinking of the times that are long enough agone.' " In those days
the stately house, with the coat-of-arms of the Rutherfords over
the door, had roofs at least on its corner turrets. But from one
turret the roof has now fallen, and on the other, at a perilous angle,
sticks a tattered conical roof, like the cap on the head of an
intoxicated man, the ivy has been stripped off, the stairs are broken
down—all is ruin. Yet this house has the sunniest aspect of any on
Tweedside . . . It was a rich house once, and there is room for a
large, merry family. Of old, about 1490, it belonged to the Kers—
the family of Ker of Faldonside, who aimed his pistol at Queen
Mary when Rizzio was slain, and who wedded the widow of John
Knox . . . In 1700 the Rutherfords bought the place, and set their
shield upon the door . . . The daughter of the first Rutherford,
who married Alison Ker, was author of "The Flowers of the
Forest," at least of one version of that song, and was the first to
detect the genius of Scott when he was a little child. She was born
in 1713 . . . She had seen the "Fifteen," the "Forty-Five," the
Terror; she had seen Burns in his prime and Scott in his glorious
youth . . . Her house is roofless and the ancient lovers' tree behind
it has fallen. There remain only crumbling, fissured walls, and the
enclosure of the pleasance—*The Flowers of the Forest are a "wede
awa'*! "[137]

Since Lang wrote thus in 1894 the old house of Fairnilee has
been "wede awa' " even more, probably by the hand of man; but
what remains has been set in order, and the decay arrested. Only
about a third of the house is left, the end furthest from the
approach, but this portion has been roofed and the windows

glazed. One of the turrets remains—that in which "The Flowers of the Forest" is said to have been written; on the ragged ends of the walls where the rest of the building has been pulled down the creeper is now draping itself, while the foundations of the house remain as a terrace wall about two feet above the ground. This picturesque ruin stands in the midst of gardens, terraced banks, and well-kept lawns, while behind it and a little to the right stands Alexander Roberts' great new house, now the seat of Lord Craigmyle.

"There are many trees crowding all round, and there are hills round it, too; and far below you hear the Tweed whispering all day. The house is called ' Fairnilee,' which means ' The Fairies' Field '; for people believed in fairies, as you shall hear, when Randal was a boy, and even when my father was a boy."

The valley of the Tweed and the lands about Fairnilee were of all the Border country the parts most loved by Lang, and it is this which gives to *The Gold of Fairnilee* its sincerity and its depth of feeling. Nearby was the old church of Caddonfoot, and here it was Lang's dearest wish to be buried: "If a Tweedside fisher might have his desire, he would sleep the long sleep in the little churchyard that lies lonely above the pool of Caddon-foot."[138] Lang even attempted to buy land for his grave in the churchyard, but it was not allowed, as he was not a parishioner. He longed to lie "like Scott within the sound of Tweed," but it was not permitted. "If I ' walk,' may I walk there! " he said, speaking of the Tweed by Fairnilee: and nowhere does one feel nearer to Andrew Lang than there.

With all this of memory and ballad lore behind him, Lang produced in *The Gold of Fairnilee*, perhaps the best prose work of his whole career. The spirit and manner of this tale differ utterly from those of all his other fairy stories, and from nearly all else that he wrote save in the most heartfelt of his poems. One can glimpse him from time to time in *The World's Desire* and *A Monk of Fife*; he is plainly apparent in the short story "The Romance of the First Radical," in *Aucassin and Nicolete*, we feel the same spirit at work; but Andrew Lang, the poet with the wistful, melancholy soul, can nowhere be seen more clearly than in this simple little tale.

The cold, clear magic of the north, austere as the hills of Ettrick and of Yarrow, is breathed over the whole piece. But the austerity is the quiet simplicity of the truest affection, and the coldness is the gentle calm of the love that is beyond passion.

The Gold of Fairnilee is quite spontaneous, quite sincere: Lang was by nature a romantic, permeated by northern fairy-lore and the deep, clear feelings of the north; and when the depths of these feelings overcame his habitual reserve—when the melancholy soul looked forth without the vizor of the gay mind—it was in the poignant simplicity of the northern romance that he found his natural and truest expression. This explains, too, his dislike of Morris's prose romances, which at first sight would have seemed in Lang's own vein. The medium, perhaps, is too near for either to have been able fully to appreciate the other's working in it: it was Morris's method that jarred on Lang, the Gothic decoration, the wealth of words, the warmth and bright colouring—the pre-Raphaelite technique applied to literature. Only in his early works, in *The Defence of Guinevere* and *The Hollow Land*, does Morris write with simple and unforced sincerity, and it was these early works alone that Lang rated so highly. That the truth is also present, and, indeed, a deeper, nobler truth, in the later romances of Morris, Lang does not seem to have been able to recognize. His own simplicity in romantic writing was increased and clarified by the classics; and the unpublished prologue and the early chapters of *The World's Desire*, although in a Greek and not a northern setting, come very near to *The Gold of Fairnilee*—thus illustrating Lang's assertion that the true fairy spirit dwelt only in Greece and the north. Morris, on the other hand, although influenced also by the classics, and later by the sagas, came to them indirectly, and saw them to a great extent as reflections in a rich medieval mirror. Nowhere is the difference in technique and temperament more easily apparent than in their translations of the *Odyssey*. Lang condemned Morris's version often and repeatedly, and parodied it on more than one occasion. What Morris thought of the "Butcher and Lang" version can only be surmised from the fact that when Lang, with whom he was slightly acquainted, sent him a copy, he ignored it completely.[139]

Lang's style in *The Gold of Fairnilee* is best illustrated by a quotation. This, a passage chosen almost at random, describes Jean's approach to the wishing well on the fatal Midsummer Eve when she goes to win back the lost Randal.

"Her feet did not seem to carry her the way she wanted to go. It seemed as if something within her were moving her in a kind of dream. She felt herself going on through the forest, she did not know where. Deeper into the wood she went, and now it grew so dark that she saw scarce anything; only she felt the fragrance of briar roses, and it seemed to her that she was guided towards these roses. Then she knew that there was a hand in her hand, though she saw nobody, and the hand seemed to lead her on. And she came to an open space in the forest, and there the silver light fell clear from the sky, and she saw a great shadowy rose tree, covered with white wild roses.

"The hand was still in her hand, and Jeanie began to wish for nothing so much in the world as to gather some of these roses. She put out her hand and she plucked one, and there before her stood a strange creature—a dwarf, dressed in yellow and red, with a very angry face.

" ' Who are you,' he cried, ' that pluck my roses without my will ? '

" ' And who are *you* ? ' said Jeanie, trembling, ' and what right have you on the hills of this world ? '

"Then she made the holy sign of the Cross, and the face of the elf grew black, and the light went out of the sky.

"She only saw the faint glimmer of the white flowers, and a kind of shadow standing where the dwarf stood.

" ' I bid you tell me,' said Jeanie, ' whether you are a Christian man, or a spirit that dreads the holy sign,' and she crossed him again.

"Now all grew dark as the darkest winter's night. The air was warm and deadly still, and heavy with the scent of the fairy flowers.

"In the blackness and the silence, Jeanie made the sacred sign for the third time. Then a clear fresh wind blew on her face, and the forest boughs were shaken, and the silver light grew and gained on the darkness, and she began to see a shape standing where the dwarf had stood. It was far taller than the dwarf, and the light grew and grew, and a star looked down out of the night, and Jean saw Randal standing by her. And she kissed him, and he kissed her, and he put his hand in hers, and they went out of the wood together."

The Gold of Fairnilee is probably the fullest example that we possess of Lang's true voice as a romantic; apart from this, the voice is heard clearly only in some of the poems, and, besides the more finite instances already mentioned, in some stray passages scattered up and down the vast concourse of his writings. Otherwise, the gay mind hides the melancholy soul almost completely; the one is seldom altogether lacking; we feel again and again that it is there, but the other is the visible, tangible part—the iron mask hiding we know not what Prince of Fairyland. "There was a touch of the elf about him," says J. M. Barrie. "Touch seems hardly the right word, because one could never touch him; he was too elusive for that."[140]

It was perhaps part of this very elusiveness that led Lang away from the depth and wistfulness of his Border fairy-tale to the light, humorous, gently burlesque court of Pantouflia.

The mildly satirical fairy-story of the Thackeray tradition is a far easier form of literature to write than anything approaching the old folk-tales and legendary romances; and it was also a type of writing that came most easily to Lang of the gay mind, who confessed once that he was possessed by "the literary *follét* who delights in mild mischief."[141] Yet in its essentials *Prince Prigio* goes contrary to Lang's own ideals, for it is a burlesque, however kindly, of the old tales. Of course, he was inventing no new *genre* when he wrote the Chronicles of Pantouflia, but merely carrying the methods of F. E. Paget, Thackeray and Tom Hood one step further, even as they had elaborated the methods of Madame d'Aulnoy and her followers. *The Gold of Fairnilee* should not be compared with *Prince Prigio*, any more than *Alice* with Grimm's tales. It is dangerous to make any very definite attempt to put fairy stories into precise categories, for most of them lie somewhere between the extremes of "primitive" (to which we would assign *Alice Learmont* and *The Gold of Fairnilee*) and "sophisticated" (to which *The Rose and the Ring* and *Prince Prigio* belong), and are best left scattered indeterminately between these extremes.

Thus, although it would be unfair to criticize one of Lang's tales by the standards of the other, we can go so far as to say that the Pantouflia stories belong to a lower and commoner form of art than *The Gold of Fairnilee*. And yet, considered solely as books for children, one would be forced reluctantly to set *Prince Prigio* first.

For lightness, humour, gay adventure have ever been the most popular with the majority of young readers. For every one child devoted to George MacDonald, there are a hundred whose faith is pledged to E. Nesbit, and the same distinction seems to hold good between Lang's two stories. The last twelve years have seen three new editions of *Prince Prigio*, but only one of *The Gold of Fairnilee* —and that has been exhausted for some time.

In its own field, *Prince Prigio* is only surpassed by *The Rose and the Ring*, but the two are sufficiently dissimilar for there to be ample room for both. Thackeray is a second Fielding—more gentle, more refined, more whimsical—but still the bold dash and the breadth of outline are there. He is the novelist at play, creating strongly-defined characters, however much burlesqued: "Angelica is a child's Blanche Amory, Betsinda is a child's Laura Bell, Bulbo is the Foker of the nursery" [142], as Lang himself observed. His scenes and characters stand out in hard outline like an illustration by Walter Crane, while Lang's recall the fine strokes and delicate drawing of Leslie Brooke. Lang has none of Fielding's violence, nor his loud-voiced hilarity; as ever, he is gentle, almost dreamy, almost apologetic. To the adult reader Lang is far more acceptable than Thackeray, for his story still amuses in its quiet, unpretentious way, while the slap-stick and the loud burlesque of *The Rose and the Ring* fail to hold the attention quite as it used to do. The child of today, if we may take the fare spread for him as symptomatic of his own tastes, delights in bright colours heavily and ruthlessly laid on, in awkward and uncouth figures from which refinement has been drained away with sentiment, and beauty with the subtler shades of the imagination. And so *Prince Prigio*, though still read and still enjoyed, hangs still on the border-line between the few real nursery classics and the oblivion that has swallowed up so much that well deserves to live.

It is the undercurrent of that power and vision which produced *The Gold of Fairnilee* that gives to *Prince Prigio*, and to much of *Prince Ricardo* also, the intangible something—one might almost call it the soul—which makes of them living works of literature that will not easily die. Although they must be regarded to some extent as burlesque, yet the sense of reality in a serious and living world is seldom lost: the characters are never overdrawn as Thackeray's tend to be, nor are they reduced to the cruel level of the everyday world as are Mrs. Gaskell's in her tale "Curious if True." Prigio's adventures are all very serious matters to him, his love for Lady Rosalind is a romantic and not a courtly passion; Ricardo and Jacqueline are more like children than grown-up people, yet they are sincere and simple in their affections, and there is no hint of the lush sentimentality over young love that defiles S. R. Crockett's otherwise excellent children's stories. It is this underlying texture of romance that serves to bring *Prigio* and even *Ricardo* near to *The Gold of Fairnilee*, for it gives something more than humour and charm, though so indefinitely that hardly any particular passage can be pointed out as possessing the magic touch. The simple love-making of Prigio and Rosalind—"So the two went into the garden together and talked about a number of things"—or Prigio's meeting with the Ladies of the Moon: all very slight touches, yet never out of place as they would be in *The Rose and the Ring*.

In whatever setting he placed his stories, Lang never failed to profit by his unequalled knowledge of the old folk-tales, and their seriousness of purpose is never absent, even at the Court of Pantouflia. "In the old stories," he says, "despite the impossibility of the incidents, the interest is always real and human. The princes and princesses fall in love and marry—nothing could be more human than that. Their lives and loves are crossed by human sorrows . . . The hero and heroine are persecuted or separated by cruel step-mothers or enchanters; they have wandering and sorrows to suffer; they have adventures to achieve and difficulties to overcome. They must display courage, loyalty and address, courtesy, gentleness and gratitude. Thus they are living in a real human world, though it wears a mythical face, though there are giants and lions in the way. The old fairy-tales which a silly sort of people disparage . . . are really 'full of matter,' and unobtrusively teach the true lessons of our wayfaring in a world of perplexities and obstructions."[143]

All this is present in Pantouflia, however much hidden by the humour and apparent flippancy. It is more surely there in *The Gold of Fairnilee*, for that, as I have suggested, is the clearer, more sincere revelation of the true mind of its maker, and greater book, even if not so successful in its appeal to its professed audience, or so much a book for constant and delighted reading as *Prince Prigio*.

The author of the Pantouflia stories is the Andrew Lang whom most people knew—the only Andrew Lang to all but the most penetrating and to all but the closest of his friends. To few people indeed was the wall broken down which he had built up between his true self and the world:

> ·"Over the wall we never could see,
> Over the wall and away"—[144]

as he wrote in a poem which did not seem to him worth including in any of his books. Two other poems, made up in dreams, he published as curiosities[145], perhaps not realizing how much they reveal his "secretest man." Another dream-glimpse, less known, but not out of place in an account of his fairy-tale writings, lies buried, like so much of his work, in the forgotten volumes of old magazines:

"I seemed to be sitting on the side of a Scottish hill, on Yarrow I think, with a fair lady of great beauty and charm. She instructed me that three times in my life she would appear to me, when I plucked a sprig of white heather. ' But do not pluck for the third time,' she said, ' till your death is approaching, and then I will come to you and be your guide and comfort through the lonely ways of Death.' So, in my dream, time went by: twice I had gathered the white heather, and twice seen the fair lady. At last I was lying on the hillside again, and by chance my idle hand broke a flower of the white heather. Instantly she appeared weeping, and told me that the last chance was wasted, and that I, like other men, must go alone down the ways of Death. Then she kissed me, and her immortal face was wet, and as cold as stone. . . ."[146]

CHAPTER X

The Approach to Romance

WHERE a writer so many-sided and voluminous as Lang is concerned, any attempt to deal with his works in strict chronology would be merely to confuse the understanding, and make even more difficult the attempt to follow him through all the various byways of his genius. While no single subject stood alone, while he could, and habitually did, interweave the most various and seemingly unrelated of his interests into the most surprising and fascinating webs of thought and illustration, it is nevertheless possible to make certain broad divisions, and follow some of these through his career. One such highway marks his development and career as a poet, and another his work as a writer and interpreter of fairy-tales. Less known, but not altogether less worthy of study, is all that Lang attempted in the field of romance: both his poetry and his fairy-tales belong primarily to this, the most potent influence in his imaginative work; but as a critic and interpreter of romance in both past and contemporary fiction, and even as a writer himself of such fiction, he well repays examination. And such a study is vital to the understanding of Lang himself, and as an illustration to his more successful and more justly famous writings in poetry and fairy-tale.

As we have seen, Lang's earliest volume of poems, besides the translations from various French romantic poets, contained many by Lang himself, most of which took the form of poetry of aspiration or regret, memories of lost love, lost youth, lost friends, and the longing for the unknown, perchance the impossible, that such contemplation breeds. That note hardly sounds in *Ballades in Blue China*, but it is the underlying *motif* in *Helen of Troy* (1882), and was to give form eight years later to *The World's Desire*.

"It does not follow," wrote Lang during this period, "that all romance is concerned with impossibilities—very far from it; but it is only the impossible that can satisfy human aspirations; we all cry for the moon; and we can only meet the moon, like Endymion,

in a dream. "Blessed I call him who sleeps and wakes not, even
Endymion," says the lover in Theocritus. The Latmian is lapped
for ever in a vision of these impossible felicities, and these adventures never to be achieved, which are in the land of Faery. Sometimes it is the function of Romance to transport us thither, and
lull us for an hour with dreams of the impossible . . . Romance
appears to be, in literature, that element which gives a sudden
sense of the strangeness and beauty of life; that power which has
the gift of dreams, and admits us into the region where men are
more brave and women more beautiful and passions more intense
than in ordinary existence. A million of novels about the Spanish
Main may not be so romantic as a dozen lines spoken on the
moonlit terrace of Belmont. A single movement or speech of a girl
in *Silas Lapham* may be as romantic as the singing of Gunnar in
his grave — while it lasts.[147]

That there was a certain element of what is now loosely called
"Escapism" about Lang's attitude to romantic literature is obvious.
An intense love and understanding of a past period or of the past
in general is almost certain to lead to a feeling that one is born out
of one's true period.

> "I would my days had been in other times,
>   That I in some old abbey of Touraine
>   Had watched the rounded grapes and lived my life
>   Ere ever Luther came, or Rabelais! "

So Lang was apt to feel, though not at all blind to the dis-
advantages of life in the various ages of the past, or of his un-
suitability to have lived in any of them. In a letter to Rider Haggard
about 1890, Lang remarks jestingly that Haggard ought to have
been born "nine hundred years ago. I might have been a monk of
Ely, and you might have flayed me and composed a saga at first
hand. It would have been a good saga, but I could not stand being
flayed, I know."[148] However exaggerated, this gives Lang's
position rather neatly.

As a natural adjunct to this love of the old, spacious times was
the sentiment for places and books that he had known and loved in
his younger days. This also is a very natural trait in a man who was
by nature a solitary dreamer, and who formed his own opinions,

his own likes and dislikes in literature without any reference to contemporary prejudice or contemporary cults, and never hesitated to state and defend these preferences, even in the face of general criticism or ridicule.

In criticism Lang spoke up for romantic literature whenever possible, but his main mission as he himself saw it was to win a fair and unbiased hearing for this type of writing. He held that it was as true and important a branch as the "realist" novels which were then winning the unbending support of the acknowledged critics, and urged only that the one form should not be exalted at the expense of the other; though with his usual frankness he was ready to admit that "if the battle between the crocodile of Realism and the catawampus of Romance is to be fought out to the bitter end—why, in that Ragnarok, I am on the side of the catawampus." Lang's best and most clearly reasoned statement of this controversy, is the essay "Realism and Romance," which appeared in *The Contemporary Review* of November, 1887, and which has, unfortunately, never been reprinted.

It was the loyalty to his earlier literary loves, and the inherent desire to champion any lost or oppressed cause, that led Lang to defend Scott against the many criticisms levelled against him, to defend Thackeray and Dickens also, as time went on; and it was this same spirit of championship that made him the defender of Jeanne d'Arc, the supporter of Homeric unity, the historian of the Jacobites.

The romance of Abbotsford had been strong upon Lang since the days of his boyhood in and around Selkirk; and in his interpretation of Scott and of Lockhart, Lang showed a deeper knowledge and a clearer understanding than in anything else which he wrote about nineteenth century literature. His *Life and Letters of John Gibson Lockhart* which appeared in 1896 has been claimed as one of the great biographies of the century; for besides knowing intimately all that had bearings on his subject, Lang understood Lockhart, in whose character he found very much that resembled his own, and was able to interpret him as few others could have done.

His work on Scott was less important, though of a more general nature. The short *Life* published in 1906 is of little importance, though not without interest of a kind; but the Introductions to the

"Border Edition" of the *Waverley Novels* (1892-94) contain much of Lang's best criticism and appreciation. And here, too, we can see how strong a hold the romantic conception had over him. "There shall still be cakes and ale," he cries, "though all the critics be virtuous, and recommend stuff rich in heartbreak. Still shall the green-wood trees be green, and the king's dappled deer shall run therein, and gallant outlaws shall slay a buck, and we shall tell our beads, and crush a flagon with the holy clerk of Copmanhurst. Out of the dim years the crashing of the Black Knight's axe is ringing yet, on oak and iron; still we are thrilled, as so long ago, when the solitary trumpet sounds, and the Disinherited Knight rides into the lists of Ashby-de-la-Zouch . . . Many a trumpet of romance has shrilled since Ivanhoe's in the list of fancy, many a spear has been shivered, many a sword-stroke and axe-stroke dealt. But while youth dwells in day-dreams that manhood does not forget, this gay and glorious pageant still holds its own."[149]

That Lang attempted to carry over into real life some of the spirit of adventure is shown in at least one amusing incident. At some time about 1885 a real treasure hunt was mooted; the "deposit," so Lang was informed, had been "put down" in some past time by a Finn. Lang and Haggard, and possibly Stevenson, were actually paying for shares in this alluring enterprise, when it was discovered that the aforesaid Finn had, at a period of no great antiquity, "lifted" the "deposit" from the altars of various South American churches.[150]

Lang's imagination seems to have been of a very active kind, though he himself considered that it was not at all the imagination necessary for a successful novelist. Besides the dreams, such as that quoted in the last chapter, and another of a very alarming kind concerning the vampire of a dead wizard, Lang was subject to very clear "waking-dreams": "I who can scarcely form the faintest mental picture, when awake, can," he tells us, "see, with shut-eyes, on the border of sleep, very vivid presentations of objects of all kinds. But I cannot voluntarily induce the presentation of an object which I want to see."[151] That he had seen wraiths and a possible ghost has already been stated; and another experience of a different kind can be added. Lang narrates how one day as he and Rider Haggard were walking together in London, the following incident occurred.

"A hansom cab with a chestnut horse ran away, that is, the horse ran away, in Westminster. The driver put the horse at a very high wooden hoarding. The horse struck it full and honestly, and I distinctly saw the cabman fly from his perch over the wooden barrier.

" ' He'll be killed! ' I remarked to my companion, ' he must have broken his neck! '

"Now my friend was a person much more ' imaginative ' than myself, luckily for him, as he is a novelist in a good line of business.

" ' He's all right,' said my friend. ' What do you mean ? '

" ' Didn't you see him pitched over the hoarding ? '

" ' Not a bit of it! ' was the answer, and as a matter of fact, though the horse's legs were broken, the driver remained unharmed on the right side of the hoarding."[152]

But this type of vivid imagination did not stand Lang in any good stead when he came to try his hand at novels and prose romances. "If he who now writes tries to compose a story," Lang confesses, "the characters never come before his mental eye: he gives them hair of this colour, eyes of that, such and such a dress, such and such things to do and words to say, but he never sees them with his mind's eye, nor hears them with his mental ears."[153]

It was not until 1886 that Lang attempted to take his place as a novelist.

This does not mean that he wrote no fiction before that date, indeed his earliest novel was written while he was a schoolboy— that story telling "why Queen Elizabeth never married," which he mentions in the essay "Enchanted Cigarettes," where also he describes a number of other attempts which never came to anything.

The most interesting of these would have been the thriller *Where is Rose?* which he began to write in collaboration with Robert Louis Stevenson. "The characters were—(1) Rose, a young lady of quality. (2) The Russian Princess, her friend (need I add that, to meet a public demand, *her* name was Vera ?) (3) Young man engaged to Rose. (4) Charles, his friend. (5) An enterprising person named "The Whiteley of Crime," the universal Provider of Iniquity. In fact he anticipated Sir Arthur Conan Doyle's Professor Moriarty. The rest were detectives, old ladies, mob, and a wealthy

young Colonial larrikin. Neither my friend nor I was fond of
describing love scenes, so we made the heroine disappear in the
second chapter, and she never turned up again till chapter the last.
After playing in a comedy at the house of an earl, Rose and Vera
entered her brougham. Soon afterwards the brougham drew up,
empty, at Rose's own door. Where *was* Rose ? Traces of her were
found, of all places, in the Haunted House in Berkeley Square,
which is not haunted any longer. After that Rose was long sought
in vain.

"This, briefly, is what had occurred. A Russian detective
' wanted ' Vera, who, to be sure, was a Nihilist. To catch Vera he
made an alliance with ' The Whiteley of Crime.' He was a man
who would destroy a parish register, or forge a will, or crack a crib,
or break up a pro-Boer meeting, or burn a house, or kidnap a
rightful heir, or manage a personation, or issue amateur bank-
notes, or what you please. Thinking to kill two birds with one
stone, he carried off Rose for her diamonds and Vera for his friend,
the Muscovite police official, lodging them both in the Haunted
House. But there he and the Russian came to blows, and, in the
confusion, Vera made her escape, while Rose was conveyed, *as
Vera*, to Siberia. Not knowing how to dispose of her, the Russian
police consigned her to a nunnery at the mouth of the Obi. Her
lover, in a yacht, found her hiding-place, and got a friendly nun
to give her some narcotic known to the Samoyeds. It was the old
truc of the Friar in ' Romeo and Juliet.' At the mouth of the Obi
they do not bury the dead, but lay them down on platforms in the
open air. Rose was picked up there by her lover (accompanied by a
chaperon, of course), was got on board the steam yacht, and all
went well. I forget what happened to ' The Whiteley of Crime.'
After him I still rather hanker . . ."[154]

In the same essay Lang describes other romances that he had
thought of writing; and in later years he had ideas for one or two
others in collaboration with Rider Haggard.

But of his own fiction that actually appeared in print, the short
stories collected as *In the Wrong Paradise* in 1886, is the earliest
example, except for the little fairy-tale *The Princess Nobody* which
had been published two years before.

The stories in the book had appeared during the previous few
years in various magazines such as *The Cornhill* and *Time*, and

Lang's original idea was to call his volume *Men, Gods and Ghosts*—
"what a Lunatic Bank holiday!" is his comment to Rider Haggard.

The book as a whole belongs to a new class of fiction which
Grant Allen described as "The romance of anthropology," to
which he assigned both Stevenson and Haggard. The stories are
certainly such as might have been expected of Lang; some of them
are rather sketches than stories proper: "The Great Gladstone
Myth" is merely a "skit" on the various schools of mythology;
"My Friend the Beachcomber" is a collection of South Sea yarns
spun from material supplied by Lang's cousin James Jasper
Atkinson; while "In Castle Perilous" is a humorous discourse by a
ghost on the worries of the haunter, and reminds one of *Phantas-
magoria*.

The longest story in the book, "The End of Phaeacia," which
appeared as a serial in *Time* from January to March 1886, is rather
a pleasant and amusing romance of a missionary wrecked on an
island in the South Seas which turned out to be the Homeric
Phaeacia, and (like the lost city in Gilbert Murray's *Gobi or Shamo*
a few years later) to have retained all the customs and civilization
of ancient Greece. To the Rev. Mr. Gowles, however, "the natives"
appear to be the veriest savages, and the great fault in the story is
that Lang seems rather to support this view by bringing together
into one small island and into the course of one year all the
barbarous rites and survivals that are recorded of the whole Greek
world from Herodotus to Pausanias. By doing this the point of the
story seems rather lost; for after gruesome accounts of the Achæan
burning alive of animals to Artemis, of the Attic "thargelion," and
so forth, one is apt to agree with the wretched missionary that the
Greeks were worse barbarians than the Polynesians! The story
is told by Mr. Gowles the missionary, and his style is amusing,
though it begins to pall by the end, where Lang appears to
have lost interest, and which is precipitated by an accumulation
of melodramatic and improbable catastrophes. But these
faults are redeemed by the living and delightful pictures of
ancient Greek life, and by the simple charm of at least the earlier
adventures.

Another tale, "A Cheap Nigger," is rather a thrilling yarn of an
American treasure hunt, and much of it came to Lang in a dream:
"I dreamed," says Lang, "about the chart branded on the negro's

I

head: the rest of it was chiefly a combination of hints from Edgar Poe, and researches in Aztec antiquities."[155]

The title story "In the Wrong Paradise," is an "Occidental Apologue" couched in Lang's most pleasantly satiric vein: taking as text that one man's paradise is another man's purgatory, it shows the sufferings of a Christian in the paradise of the Red Indians, an Arabic professor in that of the Mahomedans, and a "Neo-Grecian" *poseur* in the Classical Hades—for mistakes will occur, even beyond the grave, in such a vast postal system as the delivery of souls to their correct dwelling places.

But by far the best story in the volume is "The Romance of the First Radical," a simple, and very charming, little tale of the dawn of civilization. "The characters of our romance lived shortly after the close of the last Glacial Age in Europe . . . in the following little apologue no trait of manners is invented." The idyll of Why-Why, his defiance of the customs and tabus of the tribe, his love for Verva, and their tragic fate is told with a quiet simplicity, a vivid insight into the savage mind, and a perfect control of his medium that sets this story beside *The Gold of Fairnilee*, among the truest manifestations of Lang's genius.

"Mr. Lang's is not the sentiment that may be bawled from the roof tops," wrote Graham R. Thomson. "It is the sentiment of old romance, of dim memories, all the more beautiful for their vagueness (as the reflection is often more beautiful than the mirrored object), the sentiment of wet spring woods and birds singing in the early dawn . . ."[156]

In the same year as *In the Wrong Paradise* appeared Lang's only real contemporary novel, *The Mark of Cain*, which formed number thirteen in "Arrowsmith's Bristol Library." "The story," says an early review, "is well above its twelve predecessors, but it will not add anything to the author's renown." It is obviously the work of a beginner in the art of novel writing and suffers from faulty construction, and an over-melodramatic villain; the mystery is betrayed in the first chapter, the fate of the heroine is never a matter for concern, there is a distressing confusion of heroes, and the end for which the flying machine is introduced becomes obvious far too soon. The characters are not very deeply studied, and both they and their surroundings breathe an atmosphere of artificiality. Taken simply as a novel, the book is not a success, though even so, Horace Hutchinson's condemnation of it seems unnecessarily severe. But he must have suffered from the same disadvantage as so many readers who could see no special merit in Lang's lighter fiction: for the book is not a novel in the ordinary sense, but belongs to the rare type of fiction of which Stevenson wrote the masterpiece three years later, in *The Wrong Box*. *The Mark of Cain* is a work of a very delicate humour, of a whimsical and kindly satire. It is the gentle, wistful gaiety of the scholar and poet at play, and its charm lies more in the style and manner, in the haunting sense of literary allusion, and in the quiet undercurrent of fun which a few years later was to produce *Prince Prigio*. The scenes and characters seem to be dressed all in greys and browns; they smile, but never laugh, they languish but never love. The violent people are quite unreal, the villainous Cranley and his evil accomplice Alice; but the others are alive, even if the blood in their veins be a trifle pale. Miss Martlett the mistress of the Academy for Young Ladies may not have the vitality of Miss Twinkleton, but her school is a delightfully real place, and Margaret and her fellow pupils as deliciously vivacious and amusing as any in Mrs. Molesworth's stories. Brilliant, too, are the scenes at Oxford: Maitland, the Fellow of St. Gatien's College, has all the shyness and unworldliness, but none of the imagination of Lang himself; and not only the proceedings of the undergraduates after a "bump-supper" (which seem to be drawn from a real incident of Lang's Oxford days) suggest that "St. Gatien's" is but a thin disguise for Merton.

The late Professor George Gordon's praise of *The Mark of Cain* and of the even better *Disentanglers* of a later date, was that nobody but Lang could have written them; and if one can appreciate the Lang "touch" (and admittedly it is an acquired taste) these two books and many of the stories from *In the Wrong Paradise* can be read and re-read many times with complete and unforced enjoyment.

A novel in the modern sense Lang was not born to write: "I can do nothing with human nature," he once said to Hutchinson; and it was one of his greatest disappointments that he could not write a popular novel. "Lang never claimed to be a creator," Haggard tells us, "and whenever he sets to work to create, his wide knowledge, and his marvellous memory of everything he has read—and little

worth studying in ancient and modern literature has escaped him—
prove positive stumbling-blocks in his path."[157] But it was out of
this fullness that Andrew Lang wrote as he did, and without it such
stories as *The Mark of Cain* and *The Disentanglers* would have no
life, nor any of the strangely fascinating and lovable quality that
clings about them, bright as the dew of early dawn.

Now, apart from "The Romance of the First Radical," these
books represented Andrew Lang the scholar and *littérateur* rather
than the "disinherited dreamer" who could sing in such sad, sweet
tones of the lost love and the World's Desire. But the melancholy
soul was ever there beneath the gay mind, however seldom it
becomes apparent; and the years that produced these gentle,
bookish stories were not at all "dispeopled of their dreams" of the
romantic past.

In the year after *The Mark of Cain*, Lang edited the ancient
fairy-tale of "Cupid and Psyche," drawing parallels between the
sophisticated version of the Roman Apuleius and the primitive
tales of half the peoples of the world. But in June of that year also
he translated that most perfect of love stories, the old French song
story of *Aucassin and Nicolete*.

"My own version," he says, "was written rapidly in summer
gardens, by command of Mr. Russell Lowell, the American
scholar and ambassador."[158] Lang calls it "a labour of love," and
as he presumed "that only a limited edition could have found
purchasers"[159] the little book, which was issued by David Nutt
at The Sign of the Phoenix in November 1887, was confined to
550 small and 60 large paper copies, printed in red and black on
Japanese vellum, with etched title-page and other decorations by
Jacomb Hood. The edition was sold out immediately and very
soon became a collector's item, fetching high prices even for copies
on small paper. In 1896 it was reprinted without the frontispiece
and decorations, and has run into a great number of editions
between then and the present day.

Lang's translation in prose and rhymed verse has a delicacy and
fragrance that no other version of the lovely old song-story has
ever quite equalled. The language has a touch of the archaic,
and professes to be modelled on Malory; but it is a breath from
the Vale of Avalon rather than any servile attempt to imitate its
style, and there is never any suggestion of a forced or unnatural

diction: it is not "Wardour Street English" even to the extent
that the Homeric translations are.

This is perhaps the only book associated with the name of
Andrew Lang, that we may dare to describe as above praise.
Although he is only translating, and translating very faithfully,
Aucassin and Nicolete seems to enshrine the true Andrew Lang
more perfectly than any of his original works. "We are in love's
land today," as he says, and in that dream world of unfading
spring he can walk unmasked and unself-conscious: and going thus
all untrammelled among the woods and flowers, he can take us
with him all unresistingly:

> "Where smooth the Southern waters run
>   Through rustling leagues of poplars gray,
> Beneath a veiled soft Southern sun,
>   We wandered out of Yesterday;
>   Went Maying in that ancient May
> Whose fallen flowers are fragrant yet,
>   And lingered by the fountain spray
> With Aucassin and Nicolete."

From this gentle idyll of bright, fresh love in the world's
nonage, Lang turned to the exotic, over-perfumed passions of
Theophile Gautier. "Who satisfies the aspiration for an over-
flowing measure of love ?" he asks. "Perhaps Romvald, the
chosen of Clarimonde in *La Morte Amoureuse* . . . Life has *not* for
giving the love of *La Morte Amoureuse*. He who aspires to it is
impossibilium cupitor, and his romance will land him frankly in the
impossible."[160]

This translation appeared as *The Dead Leman* (1889), the first
in a volume of stories from the French, done in collaboration with
Paul Silvestre. Only the name tale is of much note, and that, it is
safe to say, is all the work of Andrew Lang. Gautier had always
been one of Lang's favourites, and in his Merton days he had
written an article on his poems containing translations that still
remain unreprinted; but in *The Dead Leman*, although a suitor for
"the lips that may not be kissed," Lang is not quite at home: the
element in which he finds himself is a trifle too heavy for him, and
the passions among which Gautier's lovers move are rather too
exotic and unhealthy.

But that Lang should have admired *La Morte Amoureuse* is a symptom of his longings after the impossible, and after the passions that are stronger and deeper than those of our waking experience.

And a little before this, a new "magic window" had been opened for Lang and for the whole world upon the "perilous seas" and "faery lands forlorn" of the eternal quest for the sublime, in the romances of Henry Rider Haggard.

The young barrister, but newly returned from South Africa, had then written only his first two, and at the time not very successful, novels, *Dawn* and *The Witch's Head*. Lang had read the second of these, and had been much attracted by the South African scenes, which he praises in his earliest letter to Haggard, written before their first meeting. In 1885 the manuscript of *King Solomon's Mines* was sent to him by W. E. Henley, and Lang wrote to Haggard, "I almost prefer it to *Treasure Island*." They met about this time, and a friendship began that was to grow with the years and last until death,

In 1886 Lang read *She* while it was in proof for serial publication in *The Graphic*. "I really must congratulate you," he wrote on July 12th. "I think it is one of the most astonishing romances I ever read. The more impossible it is, the better you do it, till it seems like a story from the literature of another planet. I can't give a better account of the extraordinary impression it makes upon me."

And when the book appeared at the end of the year (it was dedicated to him) Lang read it again, and reviewed it for *The Academy* at some length, tempering just praise with criticism as just, but professing himself "*incredibilium cupitor*, attached to impossible romance, an amateur of savage life, fond of haunting in fancy the mysterious homes of ruined races; a believer, too, in the moral of the legend," and recognizing that " the whole story is an allegory of the immortality of love, which death cannot destroy, nor the force of fire abolish it."

Truly moved by *She*; impressed as much by the echo of his own romantic dreams that dwelt behind the story, as by the brilliant handling of the tale itself, Lang wrote a sonnet, which has found place in most subsequent editions of Haggard's romance. It was headed simply "She," and dedicated "To H. Rider Haggard."

"Not in the waste beyond the swamps and sand,
The fever-haunted forest and lagoon,
Mysterious Kôr thy walls forsaken stand,
Thy lonely towers beneath the lonely moon,
Not there doth Ayesha linger, rune by rune
Spelling strange scriptures of a people banned;
The world is disenchanted; over soon
Shall Europe send her spies through all the land.

"Nay, not in Kôr, but in whatever spot,
In town, or field, or by the insatiate sea,
Men brood on buried loves, and unforgot,
Or break themselves on some divine decree,
Or would o'erleap the limits of their lot,
There, in the tombs and deathless, dwelleth SHE! "

And yet it was very typical of Andrew Lang that, being moved as he was by *She*, and impelled to write with such poetic feeling of the message that this "tale of adventure" brought to him, it should be in the form of parody that he was next to seek a means of showing his "loyalty to our lady Ayesha."

On 24th February 1887 the *St. James's Gazette* announces that "there is to be published immediately by Messrs. Longmans and Co. a travesty of Mr. Rider Haggard's *She*. The writer is the author of *Much Darker Days*."

This appeared as a little shilling volume bound in green paper with a design by W. Reader (parodying the Cartouche of Kalli-krates in *She*) with the title *He* (by the author of *It, King Solomon's Wives, Bess, Much Darker Days, Mr. Morton's Subtler*, and other romances); it opens with the sonnet quoted above, and a dedication dated "Kôr, Jan. 30th 1887" addressed to "Dear Allan Quater-main" and signed "Two of the Ama-Logrolla." In a copy of the large paper edition which he gave to C. M. Falconer, Lang wrote: "This volume is the child of the inspired fancy of W. H. Pollock and A. Lang, aided by the kind, but wholly impracticable advice of H.R.H."

He seems to have been written in separate portions by its two authors, Lang probably doing the first half of the book which throughout suggests his manner. Finishing first, and reading what

Pollock had written, Lang, observing that (unlike the Snark) he looked by no means gravely upon puns, swiftly re-wrote his own portion in an equally punning vein.[161]

Besides parodying *She*, the story is intended as a gentle satire on W. T. Stead, the editor of the *Pall Mall Gazette* (who appears as Pell-melli), who was then conducting one of his numerous crusades, this time against the "Log-rollers," or "Mutual Admiration Society of Authors" of whom he considered Lang and Haggard to be two of the most abject.

Such controversies and personalities have long ceased to interest; but as a parody of *She*, this little booklet still calls forth laughter unquenchable. Lang parodied Haggard's style in *Old Friends*, and in the same book lets Herodotus describe an early traveller's impressions of She-who-must-be-obeyed ; but he never surpassed the sheer high spirits and witty fooling of the first few chapters of *He*.

From *She* in those days Lang could never quite keep away, and a crude and unamusing "Interview with She" which Barrie wrote for *The St. James's Gazette* (16th February 1887) called forth an instant and delightful response. The letter is anonymous, but no one but Lang could have written it.

"Sir, It is very natural that your Kôr Korespondent (excuse the native play on proper names) should have been deceived into thinking that he had enjoyed an interview with She. But, as a matter of fact, Ayesha is really in Thibet, except when, as Madame Blavatsky, she occasionally appears in Anglo-Indian society.

"The cause of your correspondent's mistake is obvious. When She came to that accident in the place of the Pillar of Fire, there was every chance of a revolution in Kôr. The Radical party (Reds, or Red-hot Pots) projected an attack on property, and were only stopped by a stratagem of old Bilali's. He swathed up one of his wives—a tall and handsome girl—in She's wardrobe, and (as the Ama-Haggar had never seen Ayesha's face) the public were and remain under the impression that She is at home as usual. The new young lady ordered the instant hot-potting of all the Mutes: perhaps a superfluous precaution, as they were *dumb* mutes and could not write; but it is well to neglect nothing.

"Bilali's only apprehension is that, if it comes to blasting anybody, Mrs. Bilali may not carry out the programme adequately.

Meanwhile some excitement is caused by a threatened visit of M. Jules Verne, who demands a concession for working Kôr as a watering place; and it is feared that international difficulties may arise, as Mr. Rider Haggard neglected to plant the Union Jack at Kôr."

These were Lang's only important parodies of Rider Haggard, but the popularity of *He* inspired a young lawyer named Chatres Biron to write *King Solomon's Wives*, which was issued by Vizetelly in April 1887, and which has often been attributed to Lang on the strength of the title page of *He*. Lang, however, had no connection with it whatever, and, it is difficult to see how anyone could seriously have mistaken it for his. It contains some sparks of humour, but as a whole comes nowhere near the inspired fooling of *He*.

Lang did read Biron's booklet, and even wrote to congratulate him on it. To him, and to Rider Haggard he sent a set of verses that parody his own serious sonnet "She." From the version in Lang's hand which Haggard pasted into his own copy of *King Solomon's Wives* I transcribe this amusing emanation of the "gay mind":

TWOSH

To Hyder Ragged

Not 'mid the scamps who swagger in the Strand,
    The siren-haunted concert and saloon,
Mysterious *Twosh*, thou takest oft a hand
    At double-dummy with some wandering "coon"!
Not there doth *Noegood* with *Fullarder* spoon,
    Wrapped in wild music of some brazen band;
    Nay, these proceedings are not opportune,
But such as the Police would scarcely stand!

Nay, not in Kôrk ("barred" is the sacred "spot"
    Where western waves upon Hibernia wash,)
But wheresoever merriment is got
    By sportive souls that have a taste for bosh,
And *Sporting Times's* cheer the lonely lot;
    There (and well worth a shilling), there is TWOSH!

CHAPTER XI

The World's Desire

THE friendship between Andrew Lang and Rider Haggard thus auspiciously begun, grew and deepened swiftly. They saw much of each other at this time, when Haggard spent part of every year in London, discussed new stories, and even helped one another with their work.

Out of the great mass of letters which Lang wrote to Haggard, and which are still preserved at Ditchingham House, a number were included in *The Days of My Life*, Haggard's autobiography. Lang's unfortunate embargo on any collection of his letters prevents any attempt to print these *en masse*; but those included by Haggard can blamelessly be augmented with a few quotations from the unpublished letters, restricting such quotations (as Haggard does) to matters connected with literature.

Lang himself was notoriously pessimistic about his own writings: in a letter to E. Nesbit he describes one of his fairy-stories as "like everything of mine, utterly unpopular"[162], and similar expressions occur frequently in the Haggard correspondence. But with other people's writings and their success he was always ready to concern himself. "Probably I think more highly of your books than you do," he wrote to Haggard, "and I was infinitely more anxious for your success than for my own, which is not an excitement to me."

Lang read Haggard's next important work, *Cleopatra*, in manuscript, and made suggestions for improvements in style and shortening of archæological details. He also versified from Haggard's prose the "Lament for Osiris" and supplied the "Boat Song" and a song from the Greek of Meleager.

Allan Quatermain he does not seem to have read until it appeared as a serial in *Longmans' Magazine*, but the death of Umslopagaas remained one of the scenes in literature that affected him most, and he spent a whole day writing his epitaph in Greek and English, which appears in all editions of the book.

It was when *Cleopatra* was finished that Haggard and Lang decided to collaborate in a poetic romance, and began to cast about for a subject. A sequel to *She* suggested itself, but Haggard had planned to write it after an interval of twenty years (it appeared as *Ayesha* in 1905); and a scheme for a romance of old Kôr, with Ayesha's earlier adventures, also came to nothing. "Had I any ideas of Kôr ? " wrote Lang many years later when Haggard tried to revive this scheme, "She, I think is not easily to be raised again unless she drops her (veil ?) for some prehistoric admirer. I like Kôr, but have no precise conception of it, unless the Egyptians came thence."

But finally, at the end of 1887, they embarked upon the romance of Helen and Odysseus in Egypt after the end of the *Odyssey*, which finally appeared as *The World's Desire*.

Which of the collaborators thought of the idea is not stated, though the subject, Helen of Troy, suggests Lang. It was an ideal theme for them, as Lang was admittedly more at home among the Greeks of Homer's world than most other moderns, and in ancient Egypt Rider Haggard found his own spiritual home. Of another of Haggard's Egyptian romances Sir Gaston Maspero, the great Egyptologist, told him that "he could not conceive how it was possible for a modern man to have written a work so full of the true and inner thought and spirit of Ancient Egypt"; and *Cleopatra* had already shown Haggard to be well versed in all things connected with the old Egyptians.

To give a connected account of the writing of this book is difficult: Lang very seldom dated his letters, and to mention the year is, with him, almost unique. Even the order of the quotations given by Haggard is open to doubt, and as the story was written in a number of versions, and its construction was spread over at least two years, the following chronology must not be taken as final.

No beginning was made until late in 1887, or early the following year; Haggard was busy on a modern novel at the time, and seems to have varied his labours between it and the romance; but in March 1888, Lang is writing from Italy where he was on holiday, about ideas for the story. "Lang and I discussed it," says Rider Haggard. "Then I wrote a part of it, which part he altered or rewrote."

The earliest letter from Lang must be that given by Haggard as 8th March 1888. "You had better read the Helen of Euripides in a prose crib . . . It is about Helen in Egypt, and may suggest something." On 25th March he writes from Florence, "Just had your letter on the Jews. Do you think it worth while if it won't run easily ? . . . The idea of Odysseus and Helen is a good idea, but don't thrash a willing and perhaps weary Pegasus." And on his return to England: "Helen should be a priestess in Egypt, say of Pasht. You won't want much help from *me*. All the local colour is in the *Odyssey*."

After this, Haggard worked away at the story, doing a good deal of what is now the central portion. Then he sent it to Lang, who promptly lost the manuscript so completely and for so long a time that the idea of writing the book was almost abandoned. But later in the year Lang came across it, thrust into a large folio volume, and his interest revived. "There are jolly things in it," he wrote on 11th October, "*but* I fear it is too remote for this people. It isn't my idea how to do it (not that that matters), for I'd have begun with Odysseus in a plague-stricken Ithaca, and have got on to Egypt. And I'd have written in modern English. However, as it stands, I don't care quite for the way the Wanderer is introduced. He comes rather perfunctorily and abruptly on the scene, to my feeling. It is a subject that wants such a lot of thinking out. It would be jolly if we had more time in this world of ours . . . I can't help regretting my veteran Odysseus—I don't think he would have been too "grey-eyed." If we really collaborate, as we proposed originally, I'd begin with him; bring him in your way to Egypt, introduce him to the old cove who would tell him about Hatasu (as in yours) and then let things evolve, but keep all the English modern, except in highly-wrought passages, incantations, etc. I dare say it would make a funny mixture."

A few days later Lang writes: "Having nothing to do this afternoon I did a lot of Odysseus. I brought him home from the people who never saw salt, in a boat of Dreams, and I made him find nobody alive in Ithaca, a pyre of ashes in the front garden, and a charred bone with Penelope's bracelet on it! But the *bow* was at home! If you can make it alive (it's as dead as mutton) the "local colour" is all right. Then I'd work in your bit, where the Sidonians nobble him, and add local colour." And finally, on 2nd November, he writes: "I have done a little more. Taken Odysseus into the darkness and given him a song, but I think he had been reading Swinburne when he wrote it!"

After this, the next stage is uncertain. Probably Lang sent the manuscript back to Haggard, who must have written a good deal more to it, and then returned it to Lang early in 1889. Thus on 1st January 1889, Lang is commenting on Haggard's ideas: "*Splendid* idea, no two people seeing Helen the same. . . . I bar the bogles rather. They'd need to be very shadowy at least. If you have them, they should simply make room for him. But the shifting beauty is really poetical to my mind."

Here the quotations in Haggard's autobiography break off, but an undated sheet, in Lang's hand, headed "The Song of the Bow" (an early title for the book), which is loosely inserted into the manuscript in the Norwich Castle Museum, suggests Lang's reactions to the story as it was when Haggard returned it to him, probably in February 1889.

"If this is to go on, I think first the Ship of Dreams must go, too absurd, and start with a stranger *waking* in Ithaca. Leave his convoy to the reader's fancy. Then the style wants brisking up and de-archaicising—nom d'un nom, what a word! Then, at the Egyptian court, two Dervish figures must flit about and make Meneptah very anxious, and Meriamun very mad (Moses and Aaron). The night of the First Born must follow on Panauk's tale of the Incantation, which, with its terror, might almost take the curl out of Odysseus. The rabble might attack the Strange Hathor, and Odysseus rescue her and be taken for Paris by her. Recognitions, Ferocity of Meriamun. Her dodge to get at Odysseus—by pretending to be Helen—(à la Elaine and Lancelot, when she lay with him as Guinevere). Irritation and annoyance of Odysseus. Then he and Helen must come together at some time. Meriamun may make the king send him to fight the Northern Invaders, the Aquanisha, Shardana, and the rest. He can defeat them, but be shot from the sea, and, if you like, his son by Circe, Telegonus, can do the shoot, and pathetic recognition before he dies, the last of the men who fought under Troy. Helen must disappear strangely, and Meriamun go to Kôr, or blazes. We get rid of the Beni Israel, who go off on the night of the first-born. I'd have an ambush, worked by Odysseus, to catch the Aquanisha, always good, an ambush. This is a very rough sketch. I'd cut down the (*word illegible*) business very short, to "shew up" the incantation scenes, and I'd modernise the style a good deal, except in Panauk's narrative."

After this, the letters at Ditchingham show how Lang worked over Haggard's draft of the central portion of the book. Their chronology is as near as can be reconstructed.

"*March* 10 . . . I have re-written the beginning of the death of the First Born. Pharaoh. taunts the Wanderer as not drinking, and pledges him in the Cup of Pasht; the Wanderer, having lost his temper, drinks to the Strange Hathor . . . Loi (the Panauk of the foregoing, and the Rei of the final version) must *not* know the armour of Paris, the spear point is enough to annoy *him*; it would let out that Helen came with Paris . . ."

"*March* 12 . . . *You* gave Loi a white beard! I shaved it! I have not been idle. I've worked to the advent of the Jews, knocked out a lot of Wardour Street; added a heap, and re-written the first chapter plainer and shorter. In the chapter of the Baths of Natrus I have introduced a new scene, the Wanderer mending his armour with Kurri, tossing K. the bronze head of the spear. This K. uses to cut the bowstring later. Also I have made Loi bring a hiero-glyphic scroll, which stumps the Wanderer, and I have made the Apura carry Joseph's mummy-case, and made Meriamun curse them, and prophesy that not one of them shall see the Promised Land. And they *didn't*. Also I made their hymn break into Loi's story, and doesn't he curse them!"

"[*No date*] . . . Recognition Scene . . . I have written a good deal here and there, and I have a good deal of sympathy with Meriamun. Perhaps I shall re-write all that chapter once more, but *I'm* no good at fictions [? or *flirtations*?]. However, I'll try. It's the keystone of the whole affair . . ."

"*March* 19 . . . When Meriamun talks to Loi about the A(ncient) E(vil), and when she speaks to it, she speaks another tongue, a dead tongue, the tongue of ancient Kôr! That's rather nice, I hope! I've been through again and added a good deal, but I've *cut* some long speeches, and have rather a jolly scene, I think, with the W., when Loi first meets him . . ."

"[*No date*] . . . I hope you will like the new turn to the death of Pharaoh, where I give Meriamun a song, and tell the death

differently. Chess again, and 'Pharaoh is dead!' I like Helen's
song in the flames; she lets the women have it. It's rather a
misogynistic book on the whole . . ."

"*March* 25 . . . I've done about all I can to the *Bow*. I added a
tiny bit of Homeric fighting. But it was little I could do to the last
chapters, bar songs. I still wish I could modernise the style still
more. Well, it's amused *me*, and that is something! "

Thus the history of the book would seem to be that after con-
sultation Haggard wrote a small portion which Lang re-wrote or
revised; Haggard then drafted the rest of the book and sent it to
Lang, who lost it for more than six months. When found, Lang
wrote the early part of the book and revised or re-wrote much of
the rest, and Haggard wrote the final version, leaving the first four-
and-a-half chapters untouched, for they alone are in Lang's hand
in the manuscript at the Norwich Castle Museum.

The first four chapters are almost solely the work of Lang, with
certain incidents by Haggard rewritten, and a few paragraphs
incorporated. After this it is so evenly worked over that no
considerable portion can be assigned to either author, though
Haggard's style is the most predominant. Often, however, the
careful student of Lang comes upon a passage, sometimes of a few
pages in length, that is unmistakably his—just as in many other
places the manner, a turn of phrase or way of thought could only
be Haggard's. The songs, of course, are entirely the work of Lang,
though the Israelitish hymns appear to be versified from Haggard's
prose, as the Duologue of the Bow and the Snake may also be.
Helen's songs, particularly the first, second and third, and
Meriamun's song, are very charming examples of Lang's poetry,
and the third song, "Lost Love," ranks with his earlier poems of a
like inspiration.

Lang wrote also a Prologue to *The World's Desire* which is a
beautiful example of his prose. The language is quite simple and
undecorated, and the intention of the whole is pictorial and in a
sense nostalgic: and it certainly does conjure up to a remarkable
degree a vision of the heroic age, that world of unnatural light and
shade, where seas are bluer and grass is greener than our waking
experience can parallel: the temples stand white and shining among
the silver olive groves, and the woods and valleys are peopled with
nymphs and dryads; Pan's pipe sounds upon the lonely hillsides,

as in Greece today one can still hear the shepherds playing on the
grey slopes of Parnassus; and Helen's voice comes to us from
the distance, leading us willingly captive to a romance that is the
allegory of all the dreams that once were ours and that faded into
the cold light of our experience and disillusionment in the cruel
world of reality—faded, or are cherished still among the day-
dreams that age does not forget.

And yet, with the strange freakishness that was his, Lang would
not include his Prologue in the published book : "The Prologue
I wrote is better out," he remarks to Haggard, and we hear no
more of it; but it still survives with the manuscript of the book in
the Norwich Castle Museum—whence it has seemed worth while
to rescue it and print it for the first time. (See Appendix B.)

The tale itself tells of "the last seafaring of Odysseus, of
his latest battle, of his latest love; and the death that came upon
him from the sea." Sleeping in the temple of Aphrodite on
his return (from his second, unsung, voyaging) to an Ithaca
plague-stricken and deserted, he is shown a vision of Helen,
the World's Desire, whom he had three times seen in the course
of his adventures; and the goddess promises that he shall look
upon Helen again, and win her if his heart be pure and set upon
her alone.

While sleeping on the seashore, Odysseus is seized by Sidonian
pirates who bear him away to sell as a slave in Egypt; only, by
cunning and bravery he overcomes them, enslaving their captain,
Kurri, and taking their ship and its treasures. In Egypt Odysseus
finds that a time of terror and disquiet has fallen upon the land:
"the veiled, the dread, the unseen Jehovah of the Chosen People
was at awful strife with the dusky Egyptian deities, cat-headed,
crocodile-tailed, Pasht and Ra and Amen, and the lord of Souls,
Osiris." Also a strange and beautiful goddess, "the Hathor,"
dwells alone in a temple, and lures to death all men who see her
or hear her song.

Odysseus dares the dangers of the chapel perilous, and overcomes the guardians of the beauty of Helen. And there he finds
her, immortal and changeless in loveliness, innocent still of all the
deaths that were and are because of her. ("I can't feel *quite* certain
that Helen ever went to Troy," Lang wrote to Haggard. "In
Herodotus and Euripides only her shadow goes"; and acting on

this doubt, he had written "The Shade of Helen" in *Ballads and Lyrics*.)

"There was the visible Helen, the bride and the daughter of mystery, the World's Desire.. There shone the fabled loveliness of which no story seemed too strange, of which all miracles seemed true ... There sat she whose voice was the echo of all sweet voices, she whose shape was the mirror of all fair forms ... On her breast gleamed the Star-Stone, the red stone of the sea deeps that melts in the sunshine, but that melted not on the breast of Helen. Moment by moment the red drops from the ruby heart of the star fell on her snowy raiment, fell and vanished, fell and vanished and left no stain."

But the Wanderer may not win the World's Desire thus easily; and Meriamun, Egypt's queen, weaves a snare of evil magic about the heart of Odysseus, tricks him by shape-shifting, and overcomes him with desire, so that he forgets the warning of his vision, and swears by the Snake of Lust and not by the Star of Love.

Then the toils of Fate close about Odysseus: he threatens to denounce Meriamun, but is wrongfully accused by her, and is only reprieved from the tormenters to lead the Egyptian forces against the northern invaders, who are led by Odysseus' own countrymen, the sons of those who fought at Troy. He conquers in the battle, but is slain at the moment of victory by his own son Telegonus. But Helen is near him, and he dies in her arms at the last, comforted by her words, and in the belief of an ultimate union "beyond the Gateways of the West."

So dies Odysseus, and is burned on a mighty funeral pyre.

"For a while the Golden Helen stood still, looking on the dying fire; then she let her veil fall, and turning, wandered forth into the desert and the night, singing as she passed. And so she goes, wandering, wandering, till Odysseus comes again."

Lang described *The World's Desire* as "an experiment in romance," and hesitated whether to call it an historical novel; "Meneptah, the son of Rameses II, usually regarded as the Pharaoh of the Exodus, is as historical as George the Fourth," he wrote; and Meriamun was also in very fact the sister and queen of Meneptah, although, of course, "her position has no warrant in ancient legends."

But it is from mythology, from the old legendary history of
Homeric Greece and of the Children of Israel that the story is
derived. Helen was worshipped as a goddess in Egypt, as
Herodotus relates; the "Star-Stone" did indeed shine upon her
bosom, according to Servius, and Eustathius speaks of her changing loveliness. Incidents are modelled on Greek originals, particularly in Lang's first chapters: the fight with the Sidonians
from the Homeric Hymn to Dionysus and the *Odyssey*; the scene
in the Temple of Aphrodite was suggested by another Homeric
Hymn; and of course all the archæological background is direct
from Homer. The death of Odysseus is also traditional: the ghost
of Tiresias in the *Odyssey* had prophesied that it should come upon
Odysseus "from the sea," and later legends agreed that Telegonus,
his son by Circe, "did the shoot," as Lang puts it. The second
"unsung wanderings" to the people who knew not salt and had
never seen the sea, is also foreshadowed in the *Odyssey*, and may
have been dealt with in the lost epic *Telegonia*, of which Proclus
has preserved a summary. One adventure on this voyage is preserved by Parthenius, but Lang either did not know, or chose to
ignore rather a discreditable incident in his hero's career!

Other "legendary connections" are with *She*, and the underlying idea both of *The World's Desire* and of the whole "Ayesha
saga" may be found in Meriamun's vision. Many years later
Haggard re-told the vision, more clearly and at great length, in
Wisdom's Daughter, which novel is all that we have of the "romance
of old Kôr" in which Lang was to have collaborated, and which
tells the earlier adventures of Ayesha that are so often touched upon
in *She*. The idea behind all these books (with the probable exception of *She*, where Ayesha just exists without any very definite
function in the scheme of things), is of the Platonic Dual Unity of
"Complementary Souls." Haggard conceives of these as sinning in
the morning of Time when they dwelt on the divine threshold of
the world, and of being doomed to an age-long quest by the
Powers against which they had sinned: "From two be ye made
three, and for all time strive ye to be twain again," so the gods
decree in Meriamun's vision: "Pass on from life to life, live and
love and hate, and seem to die . . . work each other woe according
to the laws of earth, and for your love's sake sin, and be ashamed
and re-arise, appear to conquer and be conquered, pursuing your

threefold destiny, which is one destiny, till the hours of punishment are outworn, and, at the word of Fate, the unaltering circle meets, and the evil of blindness falls from your eyes, and, as a scroll, your folly is unrolled and the hid purpose of your sorrow is accomplished, and once more ye are Twain and One."

It is necessary to bear this myth in mind to understand how it comes that Meriamun is to be re-incarnated as Ayesha, as whom she sees herself in her vision, in the future existence where she "dwelt among the graves," girdled with the Snake, "and once more the woman and I struggled for mastery, and though I seemed to conquer, yet a sea of fire came over me." For Ayesha, in *She* and in *Wisdom's Daughter* has all the divine power of Helen, but also the evil passions of Meriamun and her magic, while the human rival (Amenartas or Ustane) has but the pale residue of the Divine Personality; while in *Ayesha*, the last book of the cycle, Ayesha herself is the Golden Helen, and more divine even than Helen was, while the human rival, Atene, is made up of all the evil that has been purged out of Ayesha, and has no part in the Three that become Two again when Ayesha and Leo, who are Helen and Odysseus, purged by the fires of death, are united once more, with the Quest accomplished.

The connection with *She* was borne in mind quite clearly by Lang and Haggard when writing *The World's Desire*. Besides the actual passage in Meriamun's vision, we find Lang writing to Haggard: "Perhaps Meriamun in her vision might have a glimpse of Kôr and the Ama-Haggars flitting about, etc. That would show the reader where he was"; and again: "Loi is Bilali, I suppose"; or later, when the original schemes are modified; "I leave it to you how much those *She* references shall stand: the vaguer the better, I think."

The World's Desire ran serially in *The New Review* from April to December 1890, and appeared in book form on 5th November of the same year, published by Longmans in an edition of 10,000, uniform with Rider Haggard's other works from the same house. The authors had originally intended to have the book illustrated by their mutual friend, W. B. Richmond, but this scheme did not materialize, and it appeared without illustrations, but dedicated to Richmond. ("I just put ' To W. B. Richmond, A.R.A.' " writes Lang to Haggard while the book was in the press, "and didn't add 'whose failures in Classic Art highly remind the authors of their own,' as I thought it would be rude!") For the edition of 1894 Maurice Greiffenhagen prepared a series of illustrations in black and white of no particular excellence, though his originals at Ditchingham House are very much better than the prints in the book.

The book had a large and immediate sale when it appeared in 1890, and has been constantly in print for the succeeding fifty years. But on the part of the professional critics its reception showed a warmth of another kind. As Lang wrote in a presentation copy of the book:

> "It did not set the Thames on fire,
> It is not quite ' The World's Desire! '
> Much rather do the public scoff,
> And yell to Nature, ' Take them off! '
> While critics constantly conspire
> To slate the hapless *World's Desire*."

The National Observer, for example, calls it a "tortuous and ungodly jumble of anarchy and culture," and the critic is "moved to curse his literary gods and die at the thought of the most complete artistic suicide it has ever been his lot to chronicle." The attack is brilliantly clever, and suggests the authorship of Henley, the editor: this "archangel ruined" was already beginning to vent his rancour at an unkind world in petty ways: his quarrel with Stevenson was of about this date, and at this period his reviews of Lang's work became suddenly most bitter.

The review takes the form of a parody of the story: The Children of Israel are neatly described as "a cross between the Salvation Army and the criminal classes." When day dawns upon Odysseus and Meriamun, "the Bow dropped into poetry, and at the sound of the noise whereof the Wanderer turned him to consult his watch and ask the meaning of that infernal row. That is to say, ' he yawned, he stretched his mighty arms, he opened his eyes '—and there beside him was She-Who-Must-Be-Obeyed! Unhappily he knew not his Haggard; wherefore he hesitated not to tell the lady that she had made a mistake. So she went forth into the Palace of Pharaoh and cried unto all men's hearing a version (carefully brought down to date) of the story of Joseph and the wife of

Potiphar. Now, the guards were simple men, and nothing they recked of chestnuts; and in those days, of fire escapes there were none in the land of Egypt. So they went for the Wanderer; and his musical box was damaged in the struggle; and they tied him fast, and, hero as he was, behold they ran him in!"

This is all very amusing, but it is not criticism. Much fairer was J. M. Barrie in *The British Weekly*—and Barrie had no special liking for romances of this type, and detested Rider Haggard's adventure stories: "The crowning misfortune of *The World's Desire* is that it is sometimes dull, a failing that we should not find in any book written by Mr. Haggard or Mr. Lang alone. The characters do not interest as human beings, because the good ones are assisted by miracles from the gods above, while the bad ones can at any moment summon the gods from below. There is a lack of Mr. Haggard's realism and Mr. Lang's humour. The imitation of Homer is capital, but it wearies. It is as an allegory that the story is impressive, and though it is at times really striking when thus regarded, the public do not care for allegories. The slaughter is terrible, but hardly tragic. Yet it should be said that the story has one singularly beautiful moment: when Telegonus discovers that he has slain his father Odysseus. This is most tragic, most pathetic, because the writing is so artistic."

Much of this is undoubtedly just; for to the critical adult reader a certain amount of the book *is* dull—or rather, it goes on too long in some places. The criticism of the characters was inevitable from such a master of character as Barrie, but he was looking for something which was never intended to be there. The story is indeed an allegory, and, like much that Haggard wrote, it depends on its large, powerful strokes rather than on any attempt at a delicate portrayal of character and emotion. It is an epic or saga rather than a novel, but it is a dream-fantasy too, in which life as we know it forms only the ground-row before a vast cyclorama of moving, shadowy shapes born from our inner consciousness, and finding an echo there and a reflection that should not and cannot be exhibited or analysed in the cold light of the world's daytime.

Judged simply as an adventure story, *The World's Desire* is not as successful as most of Haggard's romances. A schoolboy reader finds it "slow," and turns from it to re-read *The Holy Flower* for the tenth time. And yet, if he comes to read it again in a year or

two, at the time when romance has begun to mean for him something more than a succession of hair-breadth escapes and slaughters
grim and great, when the poetry of life becomes dimly apparent to
him and the clouds upon his horizon glow with the great glory of an
unseen light behind them:—then *The World's Desire* may well seem
to be the most wonderful book in the world, and the most inspiring.

We can but give our own impressions of romance; for, like
humour, it may not be judged by any canons of the art of writing,
and may move one reader to the depths of his being, while another
is merely bored.

The schoolboy who considered *The World's Desire* the most
wonderful and inspiring book in the world, did not ever go so far
as to call it the greatest. For true greatness he would turn to
Fielding or Thackeray, to Shakespeare or Morris with honest
appreciation: but he would turn from these at the year's ending for
his annual reading of *The World's Desire*, and he was never disappointed. Finding nowhere else in all Rider Haggard's fifty-eight
works of fiction, quite the same touch of enchantment, he turned
his attention to Andrew Lang, and found what he sought dwelling
like some ghost of Avalon among certain of the poems, about the
ruined towers of Fairnilee, and under the wet woods of spring
where wandered Aucassin and Nicolete.

Such a criticism is offered for what it is worth: the schoolboy
was at least a candid critic; he had no axe to grind, no one had
shown these things to him, and his reading was of a very wide and
catholic nature. To criticize it in cold blood a dozen years later is a
hard and unkind task. We can sigh over an occasional *longeur* and
mark with regret how many more passages of inflated language and
shallow thought there are than we remembered; but the book as a
whole wears remarkably well, and has still the power to stir within
the reader that unknown element of wonder and exaltation which
is the secret of romantic literature.

And apart from the readers of adventure stories, *The World's
Desire* has had its more discerning admirers. William Canton, the
poet and essayist, wrote of it as "one of the most strikingly picturesque and imaginative of recent romances"[163] and Haggard
wrote to Lang in 1907: "I think you were a bit discouraged about
The World's Desire because a lot of *ignorant* fools slated it, but in
my opinion you were wrong. That work I believe will last. It is

extraordinarily liked by many who can understand. I told you about the American Egyptologist I met, for instance, who reads it every night! "

Lang, however, was as pessimistic as usual: "*The World's Desire* took in despite of my ill-omened name: I brought you worse luck than you would have had alone."

Although so much of it is the work of Rider Haggard, the spirit of Andrew Lang is very apparent throughout the book, and it is perhaps the most definite statement that we have of his romantic aspirations towards the unattainable, his romantic love for the "Daughters of Dreams" among whom Helen was ever pre-eminent. She did not reign alone, indeed, but the other ladies of romance are themselves but incarnations of The World's Desire: "Everyone, it may be supposed, has his favourite lady in Shakespeare," wrote Lang of one of these, "among his women every man meets that soul kindred to his own, and immortally longed for, whom we do not generally find in this little life, though perhaps she may welcome us in another. It is to Rosalind that I myself, to make frank confession, have ever been hopelessly devoted, much as if Jaques had loved her in the play—the melancholy Jaques . . . Men like Jaques in Rosalind find all that is not their own, all that they have let go by them: the youth that they would not enjoy, the heart, the spring, the mirth, the courage of existence, these they find in Rosalind and hopelessly desire and know that they can never possess."[164]

Whether he tells of a love that was lost or of a love that never was found, this was ever the message of Andrew Lang the true poet, the disinherited dreamer. As he wrote one day after reading F. Anstey's *The Tinted Venus*, and recalling the old story of "The Ring Given to Venus" on which it is based:

> "We love like him who gave long time ago
>   To Venus' marble hand his wedding ring;
>   No more his love's embrace might round him cling,
> Nor heart with heart responsive ebb and flow;
> Only the goddess-ghost would come and go, ·
>   To fan him with the breath of her white wing,
>   And dull the fever, and assuage the sting,
> And comfort him a little in his woe.

"And we, like him, have given our hearts away
　　To beauty that was never clad in clay,
That puts all mortal loveliness to scorn;
　　A pale, a bitter, and a jealous queen,
With her undying beauty set between
　　Our loves and us, to make us all forlorn."

CHAPTER XII

The Romance of History

"THE WORLD'S DESIRE" did not mark the end of Andrew Lang's quest for the unattainable ideal in romance. He found an embodiment of his dreams in the legendary figure of Argive Helen, and his faith to her, and to that for which she stood, never faltered, even though he might find her living once more in the other heroines of romance, in Rosalind and in Di Vernon; but there was another lady of old time whom he loved also, though with a different measure of devotion—Jeanne d'Arc, the Maid of France.

When Lang began to interest himself in the Maid is uncertain; but it was in the early 'nineties that he began to write about her, and that she grew to be one of his most absorbing interests. In his monthly *causerie* "At the Sign of the Ship" in *Longmans' Magazine* —always a reliable indicator of the "craze" that was swaying him at the moment—Lang begins to mention Jeanne d'Arc in April 1894, when he suggests that Stanley Weyman should write a novel about her. To this same month, according to C. M. Falconer in his transcript of uncollected poems by Lang (in the Dundee Library), belongs the poem "Jeanne d'Arc," which was published in *Longmans' Magazine* three years later; and in June 1894 "The Ship" contains another of Lang's poems "How the Maid Marched from Blois." This poem, together with his best known one on the subject, "A Scot to Jeanne d'Arc," appeared at the end of the year in his volume of poems grave and gay, *Ban and Arrière Ban*, where it is illustrated by a drawing of Henry Ford's. In this poem Lang touches on the special association that the Scots have with Jeanne d'Arc, for there were Scots in her guard and near her throughout all her career, and the stigma of her betrayal and death which rests on English and French alike, cannot touch them.

"Dark Lily without blame,
Not upon us the shame
Whose sires were to the Auld Alliance true;
They by the Maiden's side,
Victorious fought and died,
One stood by Thee that fiery torment through—

· · ·

"Not upon us, dark Lily without blame,
Not on the north may fall the shadow of that shame."

Lang wrote about Jeanne d'Arc and the Scots in his "Ship" article for October 1894, and a note to the poem in *Ban and Arrière Ban* contains the gist of his researches in conveniently small space:

"Jeanne d'Arc is said to have led a Scottish force at Lagny, when she defeated the Burgundian, Franquet d'Arras. A Scottish artist painted her banner; he was a James Polwarth, or Power, or a Hume of Polwarth . . . A monk of Dunfermline, who continued Fordun's Chronicle, avers that he was with the Maiden in her campaigns and at her martyrdom. He calls her *puella a spiritu sancto excitata*. Unluckily his manuscript breaks off in the middle of a sentence. At her trial, Jeanne said that she had only once seen her own portrait; it was in the hands of a Scottish archer . . . Two archers of the name of Lang, Lain or Laing were in the French service about 1507."

Here were all the ingredients of such an historical romance as ever delighted the heart of Andrew Lang; here was a personal loyalty and a personal adoration—and out of these things Lang wove his only historical romance, *A Monk of Fife*.

The hero, Norman Leslie, is that same Monk of Dunfermline whose Latin Chronicle breaks off so tantalizingly: Lang fables that he continued it in French, and of this narrative the story purports to be a translation. Hume of Polwarth, the Maid's banner-painter, is in the book, and his daughter, Elliot, is the beloved of Norman Leslie, who is himself the artist in whose hand Jeanne once saw her portrait.

Lang's knowledge of all the evidence that has bearing on the life and career of Jeanne d'Arc was very profound, even at that date. In 1895, while *A Monk of Fife* was running serially in a magazine,

Lang issued privately a pamphlet on *The Voices of Jeanne d'Arc*, in which all his knowledge of psychical phenomena is brought to bear on the historical problem. And the "Fairy Book" for that Christmas, *The Red True Story Book*, contained a very full life of Jeanne written by him.

A Monk of Fife appeared early in 1896, printed in a type intended to suggest Black Letter, and with decorations and drawings by Selwyn Image in the style of an illustration from a late medieval manuscript or a very early printed book. "In writing *A Monk of Fife*," wrote Lang long afterwards, "I professed to have discovered the continuation, in French, of a genuine manuscript account of Jeanne d'Arc, begun in Latin by her friend, a Scot, and mysteriously broken off in the middle of a sentence. I even went so far as to forge extracts, in Old French, from the chapel register of St. Catherine of Fierbois, confirmatory of my narrative. Perhaps this was wrong. It was a blunder, if not a crime, for a learned medievalist could not make out whether he had a modern novel or a fifteenth-century document in his hands; while the novel-reading public exclaimed : ' Oh, this is a horrid real history! ' "[165]

In the following year he was to edit and translate as a companion volume to *Aucassin and Nicolete*, extracts from the genuine text of the charming old chapel register of *The Miracles of Madame St. Catherine of Fierbois:* and, alas, there is no mention in it of Norman Leslie!

The story of *A Monk of Fife* is very simple; the hero flees from his home at St. Andrews for the supposed slaying of a man in a quarrel over a game of golf, and takes service with the Scottish Guard at about the time of Jeanne's first appearance at Chinon. This young Scot, Norman Leslie, follows Jeanne through most of her career, suffering the fortunes of war, and winning for himself the love of Elliot Hume, daughter of the Maid's banner-painter. His great enemy is the villainous Noiroufle, or Brother Thomas (an historical personage, whose proceedings are quite the work of Lang's imagination) who is responsible for nearly all the catastrophes of the story—and of contemporary history. Brother Thomas, for example, wounds Jeanne under the walls of Orleans, and by him she is captured before Compiègne. In the end, Norman Leslie lays a plot to free Jeanne from prison in Rouen the day before her death, but she refuses to fly, and Norman can only be present at her burning, and ride away in adoration of the saint whose martyrdom he has witnessed.

Of the characters in the book, Brother Thomas is the most unfortunate. He is simply a piece of unnatural machinery, of a pattern common to historical fiction. Ainsworth (whose works Lang could not read) can furnish many such characters, and S. R. Crockett many more. Even Dumas could not avoid introducing in *Twenty Years After* the arch-villain Mordaunt, who alone is responsible for the foiling of D'Atagnan's plot to rescue Charles I —Mordaunt who himself strikes the fatal blow, when the Musketeers have removed all the professional executioners.

Of the rest, Leslie is a pleasant, credible character; sometimes rather shadowy, and rather too often merely the chronicler of historical events at which he chanced to be present, but well worthy the love of sweet Elliot Hume, a most winsome maid and lovable—if lacking in any great depth or penetration. Only in one respect does Norman Leslie live with a passionate intensity of feeling, and escape quite away from the slightly self-conscious artifice of the book into the "large air" of a moving and vital world, and that is in his devotion for the Maid. Here it is Lang who is speaking, Lang who is laying bare the intensity and the longing of his own heart. An early reviewer speaks of: "the kind of religious fervour that inspires it," and *The National Observer* is of the opinion that in Jeanne, Lang "has drawn a picture of her that must rank high among historical portraits."

Certainly the Maid is a magnificent piece of work. To present her as both the saint and the peasant girl was not an easy task, and perhaps Lang does not accomplish it as dispassionately as some might desire. It is with the eyes of wonder that he regarded her, that Norman Leslie regards her, and it is with the eyes of wonder that we see her too, living and moving against a background of faded tapestry, and among shadowy forms of men and women that are so much less vital than she is. Whether Lang had this contrast clearly in mind cannot be determined: but it is improbable that he had. His gift was never in the direction of depicting ordinary men and women: "I can do nothing with human nature," he remarked once to Horace Hutchinson, who goes on to say that in his historical writings Lang was interested mainly in "the activities" of the persons concerned, "in the scrapes into which they fell, and in the puzzles, as in a detective story, which they presented; but he was not really very interested in their characters and in their motives."[166] Whatever the truth of this, Lang certainly excelled in creating an atmosphere of reverence and wonder; of feeling the presence of something beyond and above our normal experience and of imparting that feeling to the reader. For this reason at least *A Monk of Fife* deserves to be read and remembered; nor, despite the faults in construction that prevent it from occupying a place in the very first rank of historical romances, is it lacking over much in the qualities that appeal to the casual reader of such books.

It has not, perhaps, the dash and glitter, the excitement and the holding power of Stanley Weyman or Conan Doyle at their best, but it is only relatively lacking in these qualities, and it has qualities of its own that neither of these authors can offer us.

In its own day it won considerable popularity, and was in a fourth edition within a few months of its appearance. *The National Observer* (of which Henley was no longer editor) gives it high praise: "To write a romance on such a subject might well give the bravest pause. Mr. Lang has done it, however, and a wonderfully fine piece of work it is. We can think of no one but himself who could have written it." And *The Sketch* was of the opinion that "this book must easily win a distinctive and honourable and permanent place." But although it was still in print at the time of Lang's death, its popularity was not such as to preserve it as a classic, and the general run of novel readers at the present day would probably endorse this opinion. Perhaps Lang was right when he wrote "The novel is not my trade; my romance . . . would turn out bitterly historical."[167] Readers of historical novels do not look particularly for careful history, any more than for beauties of style: nor do those who would appreciate Lang's qualities as a poet and a mystic weaver of romance look for them in the same shelf as Crockett and Weyman and Doyle.

Whatever our verdict may be on *A Monk of Fife*, its reception was not sufficiently warm to conquer Lang's habitual distrust of his own powers, and he never again attempted to enter the forbidden valleys of poetical romance.

But his devotion to Joan the Maid did not suffer any diminution: already in 1896 he was defending her against those historians who

sought to treat her mystic attributes as fictitious; on 5th September
of that year he wrote a long and carefully-reasoned letter to the
Academy, protesting against the reviewer of a life by Mrs. Oliphant
who sought to dismiss the Maid as an impostor. In 1906 he wrote another life for children, *The Story of Joan of Arc*, which appeared in a
series of great lives which was edited by his brother, John Lang.

But the publication of Anatole France's *Vie de Jeanne d'Arc*
early in 1908 urged Lang to a fuller and more permanent expression of his understanding of the Maid both as a character and as an
historical problem. The French work had presented Jeanne as a
weak and hysterical peasant girl, whose "voices" were hallucina-
tions, and whose proceedings were prompted by scheming priests
and prelates. Lang, despite his ardently romantic attachment to the
Maid, approached the subject as an exact and painstaking historian
(a study in which he had by then made himself as proficient as the
best), and mainly by a far more careful examination of the evidence,
was able to defeat Anatole France on his own ground.

Lang's book, *The Maid of France*, which was written in a little
over three months, became at once the standard biography, and has
not yet been superseded. "Out of the extensive literature of the
subject," says Louis Cazamian in his lecture, "we may choose other
interpretations of the Maid, equally interesting, differently
convincing; their perspective may vary widely from Lang's, their
light be more brilliant; but there is none whose authority grows
upon us with a more gradual, more gentle and irresistible touch."
"I have spoken my word for the Maid," wrote Lang to his friend,
M. Jusserand. "She was not what a vain Anatole France supposes!
He did not verify his references!"[168] And Cazamian sums up
Lang's qualifications against those of Anatole France as
exhibited in the two books: "He shows himself the better historian, the fairer interpreter of documents. Even his reading of the
texts is more accurate, when a knowledge of fifteenth-century
French is implied. His acquaintance with the international
civilization of the Middle Ages is more thorough . . . His analysis of
the Maid's character and motives is guided by a more penetrating,
because more sympathetic, perception of psychological facts."

Anatole France made some attempt to meet Lang's attack by
issuing a new and revised edition in 1909. But Lang was not yet
satisfied, and replied specifically in a rare work entitled *La Jeanne*

d'Arc de M. Anatole France, issued in Paris in the same year, with a dedication to Mark Twain—a fellow worshipper at the shrine of St. Joan. Lang describes this book of 168 pages as "a little work of historical criticism, not published in English, done into French by an eminent French critic."[169]

This was the last of Lang's writings on Jeanne d'Arc, and the monument that he has raised to his favourite heroine, with *A Monk of Fife* and *The Maid of France* forms a worthy monument also to Lang himself, and such a monument as he would most have desired. "He was always ready to champion her cause on any hint of disparagement," writes Miss Alice King Stewart. "I remember how pleased he was when a friend said to him in my hearing: ' I think Joan of Arc will be the first to welcome you in Heaven, Mr. Lang '—' I should like to think it might be so,' was his quiet reply."[170]

The consideration of Lang's writings about Jeanne d'Arc has taken us well beyond the date of *A Monk of Fife*; but the period in his career at which that romance was written marked an important new development in his labours; the beginning of his work as a historian.

Two incidents seem to have led him to take up this new branch of study seriously, of which one was the publication in 1893 of his book on the history of *St. Andrews*. He undertook it lightheartedly, without proper study, and without any experience in what he calls "the rules of the game of history": and the result, however entertaining to read, is full of mistakes and inaccuracies, which critics were not slow to point out and to condemn.

At about the same time, Robert Louis Stevenson wrote from Samoa asking Lang for materials for a Scottish historical novel of the Jacobite period. Lang examined and procured transcripts of the Pelham Papers at the British Museum, and in so doing discovered the identity of the spy who, after the "Forty-Five," kept the English court informed of all that Prince Charlie was doing or planning. Scot had mentioned, in the Preface to *Redgauntlet*, the existence of such a spy, but had not identified him. Lang discovered that he was one Macdonell of Glengarry, a chieftain of noble birth.

Here was the stuff for historical fiction, and he sent all that he could find at a first gleaning to Stevenson in Samoa, who at once embarked on *The Young Chevalier*. It was to have been a "romance of Prince Charles's hidden years," Lang tells us. "There was a treasure, an authentic treasure; there were real spies, a real assassin; a real, or reported rescue of a lovely girl from a fire at Strasbourg by the Prince." Of this proposed novel Stevenson wrote to Sidney Colvin on 9th March 1892: "The Lang story will be very little about the treasure; the Master (of Ballantrae) will appear; and it is to a great extent a tale of Prince Charlie *after* the '45, and a love story forbye: the hero is a melancholy exile, and marries a young woman who interests the Prince, and there is the devil to pay. I think the Master kills him in a duel, but don't know yet, not having seen my second heroine. No—the Master doesn't kill him, they fight, he is wounded, and the Master plays *deus ex machina* . . . My melancholy young man is to be quite a Romeo. Yes, I'll name the book from him: Dyce of Ythan . . ."

But Stevenson wrote no more than a chapter and a half, and after his death in December 1894, the transcripts were returned to Lang, who toyed for some time with the idea of writing the novel himself.

But he resisted the temptation, and after further very careful researches he produced his historical monograph *Pickle the Spy, or The Incognito of Prince Charles*, at the end of 1896. As early as May of that year *The Academy* announces that it is in preparation: "not a novel, though it contains the materials of romance"; and its popularity was such that it was in a third edition by the beginning of March 1897.

Although widely read, the book produced a storm of abuse from those readers (mainly dwelling to the north of the Border) who preferred a sentimental silence to a plain statement of unpleasant truths. But Lang did not bow before the storm: he had now learned the methods of historical research, and the criticisms levelled against the book, as against all his other books as a historian, were not based on any mistake or inaccuracy in his careful presentation of all the available evidence.

Of Lang's greatest work as a historian, *A History of Scotland from the Roman Occupation to the suppression of the last Jacobite Rising* (1900-7, 4 volumes), this is not the place to attempt any judgment: only from specialists in this very difficult subject can such a judgment be of any value, and at least four eminent scholars have dealt wtih Andrew Lang's labours as a historian, in the published lectures delivered of recent years before the University of St. Andrews. A general reader can peruse the four large volumes with interest, and find therein an excellent and compelling narrative, well, and on the whole, interestingly written: he may also turn the pages of such off-shoots of the *History* as *John Knox and the Reformation* (1905) or *The Portraits and Jewels of Mary Stuart* (1906), which are intended more for the specialist than is the main work; of the biographies and monographs on historical mysteries he may form his opinion as works of literature, may study for their intrinsic interest, may deal with as exhibiting various sides of their author's character; but to judge of these works as history would require the specialized study of a lifetime.

Lang followed *Pickle the Spy* with a sequel, *The Companions of Pickle* (1898) that elaborates the theme of the former book. The two volumes, besides being works of great importance to the historian, make most interesting reading to those with no special interest or knowledge in the historical field. "However unimportant a secret may be," writes Lang, "it is pleasant to know what Europe was once vainly anxious to discover." Indeed, these and his subsequent volumes of historical mysteries read rather like detective stories, and make one regret that Lang never tried his hand at any serious fiction of that variety.

When answering a questionnaire in *The Academy* during January 1897 as to which two books read in 1896 pleased and interested him most, Lang names *Tom Jones* and *The Report of the Lord's Committee on Layer's Case*, 1723. The second of these deals with a very minor Jacobite conspiracy which took place in 1722, and which is usually known as "The Bishop's Plot," after Pope's friend Francis Atterbury, Bishop of Rochester, who was principally concerned in it. Atterbury's agent was a certain young Irishman, the Reverend George Kelly, who in later years escaped from the Tower of London, fled to France and became one of Prince Charles's most faithful followers. Kelly was one of the "Men of Moidart," who landed with the Prince in 1745, and thus Lang would have been making a particular study of his career for one of the essays in *The Companions of Pickle*, and for the life of Prince Charles which he was preparing.

There was a certain mystery attached to the events surrounding
the arrest of Kelly in 1722, and many possibilities suggest themselves to the reader of the documents describing it. Lang
could not remain obdurate to these, and besides making his careful
historical study, he wove the story of George Kelly's arrest into a
short story. Not satisfied with this, he showed it to a new friend of
his, A. E. W. Mason, who in 1896 had won fame and Lang's
sincere admiration with his historical novel *The Courtship of
Morrice Buckler*.

Lang was ever on the lookout for new writers of romance, and
was always ready to help and encourage them. Mr. Mason's book
appeared in February 1896, and was enthusiastically reviewed by
the *Saturday Review*. Some weeks later, however, another writer,
some professor from Dublin, dealt with it again in the same paper,
but in entire contradiction of the previous review. Lang took this
up in the *Daily News* and made merry sport by printing extracts
from both reviews in parallel columns, with comments.

Not long after this, Frederick Macmillan, the publisher of
Morrice Buckler, invited Mr. Mason to meet Lang at luncheon, and
the two became friends and saw much of one another for the next
five or six years.

Very soon Lang brought forward his short story about George
Kelly and the Bishop's Plot, and they began working on it
together. The first idea was to make it into a play, which was done
in a short form, mainly by Mr. Mason. Lang, of course, took no
interest in the theatre, and did not like acting or consider that
profession as a serious art; but Mr. Mason had himself been an
actor, and his first literary work had been a play based on Stevenson's short story "The Sire de Maletroit." But neither collaborator
thought very highly of the Kelly play, and it was re-written in
the form of a full-length historical novel, Lang supplying all the
history and historical background, while Mr. Mason did the larger
share of the writing.

"As to novels, they are not bad history," wrote Lang to W. Pett
Ridge, "I wrote *Kelly* in a short form. Mason (and I a little) made
a play of it; we did not care for the play, and Mason went behind
my story, brought forward Wogan, and wrote the first third with
patches by me, and the rest is mixed."[171]

As both the collaborators were in London at the time, they could meet frequently to discuss the story, and no letters survive such as those from Lang to Haggard over *The World's Desire*. Lang was in the habit of writing in the morning, and again after tea; and Mr. Mason tells me that the amount Lang could write of *Parson Kelly* in one morning quite frightened him.

By April 1898 *The Academy* is announcing that "Mr. Andrew Lang is collaborating in a romance with Mr. A. E. W. Mason," and the story began its serial publication in *Longmans' Magazine* in January 1898, where it continued to appear until November. In December of the same year Longmans issued it in book form with a frontispiece by Gordon Browne, and its popularity was such that new editions appeared in January, February and March of the following year, and it still remains in print, though not as well known as it should be, as it was unfortunately not included in the collected edition of Mr. Mason's novels and tales, nor is it usually listed with his works.

"No one should fail to read *Parson Kelly*," wrote a critic in *The Bookman*, "and to read it twice; for on the first reading the excitement and breathlessness of it all hurries one on too rapidly to allow one to do more than think of the happenings; it should and will be read a second time for the sake of the language and the phrasing."

Apart from a certain slowness about the first few chapters, this praise of it is very just. While there are none of Lang's finer touches of poetical romance in the book, there are very many other virtues, both of his and of Mr. Mason's, that place it high among stories of this type. Mr. Mason's skill in the handling of plot and incident prevent any of the discursiveness and lack of economic construction which Lang recognized as faults in his own fiction. And although the historical detail is there in abundance, giving shape to most of the characters, and suggesting or informing many of the incidents, there is never any feeling that the book as a work of literature or of simple entertainment is overweighted or forced out of its course by it. With the exception of Lady Mary Wortley Montagu, whose part is small, and of Prince Charles and his followers in the first and last chapters—the prologue and epilogue of the story—no famous historical personage is introduced: and yet nearly every character from Kelly and Wogan down to Sam Wesley the usher and Hutchins the Bow Street runner was a real person, and in most cases performed some or all of the actions with which the story credits them.

The background of the novel is the plot of 1722, in which Kelly was Bishop Atterbury's right-hand man, and thus in the thick of the intrigue. The story centres around Kelly's love affair with Lady Oxford, an adventuress of a calculating and unscrupulous nature. After he has been fleeced of all his savings by the lovely enchantress Kelly discovers her true character, and puts her from his heart. Shortly afterwards he falls truly in love with Rose Townley, exiled in Avignon with her father. But he does not tell her of Lady Oxford. The story turns on the activities of the traitor Scrope, a former lover of Lady Oxford's, and her revenge on Kelly for, as she thinks, supplying details about her for a street ballad, whereof Scrope is the actual author. Lady Oxford betrays Kelly to the authorities, but is only saved from exposure herself when his rooms are searched and her letters to him like to be discovered among his Jacobite papers, by his refusal to take a mean revenge: (he is able to arrange with another of her ex-lovers, Colonel Montague, to have her letters destroyed). Kelly is bailed out of prison long enough to be reconciled to Rose Townley by the help of Wogan, and married to her before the trial which dooms him to perpetual imprisonment. This ends the story proper, but a short chapter describes his escape from the Tower, and the Epilogue deals most amusingly with Wogan's meeting with Lady Oxford during the '45, when she is touring the country as Elect Lady to a Methodist Preacher, and confessing her sins in public for the edification of her congregation.

Nicholas Wogan's part in the story is that of onlooker and friend, rather than of a chief character, though he has many pleasant and important functions to perform, and is at times inclined to occupy rather more of our interest than the plot requires. But he is very nicely differentiated from Kelly, to whose deep earnestness and engaging unworldliness Nick's self-assertive gaiety and humorous command of any situation act as a very effective foil. Nick is the supposed narrator of the story, but it is not told in the first person. In this it follows its only obvious exemplar, *Henry Esmond*. One could find other trifling resemblances, and indeed it would be well-nigh impossible for any subsequent romance concerned with the same period to avoid them altogether. It might be said that both novels turn on a Jacobite plot betrayed through the fascinations of a lovely and unscrupulous woman, but one can scarcely say that Lady Oxford resembles Beatrix Esmond. In one of those house parties of the imagination for which Lang so often delighted to choose the guests (only this one he called "a Seraglio of the Fancy!"), though Di Vernon and Barbara Grant are there, Elizabeth Bennet and Rose Bradwardine, "Beatrix Esmond is always queen of these gatherings."[172] For indeed she is one of the great lovers of fiction—a term which no one could apply to Lady Oxford, whose character would not make her a desirable guest at any such assembly. Beatrix is the Cleopatra of a milder age, but Lady Oxford is the Cressida. Beatrix is playing a mighty game when she deserts Esmond to captivate Thackeray's gay and dashing (though utterly unhistorical) James III; but Lady Oxford, who we must remember has an invalid husband in the country, allows her affections to rest, as best suits her petty interests, upon Scrope or Kelly, upon Colonel Montague or Lord Sidney Beauclerk.

Of the true heroine, George Kelly's charming little Rose Townley, it is more difficult to speak. Her part in the novel is small, and she is overshadowed by Lady Oxford, as Helen is by Meriamun. But when we can see her clearly, in Avignon, or at Lady Oxford's rout, perhaps even in the slightly unconvincing scene with Wogan, she presents a pleasant enough picture of simplicity and charm, with a strength of character clearly brought out that prevents any suggestion of ineffectuality.

The other characters do little more than form the background of the story, but none of them are quite lay figures, and even the villainous Scrope gives no feeling of impossible or improbable wickedness.

The historical foundation of the book is extensive and fascinating, and a delightful number of true details are woven into the story, and the most romantic incidents turn out to be strictly true. "The authors wish to say," states the Preface, "that the proceedings of Lady Oxford are unhistorical. Swift mentions a rumour that there was such a lady, but leaves her anonymous." Lang himself gives an interesting account of Nicholas Wogan in *The Dictionary of National Biography*: "In 1722 he was deep in the Jacobite plot. The report of the Lords' Commission is full of references to ' Nick,' who was on shipboard waiting for a chance to land with troops in England."

For Kelly's adventures the evidence is far more copious, and the curious may consult such documents as *The Appendixes Referr'd to in the Report from the Committee Appointed by Order of the House of Commons to Examine Christopher Layer and Others— etc.—containing . . . Papers relating to George Kelly . . . Published by Order of the House of Commons . . . MDCCXXII.* Here will be found the information of John Hutchins and Daniel Chandler concerning the arrest of Kelly; how Montague was mistaken for him; and how it came about that certain of Kelly's papers were burnt, before he finally allowed himself to be led away smiling to captivity; how Mrs. Barnes, Kelly's landlady, confessed to have had "a little Dog whose Leg was broken . . . left with her to be cured, by Kelly; and that Kelly told her that the said Dog was for the Bishop of Rochester; that the Dog was called Harlequin, a very fine spotted Dog;" how a letter was found in which this dog was referred to as a present for "Mr. Illington," and how this led to the identification of this pseudonym with Atterbury; how the dog was "the Present sent by the young Lady"—by Rose Townley, in fact; and many other points of interest in the story.

Or one may turn to the poems of Jonathan Swift, and read of this same dog:

> "His name is Harlequin, I wot,
> And that's a Name in every Plot,
> Resolved to save the British Nation,
> Though French by Birth and Education."

On all counts, *Parson Kelly* is a very successful historical novel, and one can but regret that Lang did not try his hand again at anything in the same style, with or without his able collaborator.

But after this he seems to have been content to let other people write the romances in which he was interested. "If I were king," he wrote, "I would keep court officials, Mr. Stanley Weyman, Mr. Mason, Mr. Kipling, and others, to tell me my own stories."[173]

If he could not command, Lang could at least suggest and help; and a number of historical novels of the period owe their inception to him. Mr. Mason's *Clementina*, which is dedicated to Lang, owes a great deal to him. Lang had made researches into the thrilling story of how Nicholas Wogan's brother, Charles, rescued the Princess Clementina Sobieska from imprisonment in Innspruck in April 1719, and brought her safely to Rome to be the wife of James Stuart and the mother of Prince Charlie, and he had published a long account of Wogan's adventures in *Macmillan's Magazine* (February 1895). He suggested that Mason should use this exciting incident as the plot for a novel, and supplied him with information about the Wogans and copies of Charles Wogan's various accounts, in French and English, of the affair. *Clementina*, the resultant novel, needs no introduction: it ranks with the best stories of its kind that the last fifty years has produced; and if the reader of age mature finds more to appreciate in the quieter, more humorous *Parson Kelly*, the time was when *Clementina* gave place to few indeed among the adventure stories that once held him in thrall.

Another subject on which Lang was anxious that a novel should be written was Mary Queen of Scots and the Casket Letters, and this time the author destined to deal with it was Maurice Hewlett, whose acquaintance Lang first made while staying with Mr. Mason on the island of Lismore. Lang had admired Hewlett's *Forest Lovers* exceedingly, and now he supplied him with all necessary details about Queen Mary, and a copy of his book on the Casket Letters, *The Mystery of Mary Stuart*; and the result was Hewlett's best known historical novel, *The Queen's Quair*, which also is dedicated to Andrew Lang.

Whether he was merely never again moved to enter the ranks of historical novelists, or whether he felt that his success in that direction did not warrant any further attempts, Andrew Lang turned away from fiction after *Parson Kelly*, and for the last twelve years of his life, with the exception of *The Disentanglers* at the very beginning of the period, sought for romance only in the highways and byways of legitimate historical research.

At the time when he was writing *Parson Kelly*, Lang was engaged on his life of Prince Charles, which appeared in 1900 in the sumptuous Goupil Series, and was later reprinted in a handy edition by Longmans. With perhaps the exception of *The Maid of France*, this is Lang's best historical biography.

While he had no illusions as regards the later Stuarts, and was a Jacobite only in the sentimental sense, Lang's affection for the royal exiles gives life and colour to all that he wrote about them, in verse as well as in prose. His habitual eagerness to champion a lost cause, and his delight in following the romantic fortunes, the well-nigh incredible adventures of the Prince and his followers, and in unravelling the mysteries connected with them that had remained unsolved until he came to elucidate them, explain Lang's enthusiasm. The exiled Stuarts were the symbols of that romance and adventure for which his soul craved:

> "These are but symbols that I sing,
> These names of Prince, and rose, and King;
> Types of things dear that do not die,
> But reign in loyal memory.
> ' Across the water ' surely they
> Abide the twenty-ninth of May;
> And we shall hail their happy reign
> When life comes to his own again! "

But this chivalrous loyalty never prevented Lang from revealing in his historical works the truth, often so bitter and disillusioning, that his intensive researches brought to light. Professor Mackie tells a story of Lang's meeting with a Highland gentleman at some function in Holyrood-house: "The two had had a happy evening together, recalling the old glories of the Highlands and the proud traditions of the Jacobites; but when the chief discovered that his pleasant companion was none other than Andrew Lang, the author of *Pickle the Spy*, his hand went at once to his weapon." Whatever his feelings of loyalty and attachment to the Stuarts, Lang's rectitude as a historian could never be called in doubt: "Lang was an able advocate," continues Professor Mackie, "who could be, and indeed must be, convinced by the evidence. That is why, despite his openly admitted prejudices, he takes his place as a great historian."[174]

In *Prince Charles Edward Stuart* we have a straightforward and interesting biography, an exact statement of facts, as well as a lovingly drawn portrait. Lang in his later historical works is apt to concentrate his interest on details, usually those of a puzzling nature, and to follow them up at the expense of the symmetry of the picture that he is striving to present. But in this volume he had not yet developed these disturbing traits, and he is able also to present Prince Charles as a real and living character, and not merely as the most important cog-wheel in a complicated machinery of plot and incident. Nothing is suppressed or extenuated, and he neither attempts to whitewash his hero, after the usual Victorian method, nor to hold him up to derision as so many modern biographers tend to do. Lang never falls into either of these extremes in this or in any other of his biographies, and though some of them are too weighed down with historical research and controversial detail to make them readily acceptable to most readers, none of them are lacking in charm, or devoid of interest. Of charm, Lang was seldom or never lacking, and he touched few subjects without adorning them; and his unquenchable spirit of adventure always prompted him to make the best possible use of the various ingredients of mystery, romance or surprise that characterize nearly all of the historical persons and events of which he wrote.

Other members of the Stuart family were dealt with by Lang, though in less completeness than was Charles Edward. Nevertheless he did most service, probably, to James Stuart, the Old Pretender, whose character had always been misjudged and misrepresented—not least by Thackeray in the closing scenes of *Henry Esmond*.

James was the best of the Stuarts, and had fortune favoured him, might have made the most successful king. But historians and novelists had confused his character with that of Charles II, and of Prince Charlie in his later years, and presented a dull and debauched old man, enjoying "martyrdom sweetened by indolence and luxurious enjoyment."

In *The King Over the Water* (1907), in the writing of which Lang had the help of Miss Alice Shield, James Stuart is dealt with fully and with justice, and though the work is heavier and less entertainingly written than the life of Prince Charlie, it is still of a nature that makes the reader loth to set it down having once embarked upon it: a virtue that we must regretfully deny to Lang's last historical biography, *Sir George Mackenzie of Rosenhaugh*. (1909).

Of the last of the Stuarts, Henry, Cardinal of York, Lang did not write, except as his other works were concerned with him, and in the Introduction that he wrote to the biography by Alice Shield, published in 1908.

But of the ideal for which the Stuarts stood, and of their message to those such as he, whose devotion was of the heart and of the imagination, Lang has written at the end of *The King Over the Water*.

"So the last British-born Stuart was laid to rest. With him was buried the ancient Stuart royalty. Nothing remained of it but the disappointed hope and angry protest of his elder son, the gentle but dignified acquiescence of the younger. All was over that was mortal. The old song was sung; the last drama of the awful Stuart cycle was played out. The cause and its glory remained a banquet hall deserted, whose lights were fled, whose garlands dead, and all but a little few and a mournful memory departed. But that few—and that memory! Green as the unfading pines of the Highland glens, that memory lives for ever. And for that few! We fools esteemed their life madness, and their end to be utter destruction, but they are numbered among the heroes of all time. They stood with great constancy against those that afflicted them, and made no account of their sufferings; and they shone as sparks among the stubble of their sordid, self-seeking age. As gold in the furnace were they proved, and in time there has come respect to them. In the sight of the unwise they seemed to perish in misery, but they who were faithful in love now rest in honour, and their names live for evermore where loyalty and faith are crowned."

CHAPTER XIII

The Literary Critic

THAT rather limited aristocrat of letters, Henry James, wrote to Stevenson in July 1888 his opinion that "Criticism is of an abject density and puerility—it doesn't exist—it writes the intellect of our race too low. Lang, in the *Daily News*, every morning, and I believe in a hundred other places, uses his beautiful thin facility to write everything down to the lowest level of Philistine twaddle—the view of the old lady round the corner or the clever person at the dinner party." And late in 1912 when Edmund Gosse had written a chapter on Lang in his *Portraits and Sketches*, James wrote to him on the matter in much the same vein: "Where I can't but feel that he *should* be brought to justice is in the matter of his whole ' give-away ' of the value of the wonderful chances he so continually enjoyed (enjoyed thanks to certain of his very gifts, I admit!)—give-away, I mean, by his ' cultivation,' absolutely, of the puerile imagination and the fourth-rate opinion, the coming-round to that of the old apple-woman at the corner as after all the good and right as to any of the mysteries of mind and art."[175] To which, and very much more in the same vein, Gosse—always notorious for suiting his opinions to his correspondent—replied: "Every word you say about Andrew Lang is most valuable and penetrating. Somehow his memory *irritates* me! He possessed the truth and answered to the heavenly calling, and yet always without joy, and almost always without grace. His puerility, as you say, was heart-rending." Gosse, it may be observed, had written to another friend, Floris Delattre, a couple of months before that Lang's was "the most elegant mind that the English-speaking race has brought forth in our time."[176] We need not pause for more than a moment to consider what Gosse meant by "without joy" and "without grace"; most people have admitted the grace of Lang's style and method—(and if heavenly grace be intended, that is a gift that no critic can affirm or deny with any finality): as regards his "joy" in writing, he has more than answered this criticism, both by the obvious pleasure that informs practically everything that he wrote, and more specifically by such an avowal as this: "As an old pressman, I confess that I could not write a ' leader-note ' without enjoying the doing of it—whether the public enjoyed the reading of it or not."[177] Or again: "The work, as in all arts, is a pleasure. Have we to live by writing paragraphs ? Then it is a delight to write good paragraphs, or paragraphs that seem good to us."[178]

The main indictment put forward and elaborated by Henry James is directed at Lang's methods in criticism and his tastes or prejudices in contemporary literature. Henry James, it must be admitted, wrote for a very small and select circle, and tended to regard the general reader, and all such as read for "human pleasure," as mere Philistines whose tastes and opinions were beneath any attempt at serious understanding.

It was in this view, among others, that he differed so strenuously from Lang, who held that a novel should certainly be a work of art, but that it sinned against that art if it required a dictionary and a grammar to understand it, if, in fact, it could not be read for "human pleasure," which he considered to be the object of a work of fiction.

Holding some such creed as this, Lang in his essays wrote as a popularizer and an interpreter: he wrote for readers of average intelligence, and when he dealt with the great works of the past, he attempted to impart his own enthusiasm, attempted to provoke interest, to invite a reading. Although his essays are mainly of this nature, and although the very profound and serious learning of the author is habitually disguised, is often even apologized for, yet Lang was a man of immense knowledge, and his criticisms, however lightly thrown out, usually contain a deep undercurrent of understanding, and a clear appreciation of the author's intentions.

Lang embarked on his career as a critic in the 'seventies, and by the 'eighties was established in the very forefront. He came to literature at a time when "culture" had become the fashion, and when the majority of those who read—however small a number that might seem to us now—did so with a considerable amount of taste and discretion. The novel readers were only a little in excess of the poetry readers: it was the age of *The Idylls of the King* and of *The Earthly Paradise*, and these were popular books in a way that no poetry is popular now. It was a small world, but an ever-growing one, and Lang, though fastidious and even aristocratic in many ways, believed in this growth and strove to foster and cultivate it. He "wrote down" to his audience knowing how varied that audience was becoming, with the intention not of bringing literature down to a lower level, but of raising the cultural level of his readers up to that of the great works of literature.

In a sense, his Homeric translations partake of this object, and he would certainly write of Homer or Theocritus or more generally of Greek poetry, at many levels. *Homer and the Epic* combines literary criticism with the more abstruse aspects of his subject, and indeed this insistence that Homer was primarily literature is one of Lang's most important contributions to Homeric studies. But equally willingly Lang would write an essay on Homer for *Atalanta*, the school-girl's magazine which L. T. Meade edited; or for *Blackwood's Magazine*, one of the more serious of the literary monthlies; or for *Good Words*, the family magazine that most classes were in the habit of perusing on Sundays.

Critics, both of his own time and of the present day, who find much whereof to complain in Lang's utterances on contemporary literature, find themselves forced to admit his greatness when dealing with the masterpieces of the past. "His critical essays on Theocritus, on Edgar Poe, on Gérard de Nerval, reveal an under-standing and an imaginative sympathy as delicate as they are illuminating," writes Mr. Forrest Reid in his *Retrospective Adventures* (1941); and these are the words of a critic not otherwise in sympathy with Lang's outlook on literature.

Of the Greeks, Lang wrote well and with understanding; Homer was his chief interest, but the Bucolic poets came second, and the Alexandrians were not far behind. "Byways of Greek Song," among the uncollected essays in *The Fortnightly Review* (October 1887) treats with much insight of the writers in the *Anthology*; and a paper on Lucian in the same magazine (July 1888) shows that his understanding was not confined to Greek poetry alone. Nor was he content to write merely of the most famous: who else has written with such sympathy of the sadly under-rated Quintus Smyrnaeus as Lang in *The Illustrated London News* (3rd August and 10th September 1892) and in his short *Life of Tennyson*?

In medieval French literature Saintsbury considered Lang as among the most well-versed of his time. Both the translation of *Aucassin and Nicolete* and the essay on it in *Letters on Literature* prove this; and not less do his earliest verse translations, *Ballads and Lyrics of Old France*, besides the unreprinted articles on "French Peasant Songs" (*Cornhill*, May 1876), "Three Poets of French Bohemia" (*Dark Blue*, May 1871) and "Rabelais and the Renaissance," and "Gérard de Nerval" in *Frasers Magazine*, (March 1870 and May 1873).

Lang did not write so often of early British literature, though he contributed articles to Ward's *English Poets* on Gawain Douglas and Henry Constable, and wrote at considerable length of Malory in Oscar Somers' great edition of the *Morte d'Arthur* (1891). For Malory, as was natural, Lang had a strong affection: "Malory," he wrote, "has penned the great and chief romance of his own age and of ours, the story that must endure and must move the *lacrymae rerum* till man's nature is altered again."

Elizabethan literature is seldom thought of in the same connection as Andrew Lang, and of it he wrote relatively seldom. With his intense dislike of the theatre, it is natural that Lang should prefer to read Shakespeare, and even that he should hold, like Lamb, that so only could he be rightly appreciated. Lang's love of Shakespeare and his knowledge of the plays was considerable, and always present. *Midsummer Night's Dream* "the most magical page in the literature of the world," had opened the earliest magic casement through which he had glimpsed the world of romance as a child, and it retained its place, with *A Winter's Tale* and *The Tempest* beside it. Between 1890 and 1895 Lang wrote a series of fourteen essays on "Shakespeare's Comedies" for *Harper's Magazine*, where they were illustrated by drawings made by E. A. Abbott, who later illustrated the Tragedies, for which Swinburne and Watts-Dunton wrote some of the articles. Lang's essays do not pretend to go very deeply into criticism; they are again invitations to wander among the people, among the sights and sounds of Shakespeare's world: "Like flowers pressed in an ancient book, and yet no *siccus hortus*, but blossoming with all their scent and sap, they lie in Shakespeare's pages, and you have but to throw down the penny newspapers, to open the volume, and your life is that you would gladlier have lived in the larger, airier, more kindly and congenial days, 'the spacious times of great Elizabeth ' . . . "

Light and brittle though these charming unreprinted essays are, Lang's knowledge of the more academic aspects of Shakespearean study was very considerable, though it was only revealed in his writings on the Bacon problem. To begin with, his reactions to various exponents of the "Bacon Heresy" were merely to ridicule their ignorance and lack of historical research. When Mrs. Gallup published her famous book on the cypher revelations which she professed to have found in the plays, and which proved not only that Bacon was their author, but that he was the legitimate son of Queen Elizabeth, Lang wrote with witty but scathing effect in the *Pall Mall Magazine* (July 1902). As an example: Mrs. Gallup gives the date of Robert Cecil's birth as 1550, and quotes "the encyclopædias". "I shall be happy to consider Mrs. Gallup's reasons for her date," writes Lang. "Bacon was two years at least the senior of Robert Cecil—which, unluckily, does not suit the cyphered revelations. Mrs. Gallup has been misled by the *Encyclopædia Britannica*—which could not have deceived Bacon." And, with no other remark he prints in facsimile a contemporary manuscript proving the correct date to be 1563.

But in the last year of his life, Lang produced a large volume, *Shakespeare, Bacon, and the Great Unknown*, which was published posthumously. In a field of controversy that is not worth the paper on which it is printed, Lang's contribution is a brilliant bit of work. If any intelligent reader needed to be assured that neither Bacon nor another wrote Shakespeare's works, Lang did so very conclusively and well. The book is dead now, and rightly so. Such controversies have small place in the annals of serious scholarship, and Lang wrote, one feels, mainly in the fear lest the ordinary reader might be deceived by such plausible inanities as Mrs. Gallup's book—and others of the kind—which seem to have been more common then than now. But it is a good example of Lang the historian, of his controversial methods—and of his knowledge and appreciation of Elizabethan literature.

That Lang considered *Tom Jones* to be the greatest novel in the English language, and wrote with understanding of Richardson and Smollett in essays easy of access, show his knowledge and appreciation of the eighteenth century also. With the seventeenth he had little sympathy: *Paradise Lost* is included among the "Books I have stuck in," and Gosse's successful effort to place the neglected Donne among the major poets met with only medium approval from Lang, who seemed more interested in the apparition of Mrs. Donne. Walton was among Lang's very favourite authors, and he edited *The Compleat Angler* for Everyman's Library, besides allowing a privately printed edition of an essay in the *Illustrated London News* on "The Tercentenary of Izaak Walton." He intended to write his life for his series of "English Worthies," but, like Stevenson's life of Wellington for the same series, we hear no more of it after the publisher's announcement that it is "in preparation." But Lang was himself a most ardent fisherman—and Walton has ever been the gospel of anglers.

Lang's taste in all ages of literature was catholic and individual, and in the same volume as his essay on Smollett, we find him writing fully and with enthusiasm of Mrs. Radcliffe. For mystery novels Lang always had a weakness, and in a later age he was one of the first to welcome the advent of Sherlock Holmes.

With the nineteenth century Lang's criticism enters a more controversial field. Scott, indeed, was his favourite novelist of any age, and of Scott's poetry he entertained perhaps too high an opinion, though, characteristically, he admits that this is one of the loyalties of his boyhood which he has been unable to outgrow. In the more scholarly field his best work is the *Life of Lockhart*, in which, and in related writings (mainly uncollected) he put forth both new facts and new points of view, vindicating Lockhart from many clouded judgments and moving a reconsideration of his violent reviews of Keats and Tennyson.

In another way, Lang vindicated Scott, and that was in the matter of the Border Ballads. Lang's anthropological investigations, besides his early allegiance, had made him an authority still respected on the subject of popular poetry, and he stated the case for Scott's integrity in *Sir Walter Scott and the Border Minstrelsy* (1910) with his usual learning and his usual flippant gaiety—during which he "faked" a number of ballads himself, as an example of the method of Surtees of Mainsforth who misled Scott in like manner.

Jane Austen was another novelist in whom Lang delighted, and out of which delight he wrote with particular understanding. For her he took up the cudgels against Mr. Stephen Gwynn in "The Ship" for September 1899, and at the same time expressed his own distaste for the Brontës. Charlotte Brontë, he says, "did not care for Miss Austen any more than I agree with Lockhart in placing Miss Brontë high above Dickens. Miss Brontë had neither wit nor humour. Passions in tatters, parts to tear a cat in, were her line. Well, I prefer Mrs. Radcliffe as reflected in the terrors of Catherine Morland, to the Radcliffian horrors of the house of Mr. Rochester . . . Miss Austen knew what she was writing about; Miss Brontë, when she strayed away from her very limited experience, did not. If I had the courage to say what I think about Miss Brontë, Mr. Gwynn's sufferings from critics would be nothing to mine!"

Another author whom Lang felt himself bound to defend during the reaction that set in round about the end of the century, was Dickens. Of him, as of Thackeray, Lang has written in various accessible places. One of his most interesting essays is the Introduction to the Gadshill Edition which he edited in 1897, where, after a long and very fair study of Dickens as a novelist, he admits that his own preferences in literature, but not his literary judgment, would set above Dickens only Scott and Thackeray. Lang's notes and prefaces to this edition are of no special importance, but they hardly deserved the thunderous denunciation with which Swinburne favoured them: "The prefatory importunities of a writer disentitled to express and disqualified to form an opinion on the work of an English humorist. The intrusive condescension or adulation of such a commentator was perhaps somewhat superfluous in front of the reprinted Waverley Novels; the offence becomes an outrage, the impertinence becomes impudence when such rubbish is shot down before the doorstep of Charles Dickens."[179]

On this *The Academy*, not often at that period either friendly to Lang, or outspoken against writers of settled reputation, commented: "Mr. Lang's gentle chidings of Dickens may have been a thin and unnecessary *sauce piquante* to the Gadshill banquet, but we are quite unable to discover why they should infuriate a poet who screams the very same objections!"

Now at first sight Dickens would not appear to be an author that Lang would have cared for. Lang admitted his own preferences in literature very freely, and the most important of them was for

romance, as his most constant bias was against "realism." Some
very illuminating opinions were expressed by him in one of the
most interesting of his uncollected essays, "The Evolution of
Literary Decency," in *Blackwood's Magazine* for March 1900.
He was ready to admit: "Romanticism itself (in spite of some old
French romances) is, in essence ' a delicate thing '; knights
amorous and errant are all unlike the festive wanderers of Fielding
and Smollett. The squires of romantic lovers are no Straps or
Partridges, and the knights understand ' the maiden passion for a
maid ' in a sense unknown to the lovers of Sophia and Emilia and
Narcissa." But he goes on to defend *Tom Jones*: "I presume that
Fielding was reprobated because he was humorous. Even now we
find the advanced and virtuous and earnest applauding the most
squalid horrors of M. Zola and others, while they would fly in
horror from Gyp. And why ? Obviously because M. Zola is
absolutely devoid of wit and humour (which Gyp possesses) and
therefore may be as abominable as he pleases. Has he not a lofty
moral purpose! So, in fact, had Fielding, but alas! he was humorous
—all unlike Richardson, Zola, Ibsen and Tolstoi."

Lang's exaggeratedly sensitive nature prevented him from
appreciating the more sordid or gloomy type of contemporary
novel; suffering, if brought home to him too nearly, and any hint
of squalor or any lack of good taste in the presentation of the raw
passions and facts of existence, seem to have hurt Lang to quite an
abnormal degree. He did not, one feels, find this world a very
happy place, and he had himself experienced perhaps more than
his due mead of mental suffering. Nor was he a stranger to physical
pain, whose health was frequently of the most precarious nature.
To one of this temperament an escape into a more visionary or
artificial world was inevitable, and the tenacious loyalty to his
earlier tastes in literature presented him with ready access to such a
world. Added to this he was gifted with a very strong, if somewhat
ironic and academic, sense of humour that formed another of his
shields against the *lachrymae rerum*. His friend, F. Anstey, noted
Lang's "air of languor and boredom, which quickly vanished when
anything appealed to his quick sense of humour."[180], and that
ready gift of kindly mocking laughter was Lang's saving grace as a
critic of contemporary literature.

Besides his sensitiveness to pain and unkindness that were a part of him, Lang's over-refinement of feeling was also exhibited in a sense of chivalry and decorum. He was always ready to deprecate the inquisitive or scandalous researches of the popular biographer, and his feelings with regard to the type of psyhcology which began to be prevalent and popular in the fiction of the period bring out the same kind of reactions: "One would as lief explore a girl's room and tumble about her little household treasures, as examine so curiously the poor secrets of her heart and tremors of her frame . . . Such analysis makes one feel uncomfortable in the reading, makes one feel intrusive and unmanly. It is like overhearing a confession by accident . . . It is, perhaps, science—it may be art; and to say that it is extremely disagreeable may be to exhibit old-fashioned prejudice."[181]

With these limitations it is inevitable that when Lang came to contemporary criticism, he should incline towards the current romantic writing and look askance on those who practised the art of social or psychological analysis. Another opinion of Lang's that must not be overlooked is the feeling which he seems usually to have entertained that the great ages of literature were over, and that the books of his own day were so relatively unimportant that the critic need not take any very serious view of them. In this sense he expressed himself once or twice: "Writing about contemporary books is the merest journalism. It is pleasant to praise what one thinks good, and to our deeply fallen nature it is not always unpleasant to blame what one thinks bad; but to be literature, writing about books ought to deal with classics—Homer, Molière, Shakespeare, Fielding, and so on."[182] "One kind of book pleases a man at one time and in one mood, and another at another time and in another mood . . . Late Victorian novels are not the great things of human literature, and a reader may blamelessly amuse or depress himself with them as he will. I prefer to be amused."[183] Or again, he will speak of criticism as "Reasoned and considered writing on the tried masterpieces of the world, or even ingenious and entertaining writing about new books. To have a clever and accomplished man telling you, in his best manner, what thoughts come into his head after reading even a new novel, is no trifling pleasure among the pale and shadowy pleasures of the mind."[184]

Remembering all these factors and opinions, one can arrive at a much fairer understanding and appreciation of Lang as a critic than those readers who set out to find in his writings things that were never intended to be there.

Lang's monthly causerie "At the Sign of the Ship," which appeared in *Longmans' Magazine* from January 1886 to October 1905, and which has never been reprinted, except in the form of short quotations in a magazine article, contains the largest body of Lang's pronouncements on current literature. But as a reviewer his work began in *The Academy* in January 1874, and was continued in the *Daily News*, the *Morning Post* and the *Saturday Review* for many years. When these failed him, he had *The New Review*, *Cosmopolis*, *The Pilot* and *The Illustrated London News*, in the last-named of which he carried on the "Ship" articles after the discontinuance of *Longmans'*, as a weekly column "At the Sign of St. Paul's" until his death.

With his professed preference for "more claymores and less psychology," and his usual avoidance of books with which he did find himself in sympathy, we find Lang most often extolling the works of the romance or adventure story writers, particularly Stevenson and Rider Haggard. The first of these was perhaps Lang's earliest discovery in the field of contemporary genius, and from the time of reading "Ordered South" shortly after his first meeting with Stevenson at Mentone, Lang was convinced that "here was a new writer, a writer indeed," and he made his opinion known long before Stevenson had won to fame with *Treasure Island* and *Jekyll and Hyde*—and helped with constant and unswerving loyalty to found the reputation of this one at least of the great writers of the period.

Opinions differ as to Rider Haggard's place in literature, many critics still denying him a place at all, but Lang, with his instincts of fair play, and his affection for romance and belief in its integrity and high functions, did not hesitate to make known his admiration here also, acclaiming *She* in a long and well-reasoned review in the *Academy*, and speaking highly in other places of Haggard's more ambitious efforts such as *Cleopatra*, *Nada the Lily* and *Eric Brighteyes*.

Another writer of undoubted genius, whose advent Lang was the very first to hail both in the British and American press, was Rudyard Kipling—whose Indian stories at least could not have been described as "romantic."

For Kipling's works his admiration and appreciation were intense and, on the whole, just; but his own character and tastes blinded him to the excellence of *Stalky and Co.*, and such stories as "The Mark of the Beast." But his critical writings on Kipling—the paper in *Essays in Little* and the Introduction to the American edition of *The Courting of Dinah Shadd, and other stories*—are as instantaneous and as sane a recognition of the appearance of a new major author as can be found in recent years.

He was on what is now sure ground, but was then considered as unsound as his judgment of Haggard is now, when he insisted on praising the works of Mark Twain: "I have tried in an ineffective but hearty manner, to praise Mark Twain as one of the greatest of living geniuses (perhaps it is not saying much), who now use the English language"[185], he wrote in 1888, and followed this up with an essay on "The Art of Mark Twain" in the *Illustrated London News* of 14th February 1891, where he states his belief that *Huckleberry Finn* can seriously be claimed as a masterpiece.

For the lesser writers of adventure stories Lang made no exaggerated claims, and was among the first to remonstrate with the uncritical admirers of S. R. Crockett who were for placing that worthy on a level with Scott. But Crockett, as well as Doyle and Hewlett and Weyman and Mason owed much to Lang for the praise and encouragement which he bestowed on them for their earliest books, and for the frank avowal in the "Ship" and elsewhere, that these were the books that *he* liked—with the delicate suggestion in his words that all other cultured readers should appreciate them too.

Another famous book of which Lang was the earliest admirer was *The Prisoner of Zenda*, and he followed Anthony Hope's career with appreciative interest.

But although his preferences lay in this direction, he did not hesitate to praise works of the realist variety when such seemed good to him, and did not offend against his sensibilities. Barrie was the most obvious writer of this type for Lang to acclaim, and he was also able to appreciate such writers of domestic fiction as Rhoda Broughton and Anne Thackeray Ritchie.

Later in his career, when his views on realist fiction were becoming rather an uncritical bias, Lang could still see the excellence in the novels of Mr. H. G. Wells: "I venture to hope that many people will be no less entertained than myself by *Love and Mr. Lewisham*," he writes in the "Ship" of September 1900.

Rather a more surprising conquest was *The House with the Green Shutters*: "In brief," wrote Lang, "the pessimism, the blackness, was all that my soul detests; yet I read on and on; after the clock struck the hour of retiring. Now, if a book seizes hold of you like this, there is something not common in the book. It offended, but conquered *mon naturel*."

But the most serious—and the most famous—of Lang's adverse criticisms was that directed against Thomas Hardy, more particularly against *Tess of the D'Urbervilles*. Lang had already confessed himself out of sympathy with Hardy, and after this, he refused to review any more of his books. ("To review a book when one labours under a total lack of sympathy with the author's philosophy of life, is to spin ropes of sand"[186].) But he was sometimes moved from his usual practice of avoiding reviewing books to which he was unsympathetic by what he considered exaggerated praise of them. In the late 'eighties, for example, the interest in French and Russian novels had become a fashion and a sign of "culture" among persons not able to judge dispassionately for themselves: "I am coming to suspect," wrote Lang, "that the majority of Culture's modern disciples are a mere crowd of very slimly-educated people, who have no natural taste or impulse; who do not really know the best things in literature; who have a feverish desire to admire the newest thing, to follow in the latest artistic fashion . . ."[187] Lang is aiming at critics here perhaps rather more than at the general reader, and is fighting his usual battle for a fair treatment of both kinds of fiction. But he could not win this fairness from the champions of the Russians and their followers: "Their chief admirers," he complains, "in some cases will hear of nothing but the Russians, and the glorious Frenchmen and Finns and Lithuanians. We should have merry endings and prosperous heroes now and again . . . Their gloom begets within me a certain prejudice against the gifted Muscovites. It is not exactly a literary judgment; it is a pardonable antipathy." But he goes on to confess that "the genius of Tolstoi, Tourgueneff and Dostoievsky there is no denying,"[188] and of *Crime and Punishment* he says elsewhere that it "is, to my thinking, simply perfect in its kind; only that kind happens to be too powerful for my constitution."[189]

It was what he considered to be criticism of this variety that moved him to review *Tess* in *The New Review* for February 1892. Hardy's preface to the fifth edition of *Tess* makes bitter reference to this review of Lang's and quotes certain phrases from it; but he fails to give the gist of the whole, or, one must feel, to be quite fair to his critic. After describing the novel, Lang had gone on to say: "Here are all the ingredients of the blackest misery, and the misery darkens till ' The President of the Immortals has finished his sport with Tess.' I cannot say how much this phrase jars on one. If there be a God, who can seriously think of Him as a malicious fiend ? And if there be none, the expression is meaningless. I have lately been reading the works of an old novelist who was very active between the years 1814 and 1831. He is not a terse, nor an accurate, nor a philosophic, nor even a very grammatical writer, but how different, and, to my poor thinking, how much wiser, kinder, happier and more human is his mood. But Homer is not less pitiful of mortal fortunes and man ' the most forlorn of all creatures that walk on earth,' and Homer's faith cannot be called consolation: yet there is no bitterness in him; and probably bitterness is never a mark of the greatest art and the noblest thought." Lang then goes on to criticize certain points in style, and in the conversation of the rustics; and he concludes his review: "However, tastes differ so much that the blemishes, as they appear to one reader of Mr. Hardy's works may seem beauty spots in the eyes of another reader. He does but give us of his best, and if his best be too good for us, or good in the wrong way, if, in short, we are not *en rapport* with him, why, there are plenty of other novelists, alive and dead, and the fault may be on our side, not on his."

It is difficult to see why this should have provoked such a storm as it did; but Lang was never allowed to forget it, and most adverse criticisms of him in his later years turned on the assumption that he preferred Rider Haggard to Thomas Hardy. "It is not for me to make a class list of novelists, and give Mr. Hardy a second," he remarks, without any attempt at self-justification, except to repeat that a man likes different books at different times in varying moods, and that there is room for both authors in the world of letters; but he goes on to say, with a trifle of petulance, "I know, but will never reveal, what Mr. Stevenson said about *Tess!* " But he had revealed this dark secret many years before when, in his "Recollections of R.L.S." he tells us that "Concerning a novel dear to culture, he said that he would die by my side, in the last ditch, proclaiming it the worst fiction in the world." And as he goes on to say, "I do not remember another case in which he dispraised any book," one can only assume that he is here referring to *Tess*.

Of other "serious novelists," as Mr. Reid calls them, Lang praised the earlier works of Henry James, saying that he "has done so much, so well, and in so many ways, that all readers of modern books may be grateful to the author of *Roderick Hudson*, *Daisy Miller*, *The Siege of London* and *Washington Square*, for four admirable, vivid, living studies of characters and lives extremely varied and amazingly true."[190] But of the later James, when complexity of thought and diction came to blur the excellence of the work, Lang was not so complimentary.

George Moore was another writer whose work Lang disliked: "An Irishman without humour is capable of anything, and Mr. George Moore has proved capable of writing *Evelyn Innes* . . . The story becomes a tract ; the people are puppets of the tract-writer; and the Ulick puppet is a mere study of a contemporary affectation, an isolated freak in the great business of forced originality."[191]

But the increasing severity and uncomprehending nature of the attacks to which he was subject for such reviews tended to embitter Lang towards the end of his life; and he came more and more to air his prejudices with something of petulance and bravado, and such remarks, made in moments of apparent irritation, are to be found as: "I cannot go so far as to despise the novel of character, but I do ' bar ' the novel of bad characters: idle, brainless, full-fed, lustful maids and matrons, with their appropriate males, smart stockbrokers and others who cumber the ground. There are such people, of course, but why should they be considered objects of interest ? "[192]

After 1900, though he gives rather the impression that the writing of great fiction is a lost art, Lang usually speaks of contemporary novels with amused or pitying tolerance, but seldom with unkindness or any active dislike. "It occasionally, but rarely, falls to my lot to review a group of novels," he wrote in 1903, when describing the delight with which he first chanced upon *The House*

with the Green Shutters. "One does not find many surprises in the
course of such adventures. The romances, in their bright coloured
boards, are found to fall into certain definite and familiar categories.
There is the large and artless category written for ladies, by ladies.
These probably give to the fair pillars or caryatides of the cir-
culating libraries exactly what they desire, but the male reader they
do not over-stimulate. Then there are the didactic novels. Most are
of various colours of socialism, in some cases complicated with
the problems attending the ritual of the Anglican communion. The
'love interest' in these romances is rather perfunctory; and the
hero is usually knocked on the head in a British or foreign strike,
much to my private satisfaction. Other didactic novels deal with
the problems of Belief, and the inferences to be drawn from the
Higher Criticism, as apprehended through liberal manuals of
devotion and the monthly magazines. Personally I prefer to take
my Higher Criticism 'neat,' and from the fountain heads, rather
than from didactic novels. Then there is the improper didactic, on
the merits of simple and compound adultery, and of any more·
esoteric vices which the author may have picked up in the course
of her study or practice. These fictions, to my private taste, are
unalluring. Not much more attractive are most of the novels, by
persons of genius, perhaps, but certainly not by experts in historical research. There are also slum-novels, which are a sub-class
of the didactic, and there are novels which 'stand in a false
following of' Mr. George Meredith, things of portentously
affected dullness. There are novels about the vices of society,
which, as we have the newspapers always with us, appear rather
luxuries than necessaries. There are detective novels which, unlike
the other kinds, 'are not literature,' but compared with the
others may occasionally be readable. There are other kinds. And
there are, happily, a few novels every year by the real novelists,
of whom I could gratefully mention about two dozen, but to name
them might be invidious . . ."[193]

Lang wrote relatively seldom about contemporary poetry,
though there are full and very satisfactory uncollected essays on
Matthew Arnold, Morris, Tennyson, Browning and Jean Ingelow,
besides the essay on Morris in *Adventures Among Books*, the
detailed criticisms included in his short book on Tennyson for
Blackwood's "Modern English Writers" series, and the two essays

on contemporary poets in *Letters on Literature*. "If one were to write out of mere personal preference," says Lang in the first of these two essays, "and praise most what best fits one's private moods, I suppose I should place Mr. Matthew Arnold at the head of contemporary English poets. Reason and reflection, discussion and critical judgment, tell one that he is not quite there."

One is tempted to direct any reader who has doubts of Lang's discernment as a critic to these two essays in *Letters on Literature*. They are admirably expressed and reasoned, and although written during the lifetime of the poets concerned, Tennyson, Browning and Arnold, Morris, Swinburne and Bridges, they seem to be in almost complete accordance with the more reasoned modern judgments on these poets.

Tennyson was always Lang's favourite, and perhaps he set him a shade too high; one hesitates to agree when Lang, at a later date compares him with Morris thus: "I would rather part with all that Morris wrote in prose and verse, than with Tennyson's ' Morte d'Arthur ' and ' The Lady of Shallott ' "; though he is on surer ground when he says of Morris that he "would rather part with all his later poems than with *The Defence of Guinevere*."[194] Posterity has endorsed this estimate of *Guinevere*, an estimate that Lang made unhesitatingly as early as 1882; and where Morris's prose romances were concerned, Lang had always a blind spot.

On Swinburne also Lang's views were of the sanest. He continued to admire *Atalanta* and certain of the *Poems and Ballads*:—"One's old opinion, that English poetry contains no verbal music more original, sonorous, and sweet than Mr. Swinburne wrote in these pieces when still very young, remains an opinion unshaken." But the later poems and the interminable verse dramas, he found but a weariness, and an expense of spirit.

Browning he placed second only to Tennyson, but had no very deep love for his works, save for *Men and Women* and some of the lyrics.

The fact that he includes Bridges in *Letters on Literature* shows that Lang could, and did, form and maintain his own opinions, and not confine his criticism to poets of an assured reputation. Indeed, he had perceived the importance of Bridges when he reviewed his first volume of poems in *The Academy* of 17th January 1874, and he continued to voice this opinion, although it was very many years before Bridges received much other recognition.

Among younger poets, Lang was one of the first to appreciate Kipling's gifts, and also the similar gifts of Henry Newbolt, whose "Admirals All" Lang picked out the moment he received the manuscript from its unknown author for inclusion in *Longmans' Magazine*; and a like discernment made him secure the earliest of Mr. Walter de la Mare's poems for inclusion in the *Magazine*, and subsequent production by Longmans in book form.

Any approach to arrogance or affectation annoyed Lang, and he had little sympathy with the *fin de siècle* poets of the *Yellow Book* following, such as Ernest Dowson of whom he wrote that his genius, which Arthur Symons claimed for him, "does not seem to be made very manifest unto men. Little imitative things, sad *épaves* of a life wasted on ideals out of Murger and Baudelaire; old, old outworn fallacies, and follies, and affectations, these appear to be what is left. The story is a worn piece of pathos. The ideas of life on which Dowson ruined himself have been the ideas of hundreds of boys, of whom the majority laugh at their past selves in a year or two. If this kind of existence, if these sorts of productions, be decadent, surely even boys must see that decadence is rather a mistake."[195]

Another affectation, that of the "Celtic revival," also provoked Lang's ridicule, and he makes delightful fun of a neo-Celtic poet in *The Disentanglers*, though of its more serious exponents he was well able to see the merit: "Really Celtic, as a critic not without the necessary drop of Celtic blood dares to think, are Mr. Yeats's tales in prose, and, above all, Mr. Neil Munro's stories in *The Lost Pibroch*. In these we meet genius as obvious and undeniable as that of Mr. Kipling, if less popular in appeal."[196]

But when all is said, it was always to the literature of the past that Lang turned most readily; and there he was happiest and most in his right environment. "Perhaps the only kind of criticism worth reading or writing," he admits, "is that which narrates the adventures of an ingenious and educated mind in contact with masterpieces. The literary masterpieces of the world are so rich, so full of beauties, so charged with ideas, that some or many of these must escape most readers. We wander as in a world full of flowers: we cannot gather all, nor observe all. It is pleasant and profitable to hear the experiences of another in the same paradise, of another whose temper, whose knowledge of the world and of books, are very different from our own. We may agree with what he tells us, or may differ, but even in our differences we feel that we learn much, that our mind is moved to new activities."[197]

CHAPTER XIV

Lang and his Friends

"I NEVER yet knew a man of genius who did not loathe Lang!" Theodore Watts-Dunton is said to have remarked, thumping the table to add force to his dictum, and perhaps glancing across at Mr. Swinburne to indicate which man of genius he had most in mind. And yet, though other men of genius at times agreed with the verdict of *The Pines*—Max Beerbohm, for example, Henry James and George Moore—there can have been few writers who have also been so beloved by their contemporaries in the world of letters.

In reading the biographies and memoirs of the period one comes upon writer after writer whom Lang had helped or encouraged; writer after writer who met him and, if a trifle repelled at first—for Lang was a shy man, and put up a brusque, off-handedness as a defence—bears testimony to the affection that he seldom failed to inspire among those who knew him at all well.

Of these, Rider Haggard knew him perhaps better than any, and was his best friend through all the later part of his life. Haggard was a good judge of character, and was always interested in those with whom he came in contact; and Lang's character he "had opportunities of observing through many years. Take him all in all, I think him one of the sweetest-natured and highest-minded men whom it has ever been my privilege to know, though a certain obtrusive honesty which will out, and an indifferent off-handedness of manner, has prevented him from becoming generally popular . . . Of the friend I know not what to say, save that I reckon it one of the privileges of my life to be able to call him by that much-misused name; the tenderest, the purest and highest-minded of human creatures, one from whom true goodness and nobility of soul radiate in every common word and act, though often half-hidden in a jest, the most perfect of gentlemen—such is Andrew Lang."[198]

Their friendship began when the manuscript of *King Solomon's*

Mines was shown to Lang by Henley early in 1885, though before this Lang had written to Haggard about a short story, "The Blue Curtains," which had been sent to him as London editor of *Harper's Magazine.* Lang was forced to return it (it appeared in the *Cornhill,* and was reprinted many years later in *Smith and the Pharaohs*), but he writes of it warmly, and takes the opportunity of praising *The Witch's Head.*

The friendship ripened quickly, and during the years when Haggard spent much time in London, they met very frequently. Lang read most of Haggard's work in manuscript or proof, and was always ready with criticism and praise. Circumstances tended to keep Haggard in the country for most of his time after about 1895; but though they seldom met, they corresponded regularly, and their friendship suffered no diminution. "You have been more to me of what the dead friends of my youth were, than any other man," wrote Lang, "and I take the chance to say it, though not given to speaking of such matters."

With these two a third was joined in a like measure of friendship —Charles Longman the publisher. Lang's first connection with the family was by means of F. W. Longman, who was a friend of Lang's at Balliol. Lang knew Charles Longman by the beginning of the 'seventies, and he soon became literary adviser to the firm, in which capacity he continued until his death.

At the luncheon given at Stationers' Hall, on 5th November 1924, to celebrate the bicentenary of the founding of the firm, both Haggard and Longman paid special tribute to the memory of Lang. "Charles Longman is now almost my oldest friend," said Haggard, "also there is a further and particularly intimate link between us— a mutual attachment to our late great friend Andrew Lang, to whom and to whose memory we are both devoted. Indeed, not a day goes by but I remember him." And Longman also paid his tribute: "I should like to say a word of special thanks to my friend Sir Rider Haggard. It is perfectly true that for forty years we have been bound by unbroken friendship. There is one who, of all men, he and I would most like to have been here today, to whom we are equally bound, and of whom he and I seldom cease to think—Mr. Andrew Lang."[199] And a few days after Lang's death, Longman wrote to Haggard: "The breaking of an unclouded friendship of five-and-forty years is no light thing . . . You and I will always feel a blank when we think of Andrew Lang. He was of all men the most loyal to his friends—it was one of the most marked of his characteristics, and there had been a bond between us three which nothing could break."

Probably Lang's most famous friendship was that with Robert Louis Stevenson. This began with an aversion on both sides, and there were certain things in each other that neither ever quite got over until the distance of the whole world lay between them: and then only did they realize how much their friendship meant.

> "Once we were kindest, he said, when leagues of the limitless sea
> Flowed between us, but now that no wash of the wandering tides
> Sunders us each from each, yet nearer we seem to be,
> Whom only the unbridged stream of the river of death divides,"

wrote Lang after Stevenson's death. Of "Dear Andrew with the brindled hair," Stevenson had written many years before, and also, less famously, in some verses which were prefixed to a few copies of the large paper edition of Lang's re-editing of *Cupid and Psyche*:

> "You that are much a fisher in the pool
> Of things forgotten, and from thence bring up
> Gold of old song and diamonds of dead speech,
> The scholar, and the angler, and the friend
> Of the pale past . . ."

But at first Stevenson's reactions had been of another kind, and he had written—not for publication—some amusing verses which Miss Rosaline Masson has rescued from a letter to Henley:

> "My name is Andrew Lang,
> Andrew Lang
> That's my name,
> And criticism and cricket is my game.
> With my eye-glass in my eye
> Am not I,

> Am I not
> A la—dy, da—dy, Oxford kind of Scot
> Am I not ? "[200]

But Lang could see also the faults in Stevenson, particularly the
absurd posing and posturing of his earlier years; and he told
A. E. W. Mason of one occasion when he met him in an Edinburgh
drawing room: Stevenson did not feel that he was receiving enough
attention, so he took off his coat and sat in his shirt sleeves, until
his hostess remarked: "You might as well put your coat on again,
no one is taking any notice of you."

On one occasion Stevenson arrived to dine with Lang at the
Oxford and Cambridge Club, dressed in a striped black and white
shirt; and Sheriff Machonachie told Miss Masson that on another
occasion, when he and Lang were walking along Bond Street, they
met Stevenson wearing his famous navy-blue shirt, red tie, black
brigand coat and velvet smoking cap: "No, no, go away, Louis,
go away!" cried the scandalized Andrew Lang, "My character
will stand a great deal, but it won't stand being seen talking to a
'thing' like you in Bond Street!"[201]

At Mentone Lang had also met Sidney Colvin, with whom he
remained on friendly terms, corresponding on literary matters,
and meeting at the Savile Club. Here Lang was wont to lunch on
Saturdays with Haggard, Gosse, Walter Besant, R. A. M. Stevenson, and others. Gosse was an early acquaintance, but never a very
close friend: "Today I am mourning, with a sense of shock and
loss, for Andrew Lang, my old companion and friend of 35 years,"
he wrote to Floris Delattre on 22nd July 1912: but four months
later he was writing to Henry James: "Somehow his memory
irritates me!"

Henley, too, was of these gatherings, but his opinion of Lang
does not seem to be recorded. They had worked together for
Henley's early venture, *London*, and Lang had also contributed
regularly to *The Magazine of Art*. In 1884 Lang was one of a few
friends whom Henley collected for the strange ritual of reading
Deacon Brodie "publicly," in an empty hall, to secure performing
rights, and in 1888 they had collaborated in *Pictures at Play*, the
result of their experiences as art critics.

In July 1885 W. B. Richmond's portrait of Andrew Lang was

exhibited in the Grosvenor Gallery, and Henley wrote of it in *The Magazine of Art*: "The portrait of Mr. Lang is remarkable for its potent realization of character—an effect that is none the worse but all the better for a hint of humour, a touch, a shadow (it may be) of kindly caricature. It is expressed with rare and delicate insight, and a most subtle apprehension of the idiosyncracies of the subject. This is seen in many happy touches, notably in the languorous and graceful form, the drooping *abandon* of the right arm, the characteristic poise and turn of the head . . . Again, it possesses the intellectual revelation that alone satisfies. There is a magnetism in the thoughtful and brooding face, an expression which the artist has instinctively apprehended as a characteristic veracity, transient though it be. The same felicitous sympathy is shown in the pose and the composition, which admirably express a delicate and somewhat fastidious refinement."

W. B. Richmond, to whom *The World's Desire* was dedicated, knew Lang well. "With Andrew Lang," he wrote, "both I and my boys found much in common. He loved a game of cricket! a game I never could see much merit in. He would pass whole days at it, but I fancy he always had in his pocket a book in the pages of which he could find refuge if the play were dull. What a facility of writing he had! In my studio he would pick up two or three sheets of writing paper whereon he wrote a well-thought-out article for the press . . . What a clever fellow he was! To me there is no other translation of Homer or the Idylls of Theocritus—Henry Butcher, indeed, helped with Homer, but Lang did Theocritus all by himself.

"Quite different were the two friends Henry Butcher and Andrew Lang, the one quite Irish, the other Scotch. Both were extraordinarily good-looking, both were close friends of mine. Henry was the more concentrated, Lang the more playful."[202]

Of Lang's facility in writing, many tales are told. Richard Le Gallienne records that: "Once he was staying at a country house for the weekend, and, remembering that his ' leader ' for the day was still to be written, he strolled into the billiard room, where some fellow guests were knocking about the balls, and, curling himself up on one of the settees, he began to scribble away, all the time keeping an interested eye on the game, till at last one of the players remarked that they feared they must be disturbing him.

N

"Not in the least," he answered, "but are you sure I am not interfering with your game ? "[203]

"On another occasion," records Rider Haggard, "I was travelling with him from St. Andrews to Edinburgh, and Dr. Boyd, better known as A.K.H.B., was our fellow-voyager. He was a great conversationalist, and talked to Lang almost without ceasing. Presently Lang took off the tall hat he was wearing, placed it on his knee, produced paper and pencil, set the paper on the crown of the hat and began to write like a spiritualist automatist, if that is the right word, all the time keeping up a flow of argument and conversation with A.K.H.B. At Edinburgh I saw him post the results, without re-reading, to the editor of the *Saturday Review*. The article appeared in due course without his seeing a proof, and written in his usual clear and beautiful style."[204]

Lang's love of cricket, remarked by Richmond, dated from his boyhood, and although he was not much of a hand at it himself, he always took a keen delight in watching it played. One day, in the nineteen-hundreds, his companion at Lord's was E. V. Lucas, with whom he was fairly well acquainted. "We sat on one of the front benches of the pavilion," says Lucas, "he wore an ancient top hat, which he tilted over his eyes, stretched his legs on the seat in front and talked all the while; but I had no notion of what he was saying, partly because of his careless utterance and partly because I was watching the game. Cricket demands concentration. He had a voice that did not carry—' roupy ' he himself called it— and he did something to his words too: bit them, I think, so that most of them were lost."[205]

At other times he would take some schoolboy acquaintance; for Lang had a considerable liking for boys, and wrote of them with sympathy—though often with rather a misplaced idealism. They interested him for the strange resemblance that their outlook bore to that of savages—of noble savages, one must hasten to add, though Lang could see many of their faults quite candidly. They were rough, intolerant, thoughtlessly cruel, he would admit, but he believed sincerely in their chivalry, their loyalty and in the healthiness of their outlook. This explains his attitude to boys in books, such as Tom Sawyer and Huckleberry Finn—"If these are not real boys, then Dr. Farrar's Eric *is* a real boy; I cannot put it stronger"[206]—and his dislike of *Stalky and Co.*: "As my sympathies are not wholly engaged with Stalky and Co. in their long and successful combat with their masters, I prefer to say very little about these heroes. Whatever else they may be, they are not normal schoolboys," and he went on to praise Eden Phillpotts "delightful book, *The Human Boy*," and admitted that he was "wholly captivated by those perfect little trumps, Mrs. Nesbit's characters in *The Treasure Seekers*"[207], and wrote to her thanking her for a copy of her novel, *The Red House* "and still more for the children in *The Treasure Seekers*, and the other tales. Their chivalry reminds me of the Great Montrose."[208] It was this idealization of boyhood which prompted Lang to liken Jeanne d'Arc to "a frank and loyal schoolboy"—a comparison which has excited much ridicule in recent biographies of the Maid.

With little girls also Lang was popular, though unfortunately few records remain. We cannot feel, indeed, that his letters to child-friends can have come up to the Lewis Carroll standard, but one preserved by Lady Charnwood is sufficiently whimsical and charming to increase our regret that there can be no comprehensive collection of his letters. Lady Charnwood was the Dorothea Thorpe to whom *Johnny Nut and the Golden Goose* was dedicated, and to whom the verses were written beginning "Dear Dorothea, I and you, both write, I'm told of dwarfs and fays," and some others concerning Crab, the dog "who barked at each and other, He barked at all men born," which Lady Charnwood prints in her delightful *Call Back Yesterday*. "The best of friends at any age," she says, "was Andrew Lang. I remember with the precocity of childhood feeling: "This person is as nice to me when we are alone as when he is being kind to me to please mother." From the time when he took me walks without a nurse, to the time when we dined at each other's parties, and I was the mother of a child myself, he was the most delightful of companions . . . I loved my walks with him. My mother was under the impression that I was in the fresh air; I really was in old bookshops, more insanitary then than now, for dust and germs flourished. He used to say "If you were my child you should read everything in print, but perhaps your mother —" He was very beautiful, and he did not grow less so with years. He was in very deed one of the kindest people ever known. How he helped young authors! Many men have told me what they owed to his encouragement."[209]

The dedications to the Fairy Books, to "Master Frederick Longman," to "Francis MacCunn," "To Joan, Toddles and Tiny," "To Miss Sybil Corbet," and the rest of these charming verse epistles, testify to other friendships with children. Sybil Corbet was an "infant prodigy" who made up stories and verses at the age of four: to one of her earliest books, *Animal Land where there are No People*, Lang wrote an interesting preface.

Sidney Colvin noted "the habitual preoccupation with his own ideas which made his manner, to women especially, often seem careless and abstracted, or even rude, when rudeness was farthest from his intention," and in company he was apt to be brusque or merely bored. "With strangers he was not always easy to amalgamate, especially as so many were either afraid of him, or wondered what were suitable subjects of conversation. What thoroughly irritated him was to be introduced to someone and then immediately to be asked: 'Are you writing anything at present, Mr. Lang?'—'As if I ever did anything else,' he snapped out later when airing his grievance. This was largely caused, not from rudeness, but because he was naturally a shy man and highly strung; moreover, he did not suffer fools gladly."[210] Society and social occasions were rather irksome to him, and he preferred to choose his guests with care. On one occasion when the Langs had arranged to have a large dinner party, two guests were unable to come at the last moment, and Mrs. Lang asked him to suggest someone else to fill the vacant places: "*Must* we fill them up?" he asked pathetically.

In his earlier years he was often to be met with at dinner parties in artistic or social London, and more occasionally towards the end of his life. Dining with Lord Kilbracken in the early 'eighties, he met Gladstone, whom he always detested as a politician: "I say, what a delightful man Gladstone is," Lang began as soon as the great man had gone, and continued in the same strain for some time.[211] On another occasion he was dining at the Richmonds, in company with Anne Thackeray Ritchie, Mrs. Morris, Henry James and Marie Stillman.[212]

On 6th May 1890 he was dining with the Dowager Lady Iddesleigh, where he met Lord Carnarvon and the Earl of Cranbrook (Garthorne Hardy). Lang was then writing the life of the late Earl of Iddesleigh, Sir Stafford Northcote—the nearest approach to hack work that he ever undertook—and Cranbrook was able to give him some aid.[213] Lang detested politics, and admitted that for the political chapters in the life he was forced to call in the aid of friends more capable of dealing with such things.

At some time after the beginning of the new century Lang was a guest of the Duchess of Sutherland at Stafford House. Alice Meynell was present at one of these "intellectual Friday evenings" which Lang attended, and records that the other guests included the Duke of Argyll, the Duchess of Rutland, Winston Churchill, Lord Ribblesdale, Beerbohm Tree, Laurence Binyon, Oliver Lodge and Augustin Birrell.[214]

During the later years, when much of their time was spent at St. Andrews, the Langs received visits from friends and acquaintances. Alfred Ainger stayed with them about 1902. Maarten Maartens, the Dutch novelist, was another visitor, and J. M. Barrie was staying there in March 1894. With Barrie, Lang seems to have got on well, though they were never intimate. Barrie had included Lang among the popular characters scheduled for extermination in *Better Dead*, but this was rather a compliment than otherwise; while Lang, though critical of some aspects, welcomed Barrie's writings from the start.

Another visitor was the Irish novelist, Violet Florence Martin better known as "Martin Ross," the collaborator of Oenone Somerville in the *Irish R.M.* books, who came to St. Andrews in January 1895. The Langs gave a dinner party in her honour, and Martin Ross, appraising her host, found that he was "very curious to look at, and his lemon-pale face with its black moustache appeared somewhat foxy in profile, under the white hair which grew low on his forehead." But she decided that his looks were "very quaint and appropriate." He seemed to be shy, keeping his head down, and often not looking at her when speaking, and bringing out his sentences with a jerk in a high and indistinct voice. She describes him as having "a curious silent laugh up under his nose." Meeting her at another dinner a few days later, Lang offered to take her round the sights of St. Andrews, suggesting Monday, if the weather were suitable.

Martin Ross waited vainly until Wednesday, when, despite the Arctic nature of the weather, Lang appeared, looking very bedraggled in a long coat and a deer-stalker hat. The tour was most successful, though Lang insisted on speaking of John Knox as "that scoundrel" in the presence of an officer of the Town Kirk. Martin Ross enjoyed her expedition, and seems to have been greatly impressed by her guide.

He met her again the following week in Edinburgh, and took her to Holyrood and the Castle. Martin Ross "with a vagueness of memory almost unbelievable, enquired if Mons Meg was identical with 'Muckle-mou'd Meg.' Lang well-nigh expired at the shock of the question, but managed to gasp that Muckle-mouthed Meg was his great-great-grandmother."[215]

Lang, it may be noted, was a great admirer of the "Somerville and Ross" books, had praised an early one, *The Real Charlotte*, when few people were found to care for it, and placed *The Experiences of an Irish R.M.* with Phillpotts *The Human Boy* as his two favourite books of 1899.

After 1900 Lang made few new friends, and he seems to have seen less and less of the older friends who remained to him. But in the 'nineties, he was still adding to the list of those who knew him to a greater or less degree, and many writers, who were his friends at that time, testify to his kindness, and to the interest that he took in their work.

An older friend, Grant Allen, had introduced Yorke Powell to Lang, and Powell writes of him in a letter to Edward Clodd (28th March 1900): "What a good creature Lang is! How generous he is, and how fair!"[216] Among his younger acquaintances was Richard Le Gallienne, whose early poems, like those of May Kendall and Graham R. Thomson, reveal that Lang's influence reached beyond that of personality, and was apt to show traces in the writings of the new generation. Le Gallienne was never one of his more intimate friends, but Lang wrote frequently to him about literary matters, including the proper method of presenting *A Monk of Fife* to the public. "Above all things Lang hated to seem to take himself or his work seriously," writes Mr. Le Gallienne. "His dread of rhetorical gesture seems to have extended to the sound of his own name, which he always signed ' A. Lang,' as though ' Andrew Lang ' were too melodious and romantic . . . His later portraits look as though he were trying to be as prosaic as possible—as much as possible ' A. Lang.' He was, I think, a ' too quick despairer' about his own poetry, and, charming as is such prose of his as *Letters to Dead Authors, In the Wrong Paradise* and *Old Friends*, I believe that it is his poetry that, after all, will keep his name alive, for his best ballades and lyrics have a fragrance and a *légereté* nearer to the charm of his master Ronsard than anything else we have in English—not to forget his one great sonnet on 'the surge and thunder of the Odyssey.' — "[217]

With the young people of the *Yellow Book* circle, Lang did not feel himself at home, and looked upon much of their writing as mere affectation—though he was quick to recognize and acknowledge the genius of the greatest of that group, Kenneth Grahame, who himself had always an affection for "St. Andrews Lang," as he called him.

Another famous writer of this circle, though in a very different vein, Max Beerbohm, was among those who neither liked Lang, nor admired his work. When Quiller-Couch registered his opinion in his *Pall Mall Magazine* causerie "From a Cornish Window" (July 1897) that Lang was the master of the best style in English prose for the last ten years, Max Beerbohm expressed his horror and derision of such a pronouncement. The following year he made the acquaintance of Lang for the first time, at the house of Edmund Gosse. On entering the drawing room he beheld Lang: "He was leaning against an angle of the wall. One might almost have supposed that he had been placed there as an ornament like a palm in a pot. From the buzzing human throng he seemed to be quite as detached, as any palm in any pot. Slender and supereminent, he curved, he drooped, he was a very beautiful thing in the room. And it was even more in colour than in form that he was so admirable . . . The long nut-brown neck was not more sharply relieved by the white of the turned-down collar than was the nut-brown forehead by the silvery hair that wavily caressed it, than were the nut-brown cheeks by the silvery vapour they had of whisker. And the moustache was jet-black, and jet-black were the eyebrows and the eyelashes. In such surroundings the whiteness of the eyeballs and the darkness of the brown eyes 'told' tremendously, of course. But in a spiritual sense the eyes told nothing at all. They shone, they flashed, but with no animation to belie the general look of inanimateness. Their lustre was as lovely and as meaningless as that of jewels . . . Now and again, as he stood propped against the angle of the wall, he inserted with long brown fingers a monocle through which the rays of the eye were refracted with surpassing brilliance. And his manner of doing this seemed to indicate, not that there was anyone whom he particularly cared to inspect, but that he took a languid pleasure in the gesture. If to superficial observers the fixing of that monocle might have convicted him of curiosity, the marked way he had of letting it drop promptly down again to his waistcoat must have acquitted him of having found the slightest profit in the investigation."

On being introduced, Sir Max was chilled and repelled by Lang's tone of bored superiority, and by what he describes as the perfection of the Oxford manner. "And yet I daresay he meant to be kind. I have heard from people who knew him intimately that he was a really kind man. He may even have had the wish to please. But it is certain that one had to know him intimately before his wish could, in regard to oneself, be gratified . . . I merely shared the common lot of men who met him for the first time: I did not like him."[218] Sir Max met Lang again some years later at a dinner in aid of the Printers' Pension Fund. Lang made a speech of a witty kind: "Public speaking seemed to galvanize not merely Lang's manner, but also his mind: his speech was as delightful as one of those *causeries* or those leading articles with which, many years before, he had made his name in journalism, and by virtue of which he had so long thriven, in journalism, on his name." But on the whole, Sir Max felt little more kindly disposed to Lang than at their first meeting, and they did not meet again. There was obviously some natural antipathy at work between these two:— perhaps the old adage of Greek meeting Greek had something to do with it, as both were *alumni* of Merton! But indeed their outlooks were very dissimilar, and Sir Max could never forgive Lang for his views on Hardy and the younger writers of the newer tradition.

And yet with young writers of another type Lang was always popular, and they were ever ready to admit their debt to his help and encouragement, to his kindness and personal charm.

Besides Stevenson and Haggard, Kipling and Barrie, there was F. Anstey, the humorist. Lang read *Vice Versa* in an advance copy, and wrote enthusiastically of it in the *Daily News* and *Saturday Review*, quoted it in his essays and praised it in private and in public. His telling of the story of *Vice Versa* to George Saintsbury

reduced that sedate scholar to a state of helpless laughter, for Lang
was very brilliant as a *raconteur*. Later Lang and Anstey collaborated in a short tale of a light but psychical nature, "From a
Ghost's Point of View," which appeared in *Time* (January 1886).

Conan Doyle was another writer who owed much of his early
success to Lang. *A Study in Scarlet* had been issued in a Christmas
annual, without then attracting much attention, and Doyle's first
serious work, *Micah Clarke*, was touring the publishers in vain.
Lang read it in the capacity of adviser to Longmans, and persuaded that firm to publish it. He wrote of it in the "Ship," and
was even more enthusiastic when *Brigadier Gerard* appeared.
In April 1903 he wrote: "Were I a schoolmaster in possession of
wealth, and about to found a library for boys, my corner-stone
should be a large mass of the works of Sir Arthur Conan Doyle:
The White Company, *Micah Clarke*, *Brigadier Gerard* (the best),
and *Sherlock Holmes*."

Stanley Weyman's earlier books were issued by Longmans also,
and at least one of Anthony Hope's.

Another would-be novelist, now famous in quite another sphere
of literature, owed his first publication to Lang. This was Professor
Gilbert Murray, whose delightful romance of an ancient Greek
city which he fabled to be still existing in Central Asia, *Gobi or
Shamo*, Lang advised Longman to publish in 1889—though it did
not achieve very much success. "The *Gobi and Shamo* man is *very*
clever, but has read *She*," Lang wrote to Haggard: and we feel
inclined to add that the author of *Ayesha* had read *Gobi or Shamo*!

Unlike the more uncritical admirers of his work, Lang wrote
pleasantly and sensibly of S. R. Crockett: of *The Raiders*, for
example, in the *Daily News*: "Mr. Crockett has all the materials
for such a book as boys delight in, and wise men do not despise.
It is good, now and then, to read of a hero who marries his first
love, and does not ' ware his heart ' on other lassies. To have an
island of one's very own, with caves in it, to love a pretty girl, to
defend her against all comers in a cave, to chase her and them over
burn and hill, to sleep in a robber's hut, to escape, and just escape,
are thrilling circumstances," and, as Lang went on to point out,
make the pleasantest and most blameless form of light reading.
Lang knew Crockett, though probably not well, and visited him at
Bank House, Penicuik, where Barrie was also a guest, and where

Stevenson is said to have come during one of his last visits to
Edinburgh.

A far closer friend was Arthur Quiller-Couch, and it is much to
be regretted that his death cut short his autobiography before it
reached the point referred to in Chapter I "my friend Andrew
Lang . . . but see *infra*."

Closer still was Mr. A. E. W. Mason, whom Lang first met in
the spring of 1896. For the next six years, both before and after the
writing of *Parson Kelly*, they saw much of each other, Mr. Mason
dining frequently with the Langs at Marloes Road, in company
with Sir Ian Hamilton, Lady Elspeth Campbell, and other of
Lang's friends; and Lang going each summer to stay with Mr.
Mason at Kilcheran, the house which he rented for some time on
the island of Lismore. This house had the peculiarity of a window
over the fireplace in the drawing room that formed a similar
window in the dining room. It was a great source of amusement to
watch new visitors go towards this window, under the impression
that it was a mirror. On one occasion two guests did so at the same
moment, one in each room—much to the delight of the onlookers—
and Lang murmured the following extempore lines:

> "When Smith his tie adjusted
> And Brown arranged his hair,
> Each cried in tones disgusted:
> ' I thought, I hoped, I trusted
> My face was far more fair! ' "

On one or two occasions Mr. Mason stayed with Lang at St.
Andrews, and they played golf together.

But after about 1902 they began to see less and less of each other,
Mr. Mason being occupied with his parliamentary career, and
Lang growing more and more of a recluse, and spending more and
more of his time at St. Andrews.

An early friend, of whose judgment in literary matters Lang
thought very highly, was Mrs. Herbert Augustus Hills, to whom
The Disentanglers was dedicated. Lang sent her copies of all his
books, with grateful inscriptions in them, and occasionally
humorous verses. Her daughter-in-law, the Hon. Mrs. Eustace
Hills, remembers visiting the Langs at Marloes Road just after she
was married: on one occasion Henry Ford was there, and the

evening was spent in discussing the Fairy Books, for which he did nearly all the illustrations.

In earlier years another constant friend was Lang's aunt, E. M. Sellar. Lang wrote the memoir of her husband, Professor William Young Sellar—a piece of work which E. V. Lucas ranked very highly—and she was always a welcome guest at Marloes Road. On one occasion, when Mrs. Lang was away, Mrs. Sellar dined with him and Rider Haggard, having received an invitation couched in the following terms:

> "A weary lot is mine, fair maid,
>   A weary lot is mine,
>   When dinner but for one is laid,
>   And I alone must dine.
>   I'll ask my Rider to the feast,
>   Uncork the oldest wine
>   (Which you'll not care for in the least!)
>   If you'll but come and dine, my dear,
>   If you'll but come and dine! "

Richard Whiteing, who had been his colleague on the *Daily News*, stresses the fact that Lang "seemed to dread boredom above all other things. Chance acquaintances met at dinner, hostesses who wanted to use him as a nice man for afternoon tea, found him trying. He would slip away from the front drawing room with its buzz, on pretence of looking at a picture in the antechamber, and thence make his escape."[219]

At a garden party Professor Murray recalls seeing Lang seek the seclusion of the shrubbery to sit down and write an article! Indeed, towards the end of his life, writing became almost a disease.

Richard Whiteing was also impressed by Lang's good looks: "In his day, and to the last in his own way he was one of the handsomest men I have ever seen. There was so much distinction in the face; and when its time came the snow-cap of grey hair was an added charm for the lofty brow. He was of a melancholy cast in his innermost recesses of being; and his boundless activities were but restless attempts to make the best of a bad job— existence. He was no tuft-hunter, yet I think he sometimes suffered lords beyond the requirements of the case."

Of this last characteristic, Edmund Gosse tells quite another tale, depicting Lang in one of those petulant moods that led Horace Hutchinson to describe him as a "spoilt child." It was on 16th May 1905, while Gosse (who *was* a tuft-hunter) was librarian to the House of Lords; "Andrew Lang's manners are always amusing, if a little exasperating," Gosse wrote in his diary that day: "He came here with me today to talk over Jacobite history with Evan. By the way, I asked him if he was going to dine tonight with the St. Andrews University Club, of which he is a vice-president. He said: ' No! I hate dinners, and I hate clubs, and I hate Universities! ' I asked rather tartly: ' I believe you hate everything in the world! ' ' No,' he replied, ' I don't hate Mary Queen of Scots! ' Evan left us alone in the smoking room, and in came well-groomed, smiling Lord Monk Bretton. As he looked very curiously at Lang, I introduced them, whereupon Lang violently, after bowing, turned his back on poor Monk Bretton and buried his face in some old newspapers. Presently the Duke of Northumberland came in, and recognizing Lang, bowed and smiled. Lang glared at him like a basilisk through his eye-glass, and the Duke, abashed, presently went out. I said: ' The Duke bowed to you.' ' What Duke ? ' said Lang. ' Northumberland.' ' Oh, was that he ? I never recognize anybody. He belongs to the Roxburghe Club.' That was all he vouchsafed; he behaved like a bear, like a white ant-bear or coati-mundi, but he can be charming company if he chooses."[220]

The best description of Andrew Lang in his later years is given by Alice King Stewart, who was a most intimate friend of both Lang and his wife, and who saw much of him at a time when few others did so.

"Andrew Lang was tall and inclined to stoop, with a rather slight figure. He was very active for his years. In my mind's eye I see him slouching easily along with his hands in his pockets, but I think this attitude was to get a better view of things as he walked along. He was supposed not to have the use of one eye, and in the other he wore an unmounted monocle, which always seemed to be popping in and out, and only restrained from loss by a black elastic cord. Certainly with his one good eye he saw more than most people with two. His eyes were dark brown, matching his moustache. He had a fine intellectual head, sometimes held rather to one side when looking at objects, partly because of the blind eye.

His hair never looked as if he had recently seen a barber, and the brindled locks which Robert Louis Stevenson described were white when I knew him.

"His voice was high-pitched and rather thin in quality, and he had a slight burr in pronouncing the letter 'R.' He had a habit of cutting short his sentences and moving on to an entirely different topic and, as he was also apt to murmur his words into his moustache, one had to be alert in following his talk. He had a quaint habit of twirling a certain waistcoat button as he spoke, and there is a tradition of his schooldays that once, when the button had been removed, he became speechless . . .

"Every year he and Mrs. Lang used to stay with me, and I always found him a most charming guest, easily entertained, and interested in such a wonderful variety of subjects . . . As a couple, Andrew Lang and his wife were absolutely unlike, and yet were admirably suited to each other. She was of incalculable help to him, not alone in his writings, but in his everyday affairs of life. As she once laughingly remarked: ' I have an imbecile child of three to look after! ' He was completely helpless without her, as we found if at any time he happened to visit Cowden alone."[221]

A man is known by his friends, runs the old saying, is known by the company that he keeps: and we who never met Andrew Lang in person, can yet draw near to him with those who knew him. With the possible exception of Edmund Gosse, whose opinions were so apt to be swayed by other people, and of Henley in those last years of bitterness and revolt, all those who knew Lang well seem to have loved him well. Their testimonies in verse and prose are many; and those still living who knew him tell the same tale. One thinks of his kindness and of his chivalry, of his readiness to help all other writers without ever a trace of jealousy, of his generosity to all in need: and in thinking of these things one forgets the affectations and the petulance, the air of superiority that was so little more than a barrier to shield the shy, the over-sensitive soul of Andrew Lang.

And I can never forget the tone that came into the voice of the late Mrs. Florence MacCunn, Lang's cousin, who had known him since the 'sixties, known him as perhaps few other people did, as she spoke to me of him: "My dear Andrew," she said, "my dear, dear Andrew . . ."

CHAPTER XV

The Last Years

From the time that he settled in London at 1 Marloes Road, in the 'seventies, until his death in July 1912, Andrew Lang's life was set in a very uneventful, even a humdrum course. He did not travel often, or at least not outside the British Isles, though in his Oxford days he had passed much time in the south of France and had spent at least one holiday in Austria. In 1888 he and Mrs. Lang visited Italy; Monte Carlo for a little while, Florence for a longer spell, and Venice. But he does not seem to have been particularly impressed by the country, his main occupation being rummaging in antiquarian shops. "My wife has evolved a knowledge apparently minute of the Italian language," he wrote to W. B. Richmond, "I can't patter a word of their lingo. I am a bluff John Bull—that is the kind of man I am!"

Probably the Langs paid more visits to the Continent than are recorded, though they never seem to have gone further afield than Italy.

But Scotland was Lang's chosen country, and thither he fled more and more frequently from London. He visited Ireland on one occasion, and hoped very much to see fairies—but he failed even to meet peasants who had seen them, and declared himself disillusioned.

Fishing was Lang's favourite sport, though, as he himself admitted: "my labours have not been blessed, and are devoted to fishing rather than to the catching of fish." Of angling Lang wrote often, and "At the Sign of St. Paul's" is full of fishing stories, his own and others. There are poems too—such as the parody of Morris's "Shameful Death," and other verses in the Scots dialect. His only book on fishing, however, is *Angling Sketches*, which appeared in 1891. Many fishermen still think highly of this volume (which is delightful reading, even for one who is "no fisher, but a well-wisher to the game"), and the sporting poet Patrick Chalmers, himself an angler and a writer on angling, kept a copy in nearly every room in his house.

Although it was to Scotland that Lang turned whenever possible, he did not disdain to cast a fly in southern waters. "Andrew Lang and I shared a rod on a little dry-fly trout stream in Hertfordshire," writes John Buchan, "where I spent many pleasant Saturdays, and he used to laugh at my new-found enthusiasm for lowland waters."[222]

Thinking perhaps of weekends spent beside this very stream, Lang wrote of the trials of the town dweller in the country: "The little angling inn in the village or country town is perhaps the most wakeful place of any. The beds are strange indeed, with exquisite varieties. The ancient four-poster couch may have witnessed the fevers of Richard III, and his celebrated military treasure-chest may be concealed under the bed, where a broom has not come, apparently, since the battle of Bosworth. The heavy red curtains might harbour all the spectres that haunted the wicked king, and also persecutors more normal but as disturbing . . . The mattress is apparently stuffed with billiard balls at irregular intervals . . . Meanwhile clocks, dogs, cocks and cats keep up their wonted turmoil . . . Worse than in town are rural dogs, especially the honest watch-hound. In the deeps of Worcestershire, say, a watch-dog is awakened and bays. He wakens a dog a mile away, and another dog takes it up from the second dog, and before dawn dogs are howling in the Cheviots and at the Land's End. Cats, when noisy in the garden, are amenable to the Bible which lies in the bedroom, or to anything else that you can hurl among them. But nothing short of arsenic will stop a dog once he begins to bark, and arouses seven other dogs worse than himself . . ."[223]

To this, or another country village, came George Moore in the summer of 1897: and he tells the following tale in the likeness of a fable whereby to express his opinion of Andrew Lang as a critic:

"As I drove from the railway station to the lodging which had been hired for me, I noticed a pleasant river which seemed to promise excellent fishing. I mentioned the river to my landlady.

"Oh yes, sir," she said, "there is very good fishing here—many people come here for fishing."

"What kind of people come here?" I asked distractedly.

"Literary gentlemen come here very often, sir; we had Mr. Andrew Lang staying here."

"Oh, really—does he fish? Is he a good fisherman?"

"Yes, sir, he fishes beautifully."

"Really! Does he catch much ? "

"No, sir, he never catches anything, but he fishes beautifully."[224]

Fishing was Lang's only sport of the kind, and he held strong views about blood sports, though he did not condemn fox-hunting: "I don't much bar fox-hunting," he wrote to Haggard in 1911 during a correspondence on Haggard's latest book *The Mahatma and the Hare*, an attack on the hunting and shooting of hares, "it needs pluck, and the fox, a sportsman himself, only takes his chances and often gets away. It's all a matter of thinking. Scott was a humane man, but devoted to coursing, which I abominate. Wordsworth never thought harm of trout fishing, with fly. Now I was *born* to be ruthful to trout, as a kid, and sinned against light, but I could not use the worm."[225]

"He was really tender-hearted to a degree," writes Lady King Stewart, "even to the fish dangling on his hook when fishing. I saw him so often in the Japanese garden lake at Cowden gently disengage a small trout with his finely shaped fingers, and slip it into the water with the words, ' Poor little thing, put it back' "[226]

Lang was fond of animals, and had a particular liking for cats. No stray who came to Marloes Road was ever turned away, and Lang wrote charmingly of his feline friends in many of his *causeries*; nor did he take it amiss when Semiramis, his black cat, came and settled herself on the copy that he was writing.

At one time Lang is said to have had a dog called Oscar, of whom it was his delight to tell the most charmingly improbable stories. This intelligent Newfoundland, so Lang was wont gravely to relate, was in the habit of gazing with silent adoration at an engraving of Landseer's "Member of the Humane Society" of which there was a copy in the house. And one day Oscar decided to emulate the hero of the picture; so he proceeded to push a child into the sea, and then after barking loudly to make sure that his master was watching, sprang into the depths and saved the little boy with great heroism. On reaching shore, Oscar went straight to the nearest photographer, with the child still in his mouth, to ensure that his brave deed should not go unrecorded! Oscar, so ran another legend, did not like the Rev. A. K. H. Boyd, whose works he was in the habit of begging Lang to review unfavourably: this request was conveyed by laying a copy of the minister's latest book at his master's feet, and then returning with a carving-knife in his mouth.[227]

About 1891 the Langs began spending much of the winter in St. Andrews, in a house which they took standing on the cliff edge with the castle ruin to the east, and a fine view over the Firth of Tay and to Forfarshire.

Lang found that the University library was far more convenient for his research than the British Museum, and spent much of his time there. Nor did he neglect the only game in which he took part—golf. Lang wrote some amusing sketches about this game: "Herodotus at St. Andrews" and "Dr. Johnson on the Links," which appeared in *College Echoes*, the University magazine, and were collected in *A Batch of Golfing Papers* (1891), are the most amusing. "Especially he wrote well of golf," says Horace Hutchinson, who was himself of championship standard, "— so far as a man can write well of a game which he cannot play at all. Even a stroke a hole handicap would have complimented him too highly!"[228]

Though he probably never played it himself since his Oxford days, and was never a member of the Allahakbarries, of which his friends Barrie, Mason, Doyle and Henry Ford were staunch supporters, Lang's third and only other sport was cricket. His most considerable writing on this game is the chapter on the "History of Cricket" in the Badminton Library; but he wrote a number of poems on the subject (including the parodies "Helen, thy bowling is to me," and that on Emerson's "Brahma"), probably the least known of which is the uncollected "Confessions" which appeared in the *Independent* of New York in January 1887, and which ends like this:

"Well, there's one word that moved me when a boy,
        That moves today:
    It's when the Umpire, to the general joy,
        Pronounces ' *Play* '!

"May I, ere time with all that he can bring
        Of sorrows serried,
    Takes *that* delight from the delight of Spring,
        Be dead and buried

o

"By some field path where cricketers may pass
Along its mazes,
And over me the green short English grass,
The English daisies! "

Lang's miscellaneous writings are more numerous during the
earlier part of his life than during the last twelve or fifteen years,
when historical studies were occupying so much of his time. The
volume of *Essays in Little* of 1891 was practically his last work of
the kind, and in some ways the best. Many of the essays had
appeared before in various magazines, but the shorter ones were
rewritten for the volume, and a number of entirely new ones
added, including that on Kipling, which is the first study of his
work to be published in this country. It is the counterpart of the
introduction which Lang wrote for an American selection of
Kipling's stories which came out in 1890 as *The Courting of Dinah
Shadd*, which was also the first essay on Kipling to appear in
America.

Other papers in the volume include the appreciations of Dickens
and Thackeray which he had written for *Good Words*, and a very
pleasant paper on "The Buccaneers of America."

The next and last collection of essays was *Adventures Among
Books* (1905) which is composed entirely of articles from magazines, dating from various times during the previous twenty years
or more. Some of Lang's best essays are contained in this volume,
including, besides the title essay, the "Recollections of R. L.
Stevenson," "Boys," "Paris and Helen" and "Enchanted
Cigarettes."

The volume is dedicated to C. M. Falconer of Dundee, a rope-
spinner, whose main interest in life seems to have been the works
of Andrew Lang, of which he had a collection that has never been
rivalled. Falconer's ambition was to issue a bibliography of Lang's
works, and he produced "Specimens" in 1889 and 1894, and a
short-title *Catalogue of a Library chiefly the writings of Andrew
Lang* in 1898. Falconer also had printed privately (sixty copies)
A New Friendship's Garland (1898) which consists of a collection
of poems by various hands, written to Lang, illustrated with
copious notes. Falconer died in 1907, and his collection was sold
at Sotheby's for £150, when it was described as "Probably a

complete collection of the writings of Andrew Lang, comprising
his own works, works edited by him, and works containing contributions by him, as well as magazine and newspaper contributions, including first and other editions, and large and small paper
copies of most of his publications, in various bindings, 1863-1906.
Formed by one of Mr. Lang's most enthusiastic admirers, Mr.
C. M. Falconer, whose printed and interleaved bibliography with
MS. additions accompanies the lot." This collection, which
contained the unique copy of the printed *St. Leonard's Magazine*
(1863) and a copy, almost as unique and quite as untraceable of
The Black Thief, was sold as a single whole: but its whereabouts
remains a complete mystery. Only one item has come to light, and
that is a manuscript volume now in the Dundee Library, "Poems,
Songs and Verses by Andrew Lang, hitherto uncollected. Trans-
scribed by C. M. Falconer and revised by Andrew Lang 1906."
This contains 199 items, ranging from long poems to couplets
written in presentation copies of books. Most of the poems
appeared in magazines, and a large number were included in the
Poetical Works of 1923, but about eighty remain uncollected.

Some of the poems transcribed by Falconer were included by
Lang in *New Collected Rhymes,* 1904, which is his last volume
of verse. The newness was of collecting rather than of writing,
for most of the pieces had appeared in magazines, some as
early as 1876. For after 1900 Lang almost gave up writing
poetry, in spite of the encouragement of George Saintsbury who
tried to persuade him to continue. But Lang had long ceased
to take himself seriously as a poet, and had written of his Muse
as early as 1890:

> "So she's cut the whole concern—
> Lute and Lyre, and Torch and Urn,
> Thoughts that breathe, and words that burn,
>   Joys and woes.
> For Parnassus is ' too steep,'
> And the only Muse I keep,
> And that keeps me, writes a heap,
>   But—it's Prose! "[229]

Even in prose Lang wrote little besides history, anthropology and

Homeric criticism after 1900. His last work of fiction (apart from
Tales of a Fairy Court in 1907) was *The Disentanglers* which
appeared late in 1902, with illustrations by Henry Ford, after
running anonymously in *Longmans' Magazine* from January to
December of that year. This is the most successful of Lang's
attempts at humorous fiction, and is written in a fashion that is all
his own. It belongs to the class of *The New Arabian Nights* in that
it is a series of fantastic adventures set in a real-life setting, and
told with humour: but Lang's touch is lighter and more whimsical
than Stevenson's, and more full of literary allusion: it shines with
a brittle brilliance, it is charming and aggravating by turns, the
humour is witty but never boisterous, and its appeal is very
limited, more so even than *The Mark of Cain*. The book consists of
a series of stories narrating the adventures of a group of young
people, men and women of good birth and university education,
who, finding themselves in a destitute condition, form themselves
into a society, headed by its two inventors Merton and Logan,
whose object is "by a scientific and thoroughly organized system of
disengaging and disentangling . . . to get the undesirable marriage
off without the usual row." The fortunes of the various members
of the society are followed through a series of adventures until all
of them are themselves happily married and settled. The ingredients of the stories are of a very wide variety, and connect with
Lang's multitudinous interests in a delightful way; there are
anglers and psychical researchers in the book, anthropologists and
neo-Celtic poets; there are anti-vaccinationists who burn Mr.
Rider Haggard in effigy as the author of *Dr. Therne*; there is a
submarine, of which Jules Verne is spoken of as the inventor, the
magical practices of an obscure South Sea island play a part, and
the traditional spectres of two Scottish castles. The whole is a
delightful blend of reality and artifice, the characters of truth and
caricature; there is parody in it and gentle satire—the lecture given
by the Lady Novelist, the jargon of the neo-Celtic poet—and there
is the charming use of the *clichés* of fiction in exaggerated or
unexpected guises. It is strange to find Lang, who professed to
loathe all things mechanical, introducing submarines and wireless
telegraphy at a time when these were in their infancy—just as in
The Mark of Cain he had anticipated the invention of the flying
machine—but he seems to have been among the earliest story-

tellers to hit upon the idea of using the latest scientific developments to replace the magical devices of the fairy-tale.

While some of the adventures suggest a comparison with
Raffles, the last in the book is an excellent detective story, and in
reading it, one regrets that Lang did not attempt this type of fiction
more seriously. It illustrates, too, an interest that became very
pronounced in the last years of his life; the solving of mysteries,
whether historical, literary or even archæological. The last is
illustrated only by the purely ephemeral *The Clyde Mystery* (1905),
which is concerned with the genuineness of a hoard of prehistoric
remains discovered near Glasgow. Historical mysteries were,
however, Lang's speciality. *Pickle the Spy* had been his first
venture in this field of research, and after triumphantly clearing up
this dark corner of history, he turned his attention to others as
obscure. *James VI and the Gowrie Mystery* appeared the same year
as *The Disentanglers* with which indeed it has affinities, as Logan,
the hero of the novel, is a descendant of the Logan concerned in
the Ruthven plot against "gentle King Jamie," and the secret
passage in the House of Restalrig, plays a part in both.

Of more interest to the general reader are the collections of short
mysteries. The first was *The Valet's Tragedy, and other Studies in
Secret History*, 1903. The title mystery is that of the identity of the
Man in the Iron Mask, whom Lang proved to be merely a valet
who knew too much, and not by any means the brother of Louis
XIV in whom Dumas would have us believe. Another mystery is
that of the murder of Amy Robsart, and although Lang quotes
"No scandal about Queen Elizabeth" (*The Critic*, incidentally,
seems to have been a favourite of his), he cannot acquit her of
guilty knowledge. There are, also, papers on "The False Jeanne
d'Arc"—the peasant girl who claimed to be Jeanne, and to have
escaped, unburned, from Rouen—on "The Bacon Mystery,"
and others.

In the following year appeared *Historical Mysteries*, which had
been published in the *Cornhill Magazine*; and Lang ranges from
Gowrie to the Chevalier D'Eon, and from Sir Edmund Berry
Godfrey to the Cardinal's Necklace.

These mysteries are among the most readable of Lang's historical
works, and do at times approach very near to the excitement of an
ordinary detective story.

Another mystery which Lang strove to solve was that of Dickens's last and unfinished novel, *Edwin Drood*. As an ardent Dickensian, he had always been interested in the subject, but was stung into action by Mr. Cumming Walters's little book on the mystery which was published in 1905, and which supported the view that Edwin was indeed dead, and made the startling suggestion that Datchery the detective was none other than Helena Landless in disguise. Lang criticized the book in "An Interview between Sherlock Holmes and Dr. Watson on the Drood Mystery" in *Longmans' Magazine* of September 1905, and before the end of the year published his own contribution to the solution of the mystery, *The Puzzle of Dickens's Last Plot*, in which he championed the theory that Edwin escaped, returned in the disguise of Datchery to spy on Jasper, and was waiting in the Sapsea vault in his own likeness to frighten the murderer into an admission of his guilt.

Lang returned frequently to this subject in articles and letters which appeared in various magazines; almost the latest, and the most important, was "A Mystery of Dickens" in *Blackwood's Magazine* of May 1911, where he so far concedes to the popular theory as to admit that "Helena Landless *may* be Datchery, but she ought not to be!" One regrets that Lang was not alive to be present at the mock trial of Edwin Drood in 1913, at which a number of well-known writers attempted to solve the mystery. Lang's final attitude was, that while he felt himself unable to accept any of the theories put forth, he could not suggest one himself; and G. K. Chesterton, as staunch a Dickensian as Lang, professed himself of the same opinion.[230]

G. K. Chesterton was associated with Lang on *The Illustrated London News*. From 4th November 1905 until the day of his death, Lang contributed a weekly column "At the Sign of St. Paul's," which formed a sequel to "At the Sign of the Ship" when *Longmans' Magazine* was discontinued. In the 'nineties Lang had become a regular contributor, being responsible for two hundred and fifty short essays between 1891 and 1896, and for a weekly *causerie* "From a Scottish Workshop" during most of 1896. His discontinuance from 1897 to 1905 corresponds with the writing of his *History of Scotland*, and he also retired from the *Daily News* and the *Saturday Review* at much the same time.

His labours as a historian took him more and more to St. Andrews, but his connection with that University had been recommenced in 1885 when he was made an honorary doctor of laws, and had been strengthened by his appointment in 1888 as the first Gifford lecturer, in which capacity he delivered forty lectures on primitive religion, which formed the basis of his book *The Making of Religion*.

Although his voice was ill-suited to it, lecturing was no new departure for Lang. He had lectured occasionally at Oxford during his Merton days, and W. L. Courtenay, who had been his colleague there, had invited him to give a public lecture at the Assembly Rooms in Bath about 1875, and Lang had "talked delightfully about the poetry of Sir Walter Scott with that charm of manner, and gentle deprecating modesty which made him universally popular."[231]

Some years later Lang was in much demand as a lecturer; William Rothenstein remembered hearing him address the Philosophical Society in Bradford; he was lecturing at Edinburgh about 1889 when Professor Nichol Smith was among his audience; and Lady King Stewart heard him discoursing on historical subjects at Glasgow.

On 28th November 1889 he lectured at the South Kensington Museum on "How to Fail in Literature," and his discourse was later published as a booklet, whence we may gather something of his charm and unconventionality as a lecturer.

The following year he delivered three lectures at the Royal Institution on "The History of Society," and he was often called upon to give lectures on kindred subjects to the Folk-lore Society (of which he was part founder, and president in 1888) and the Society for Psychical Research.

On another occasion his audience included Mr. Bernard Shaw, who writes:—"I saw Andrew Lang only once in my life, at a lecture which he delivered. His white hair and *voix criarde* gave him a personality as agreeable as his very pleasant literary style. I never met him privately; and when he ridiculed the Society of Authors and took the side of the publishers in one of the conflicts that raged between the two, I denounced him at the Society's annual dinner as having sold us for thirty pieces of silver. As he meant no harm, this took him aback considerably. My relations

with him can therefore hardly be described as friendly; but I liked
the man, and in my youth had delighted in his ' middles ' in the
Daily News, which were far ahead of anything of the kind before or
since in point of amusing readableness, high literature, and good
breeding."

Lang was also sought as a speaker at various dinners and functions. One of these occasions is described by Sir Max Beerbohm;
at another, the Booksellers' Dinner, at Holborn Restaurant on
7th May 1898, he responded to the chairman, James Bryce, and
was supported by Joseph Conrad, William Archer, I. Zangwill,
and others.

But in the same year he declined a lecture tour to the United
States, pleading the poor quality of his voice. "It is not necessary
to talk, my dear Mr. Lang, come and let us look at you—we will do
the talking! " was the American comment: "How little they know
Mr. Lang! " remarked a writer in *The Academy*—"America's
talking powers are just what he dreads! "

St. Andrews was not the only place to honour Andrew Lang:
on 25th May 1889 he opened the new Public Library at Selkirk,
and was presented with the freedom of the borough. The ceremony
known as "licking the birse," was performed by his friend, Provost
Roberts, and he was presented with the "burgess ticket" in a
cabinet of oak on which was a silver plate bearing the borough
arms and an appropriate inscription: and his name was entered on
the burgess roll where Sir Walter Scott's was before him.

With Oxford also Lang kept up his connection, attending the
Merton "Gaudy" in 1888, where he sat next to W. L. Courtney,
and being made an honorary fellow a couple of years later.

On G. C. Broderick's death in 1903, certain members of the
college wished to appoint Lang as the new Warden, but the motion
was defeated by Francis Bradley, who had a deep-rooted dislike
for Lang, and mistrusted the depth of scholarship that so popular
a journalist might possess.

It is probable that in 1885 Lang had tried for the newly-
constituted Merton Professorship of English Language and
Literature: certainly he replied with some asperity to Henry
Sweet, who had published a letter in *The Academy* to the effect
that "popular writers" had no right to such a position. "Are the
claims of mere literary persons to the chair of English language and

literature therefore mythical ? " Lang had replied, "A man of real capacity and knowledge, and worthy to be endowed, is sometimes driven into periodical literature just because he is *not* endowed. He must write what people at large can read, or he must starve; and this necessity sadly limits the time and energy he can bestow on unremunerative labours of a more solid and serious description."[232]

When one reads the faded, weary journalism that Lang wrote week after week "At the Sign of St. Paul's" from 1906 onwards, one regrets that it was not made possible for him to retire gracefully and take up his abode in the Wardens' Lodgings at Merton. He might have retired before the end, even without this, for although never a wealthy man, his writings (on which he had to depend entirely) enabled him to leave about twelve thousand pounds at his death. But it would have needed some definite call to make him do so, for by the end writing had become almost a disease.

Lang never knew that he had been proposed for the Wardenship of Merton, but on 22nd June 1904 he received the honorary degree of Doctor of Letters from the University, in company with Walter Leaf, his collaborator in the translation of the. *Iliad*, Lewis Campbell, the Edinburgh Professor of Greek, and the American novelist, W. D. Howells, with whom Lang had crossed many a literary lance on the subject of realism and romance in fiction. Following this, Lang was appointed Ford lecturer in English History, and delivered his six lectures on "Anglo-Scottish Relations" between 24th October and 4th November 1904.

In 1908 R. R. Marrett, soon to become first Reader in Anthropology at Oxford, arranged a course of lectures on "Anthropology and the Classics" (published 1908), in which Lang participated (with a lecture on "Homer and Anthropology") in company with Sir Arthur Evans, Gilbert Murray, and others.

A more unusual occasion at which Lang was present was the day (7th June 1910) when Theodore Roosevelt, President of the United States, gave the Romanes Lecture in the Sheldonian Theatre at Oxford. Herbert Warren, president of Magdalen (who had known Lang since his own undergraduate days), had arranged for Roosevelt to give the lecture, and had asked him whom he would like to meet. Roosevelt's list consisted of Rudyard Kipling,

Andrew Lang, Gilbert Murray, Kenneth Grahame and Sir
Charles Oman.

As they walked, clad in all their academic splendour, to the
Sheldonian, Roosevelt buttonholed Professor Murray: "Are you
on speaking terms with Lang ? " he asked, for Murray and Lang
were in the midst of a heated controversy on the Homeric problem
at the time,—"Oh, yes! " replied Professor Murray as seriously as
possible, "we say simply frightful things to each other! "
"Splendid," said Roosevelt, "I want to be introduced! " So the
introduction was effected, and presently Roosevelt said: "You
know, Mr. Lang, I have a dreadful thing to confess to you: I used
to believe that you were right about Homer, but Murray has
converted me! " Whereupon Lang remarked in a depressed voice
to the world in general: "*I* converted somebody *once!* " Perhaps
to make up for this confession, Roosevelt, quite regardless of the
fact that he was holding up the whole proceedings, went on to
tell Lang a story of how, when on an exploring expedition in South
America, he had taken with him a volume of Lang's poetry, which
he was in the habit of reading by the camp fire of an evening. The
guide to the expedition, said Roosevelt, was always quoting
"Andrew Lang the Anthropologist," or "Andrew Lang the
Psychical Researcher," or "Andrew Lang the Historian." At last
Roosevelt had exclaimed: "You mean Andrew Lang the Poet ? "
"Oh no! " the man had replied, "he only writes serious stuff! "[233]

At the party after the lecture Warren says that "Andrew Lang
was, I remember, in very good form. It was the last time I saw him
in Oxford or spoke to him. I saw him once again in the Pavilion
at Lord's looking very much aged and blind. I was not surprised,
though saddened, by his death very shortly after."[234]

But Lang did visit Oxford again;—in 1911, when he sat next to
Ernest Myers at the Balliol College Gaudy; and on 29th June of
the same year he was at the Merton Gaudy also, in company with
George Saintsbury and Professor Walter Raleigh.

In St. Andrews that year the five hundredth anniversary of the
foundation of the University was celebrated—and there Sir
Herbert Maxwell came across Andrew Lang: "In the brilliant
September sunshine, gowns and hoods of scarlet and white, orange
and blue, purple and green, presented the appearance of a great
parterre crowded with huge, gaudy flowers. Making my way

through this august assembly, I was not well pleased to find
Andrew Lang seated on the grass in a suit of mustard coloured
tweed, over which he had donned a shabby gown of black bom-
bazine and a red hood all awry. I felt displeased, and told him so,
for surely he, of all men, should have been more scrupulous in
doing honour to 'The little city grey and sere ' . . ."235

He was president of the Society for Psychical Research that
year, in which capacity he delivered the Society's annual lecture.
His published work was little, a pamphlet on Totemism, and *A
Short History of Scotland*, condensed from his longer work. But he
wrote also the Introductory Essay to the Swanston Edition of the
Works of Robert Louis Stevenson, of which Sidney Colvin says:
"There are few finer tributes by any one man of letters to another,
his contemporary."

But he was at work on his *History of English Literature from
Beowulf to Swinburne:* and when he grew bored with parts of this
study he would wander about the streets of St. Andrews making up
limericks on the names of his authors, such as:

"There aince was a poet ca'd Caedmon,
  As we ken frae the worthy auld Bede, mon:
    He made sangs on the Word
    That are kind o' absurd,
And he's no interesting to read, mon! "

or as this:

"There was an auld regicide, Milton,
  That hated a lad wi' a kilt on,
    Gied Colkitto a rasp,
    Ca'd Gillespie ' Galasp,'
A tousy auld tyke was John Milton."

The book appeared in July 1912, a few days before Lang's death,
and in many ways ranks among his most successful literary works.
It is the result of a lifetime of reading, and nearly all of it is written
with the delight of an enthusiastic reader, discovering author after
author and striving to show his discoveries to others. Though not
a great work, it is an excellent one: an example of its author's
sound criticism, faultless taste and beautiful style; it has its
personal biases, but these are owned to in a manner that adds to

its charms. For a young reader at least, no better introduction to English literature could be devised.

Henry James, however, thought quite otherwise, and damned it with not even the faintest praise in the letter to Edmund Gosse quoted earlier:

"The extraordinary inexpensiveness and childishness and impertinence of this gave to my sense the measure of a whole side of Lang, and yet which was one of the sides of his greatest flourishing. His extraordinary *voulu* Scotch provincialism crowns it and rounds it off; really making one at moments ask with what kind of an innermost intelligence such inanities and follies were compatible."

A reader who has used it as a handbook both as a schoolboy and during an honours course in English literature at Oxford, would humbly suggest that it requires a genius of Henry James's calibre to discover what is childish, inane, foolish or impertinent about this charming and unpretentious bit of work.

Although showing signs of weariness, Lang's faculties shone as brightly as ever, as his last book, *Shakespeare, Bacon and the Great Unknown* (finished in May 1912) can show. His next work was *Highways and Byways on the Border*, in which his brother John was collaborating, but Lang lived only to write about a sixth of the book.

For Lang was failing in health and constitution during his last years, and the threatened blindness—one eye had long been useless—was creeping upon him.

He had never found it easy to recognize people—"between short sight and some more mysterious faculty I see people quite differently on different occasions"[236], and this disability was increasing rapidly.

He became morbidly depressed by and unnaturally sensitive to current events: "there was this strange depression about public affairs, which seemed as though it might grow worse. In the old days, when he was bright and cheerful it is little he troubled himself about strikes and such like," wrote Charles Longman to Rider Haggard. These two friends were much concerned about Lang's health in the winter of 1911-12, and W. B. Richmond considered his condition even more serious. However, a doctor was consulted, and could find nothing particularly wrong.

Early in 1912 Lang seems to have seen the death omen of his family, though apparently he did not consider that any warning was intended to himself. He writes about it in "At the Sign of St. Paul's" for 27th January: "It is black, the brute, and more like a cat than anything else; but horrified percipients add, with a shudder, that, whatever else it may be, it is only superficially feline, and of no known species of the animal kingdom. I heard of it fifty years ago, having seen a very peculiar cat. I then heard of this death warning, which is of very respectable antiquity. Later examples have been frequent and up to date, and truly they are inexplicable to myself, except on the theory of a hereditary hallucination, which happens to coincide with deaths. My own latest experience did not. A black cat, obviously hallucinatory, ran across my study at 10 a.m. . . . Our death omen means business—at least when women see it."

Later in the year, however, he was more cheerful, and wrote quite in his old jesting vein to Rider Haggard, whom he addressed as "Cher Monsieur le Chevalier."

On 10th July he was dining in London in the company of Sir Henry Lucy, who had been his colleague for thirty years on the *Daily News*, and seemed in his usual state of health. "At table the conversation chanced to turn to the probabilities of future life: ' My idea of Heaven,' Lang said with his lackadaisical tone and manner, ' is a place where I should always find a good wicket and never exceed the age of twenty-four! ' "[237]

While staying at Tor-na-choille, Banchory, near Aberdeen, on 20th July, he was taken suddenly ill with a heart attack. "He was only ill sixteen hours, but in frightful pain all the time," wrote Mrs. Lang to Miss Ella Christie two days later. "We had two doctors and a nurse and an Aberdeen specialist, and after becoming unconscious at 4.30 he rallied, and even made a joke to the doctors about 8.30. Though still in great danger, they thought him much better, and then at 11.50, just as I had undressed, he gave a sigh and that was all. It was really the strikes that killed him."

He died on the Saturday, and on the Wednesday his body was taken to the English church at St. Andrews for the night. Mrs. Lang stayed with Miss Christie, who describes the funeral, which took place at two o'clock on the Thursday: "Together she and I made that ' via dolorosa ' to St. Andrews, there to take our place in a walking funeral through the main streets of the classic town that knew his footsteps so well and that he had loved so faithfully. Many were the tributes paid to him. The following stream of cars was so lengthy that its speed could only be regulated with the greatest difficulty; and when the coffin was lowered into the flower-lined grave, it bore a wreath of red roses from Abbotsford."[238]

"And so to Andrew Lang, among men my best friend perhaps, and the one with whom I was most entirely in tune, farewell for a little . . . There are few such, and today the world is poorer and greyer for the loss of a pure and noble nature," wrote Rider Haggard in the chapter of his autobiography that he was writing on the day the news of Lang's death came to him.

And while Andrew Lang was being laid to rest in the buryground of St. Andrews, in the grave which he himself described as "so dull, you can't see over the wall!" another of his oldest friends, George Saintsbury, took down his copy of *Old Friends* and read the letter of Piscator to Christian:

> Sir,—I do indeed remember thee; and I trust thou art amended of these gripings which caused thee to groan and moan, even by the pleasant streams from the hills of the Delectable Mountains. And as for my " burden," 'twas pleasant to me to bear it; for, like not the least of the Apostles, I am a fisher, and I carried trout. But I take no shame in that I am an angler; for angling is somewhat like poetry; men are to be born so, and I would not be otherwise than my Maker designed to have me. Of the antiquity of angling I could say much; but I misdoubt me that thou dost not heed the learning of ancient times, but art a contemner of good learning and virtuous recreations. Yet it may a little move thee that in the Book of Job mention is made of fish-hooks, and without reproof; for let me tell you that in the Scriptures angling is always taken in the best sense.
>
> Touching my flight from the City of Destruction, I love that place no more than thou dost; yet I fear not its evil communications, nor would I so hastily desert it as to leave my wife and children behind therein. Nor have I any experience of conflict with the Evil One; wherefore, I thank Him

that hath set me in pleasant fields, by clear waters, where come no wicked whispers (be they from Apollyon or from our own hearts); but there is calmness of spirit, and a world of blessings attending upon it. And hence can no man see the towers of Doubting Castle, for the green trees and the hedges white with May. This life is not wholly vile, as some of thy friends declare (Thou, who makest Thy pilgrims dance to the lute, knowest better); and, for myself, I own that I love such mirth as does not make men ashamed to look upon each other next morning. Let him that bears a heavy heart for his ill-deeds turn him to better, but not mourn as though the sun were taken out of the sky, What says the song ?—nay, 'tis as good balm for the soul as many a hymn:

"A merry heart goes all the day,
    Your sad one tires in a mile—a! "

He that made the world made man to take delight in it; even as thou sawest me joyful with the shepherds—ay, with godly Mr. Richard Hooker, "he being then tending his small allotment of sheep in a common field," as I recount in a brief life of a good man. As to what awaits me on the other side of that River, I do expect it with a peaceful heart, and in humble hope that a man may reach the City with a cheerful countenance, no less than through groans and sighs and tears. For we have not a tyrant over us, but a Father, that loveth a cheerful liver no less than a cheerful giver. Nevertheless, I thank thee for thy kind thought of one that is not of thy company, nor no Nonconformist, but a peaceful Protestant. And, lest thou be troubled with apparitions of hob-goblins and evil spirits, read that comfortable sermon of Mr. Hooker's to weak believers, on the *Certainty of Adherence*, though they want the inward testimony of it.

But now there falls a sweet shower, "a singing shower" saith old George Chapman, and methinks I shall have sport; for I do note that the mayfly is up; and, seeing all these beautiful creatures playing in the air and water, I feel my own heart play within me; and I must out and dape under yonder sycamore tree. Wherefore, prithee, pardon me a longer discourse as at this time.—Thy friend, PISCATOR.

CHAPTER XVI

Before and After

APART from that strange, intangible gift which we call genius, a
writer's mind is in most things formed and directed by his
circumstances and surroundings. Influences from within, such as
health, and, less easy to define, temperament; and influences from
without, such as social conditions, environment, and the impression made in youth by certain books or certain personal contacts,
—these direct and clothe the gift that is born in the writer—and the
rarer gift that is born in the poet.

These things are less easy to estimate in the case of Andrew
Lang than in that of many other writers, for of intimate biographical details we have so few. His boyhood spent in the
romantic Border country; his early reading which led him to
the fairyland of Shakespeare and of Madame d'Aulnoy, and to the
romance of a past age in Scott's poems and in the Waverley Novels;
his schooling that spared him the ordeal of the ordinary boarding
school which proves inimical in most cases to any early touch of
genius:—these are the main formative elements in Lang's character
of which we can speak with certainty.

There was also the matter of his health, which was precarious,
certainly from the time of his Merton Fellowship onwards, though
the threat of consumption which sent him to Mentone in the early
'seventies did not materialize to any extent, and he died at the age
of sixty-eight—of heart failure. "His health was always delicate,"
writes Horace Hutchinson, who knew Lang well, "so that the life
even of the ordinary athletic man of civilization was forbidden him.
He had to be very careful of his diet; he could not travel very long
distances in a day, I think because the rattle and jolt of a long train
journey were too much for his head. It was all a very delicately
balanced organization of the very finest constituents."[239]

But as a boy, Lang was sufficiently strong at least to join in the
usual games at school and at college. Football he disliked, and was

probably unable to play, but cricket appealed to him very strongly, and he took an almost pathetic delight in it, as the only athletic exercise in which he was able to reach any height of proficiency. Generally speaking, however, he was unfitted, even as a young man, for any but a sedentary life; moreover, his shyness and diffident reserve prevented him from mixing in any but the politer forms of society.

Now in many ways Lang's case resembles that of Robert Louis Stevenson: Here was a man of genius growing from delicate boyhood into manhood still more delicate, whose health, whose life even, was not sure from day to day. He was doomed to a life of inaction, but his greatest regret was that he could not be a soldier, —his favourite hero was the Duke of Wellington, whose life, indeed, he once intended to write; and his happiest years were those spent, with health comparatively restored, on his estate at Vailima—whence he wrote to Sidney Colvin, with almost pathetic pride, of how far he had ridden, or how many trees he had cut down in a morning.

And when we turn to Stevenson's fiction, we find him writing historical romances that abound in deeds of valour or daring, wars, rebellions, shipwrecks, duels; hairbreadth escapes, where nerve and courage and strength are the very life-blood of his characters. Even his modern novels have for their heroes gay, dashing adventurers, Prince Florizel or Michael Finsbury, Louddon Dodd or the desperate beachcombers of *The Ebb-Tide*. There is no character that recalls Stevenson as he actually was; neither Prince Otto nor Will o' the Mill come within a mile of him.

But Stevenson as a young man had found an outlet for the mental energy that demanded the life of action which his physical powers denied him—in the wild "Velvet Coat" days, when the "Stevenson cousins" were the plague and the despair of the respectable people of Edinburgh. Louis and Bob with their ponderously humourless practical jokes and their boyish desire to shock; and Louis by himself frequenting the least reputable inns and eating-houses of the city, mingling with rough sailors and labourers, with thieves and prostitutes; although all this partook largely of the nature of a pose, and of a conscious reaction against the restrictions of ill-health and of respectability, it served also the purpose of broadening his outlook, extending his sympathies, and

P

bringing him into intimate and wide-awake contact with life in its more crudely essential aspects: Stevenson the invalid of Davos and Skerryvore and Saranac might seek for the life adventurous among the pirates and the Jacobites of fiction, but never was he out of touch with that reality of experience and observation.

Yet with Lang most of this was different: he lacked the impetuosity of soul which at times seemed almost to shake into disintegration the frail body of Robert Louis Stevenson—he lacked the wider and more comprehensive genius, we might say, of the greater artist. As his health was less precarious, in like measure his need for such an outlet was less acute, and the greater capacity for mental detachment, which is the scholar's gift, steadied him and was itself an outlet.

To this was added his inherent shyness, fastidiousness and reserve that would in themselves have prevented any such adventures as those of the young Stevenson in Edinburgh and Brabazon. Lang was not among those members of St. Leonard's College who were expelled for taking an undue interest in the night life of St. Andrews: and had he wished to participate in such exploits, the practical side of his worldly position must have had a powerful influence upon his actions. Lang's parents, though people of influence in Selkirk, and cultured after the fashion of Scots of all classes with that deeply inherent culture that requires so many generations to implant in the Southerner, were yet not possessed of any great wealth. Lang's Snell Exhibition was vital to his future, and the winning of first-class honours at Balliol, qualifying him to compete for a fellowship, was his only chance of obtaining those seven years of security at Merton wherein to stock his mind with the vast stores of learning that were to stand him in good stead in after-life.

The result of these factors in Lang's personal development was to drive him towards a more and more rarefied outlook on life, and to the inevitable attempt to seek for peace and escape in a dream-world of his imagination.

A missing chapter in this development of his personality is that concerned with his emotional relations with women at the time when his character was still forming. Probably his whole-hearted pursuit of the academic stability which was so necessary to him, prevented this element from playing very much part in his life until a comparatively late period. He won his Merton Fellowship at the age of twenty-four, and this marked the first stage in his career at which he can have been able to relax in his ceaseless struggle to pass examination after examination, save for the brief golden months of a first summer term at Oxford "when freshmen are heedless of Greats."

Here, however, we are on forbidden ground, and must respect Lang's wishes that caused to be destroyed all the usual aids to biography in the form of personal papers and letters. There is no evidence, and there probably now could never be, of any love affair; only the very obvious sincerity of the "lost love" poems, both in Lang's first book, *Ballads and Lyrics*, and in isolated poems throughout his later life; and in the note of personal feeling, almost of pain, that creeps into any utterance, however trivial or unimportant, that touches on the subject of a "first love," of a lost or shattered ideal, seem to tell us beyond a doubt that:

> "Each must deem, though neither knows,
> That *neither* found the Singing Rose."

Whatever romantic picture we may weave for ourselves out of themes and motives in Lang's poetry and of stray references in prose, and whatever of truth or fiction there lies in his recurrent suggestion that

> "within a fair forsaken place
> The life that might have been is lost to thee,"

the rift was closing in the later Oxford days—though it is significant that at some date which cannot have been much earlier than 1874, he proposed to his cousin Florence Sellar, who must then have been about seventeen years old—for at the end of that year he was engaged to Leonora Blanche Alleyne, whom he marrried in 1875.

That it was a happy marriage, we have no reason to doubt; and although it was childless, it was no devotion that passed with the passing of youth. Lady King Stewart and Miss Ella Christie, who were intimate friends of the Langs, describe how completely dependent Andrew was on his wife, when they knew them from about 1890 onwards.

But whatever the foundation, or lack of foundation for it, this element of an unforgotten sadness, for an unrealized dream, coloured Lang's deeper feelings throughout his life, and thus influenced his work.

Running parallel with this was that other unattainable desire for an active and adventurous life. That Lang was totally unfitted to grapple with any such career, mattered not a jot: "If one cannot be a soldier, a missionary, an explorer, a man of one's hands: if one has to live a tame life and die ' a cow's death ': then one prefers to scribble"[240], he wrote at the age of forty-five: and this was not the only occasion on which he spoke in this strain.

In time this feeling was developed and explained away as a kind of pose: "Mr. Lang, perhaps the most literary temperament that ever lived," wrote Richard Le Gallienne at the end of the century, "would have you believe that to write a good book is nothing compared with playing a good game of golf."[241] But the fashion was quite the opposite in the 'seventies and the 'eighties, when "culture" professed to look down upon the merely physical.

It was something of this wistful regret that stirred Lang so in the deeds of men in contemporary life: General Gordon at Khartoum, Melville and Coghill at Isandhlwana, Colonel Burnaby, whom Lang may have met, Sir Ian Hamilton, whom he knew well and who survives to bear testimony to Lang's "extraordinary sympathy and kindness extended to a young Scottish soldier with no sort of call on him of relationship or blood."[242]

It was this also that helped to produce Lang's love for adventure stories, the almost passionate love that could embrace even the most lacking in literary style or taste. This, with the shyness that made it so difficult for him to mingle happily with the majority of people and the sensitive nature that made him shrink from the unlovely and disillusioning reality of contemporary events as mirrored in the daily papers, drove Lang more and more to seek his asylum in the fancied Elysium of an idealized past.

"We are more at home under some departed Henry, James or George," he says of himself and of those like him, "than under her present Majesty who is so much better than any George, James, Charles or Henry. We are more intimate with Falstaff, Hamlet, Athos, Dugald Dalgetty or Colonel Esmond than with Mr. Chamberlain or Me. Labori; more interested in Strafford than in Colonel Dreyfus."[243]

And it was not only the more romantic aspects of a past age that Lang craved for, and in which he felt that he would have been at home: however the rougher and more sordid things of contemporary life jarred upon him, distance lent a halo of deceitful enchantment to the far more squalid and unrefined surroundings of life in Fielding's England, and he longed to mingle with "the maids at the inn, the parish clerk, the two sportsmen, the hosts of the taverns, the beaux, the starveling authors—all alive; all (save the authors) full of beef and beer; a cudgel in every fist, every man ready for a brotherly bout at fisticuffs. What has become of it, the lusty old militant world ? What will become of us, and why do we prefer to Fielding—a number of meritorious moderns ? "[244]

The world of Dickens also seemed to Lang as a choice resort, for the humour and the large kindliness, even the satire which though biting is never bitter, made it acceptable to him: "In real life we shrink from Sairey and condemn her. In fiction we take her to our bosoms. For art is not life, and a 'realistic' Sairey or Squeers would not be art, any more than is real water on the stage." "In what sense," asks Mr. Gissing, "can this figure in literature be called a copy of the human original ? " Why, in the only sense— the sense of art. The Gamp of actual existence, reflected in art, is Sairey. Art is not life, but a reflection of life under certain pleasurable conditions. Nature never made a Sairey, any more than she made a Clytemnestra or a Lady Macbeth. But she strove towards these ends; and art—in the form of Dickens, Æschylus and Shakespeare—helped her to her aim.[245]

This view of literary creation goes back, in its essence, to Aristotle, and forms Lang's most serious argument against the trend which modern fiction was taking in the later part of his life towards substituting science for art. It is perhaps this increasing tendency to judge the novel from the standpoint of the social student or the scientific psychologist, that has prevented any novelist of undoubtedly the first rank from arising in this century. Modern fiction, as Lord David Cecil points out, strives to produce a photograph and not a painting—the specialist has usurped the place of the artist.

It was the early stages of this tendency that Lang saw and fought against. He did not advocate the hampering of the novelist's material by the conventional restraints of society—lamenting with

Thackeray that since Fielding no one has dared to portray a full man, and speaking ironically in his letters to Haggard on the possibility of a public outcry against a too prominent use of "Pharaoh's great bed" in *The World's Desire*; but he did oppose the more radical views and practices that would have the novelist, in a mistaken zeal for truth, present only the squalid, the obscene and the unlovely as the essential background to life. It was not so much the work of Tolstoi and Hardy, Zola and George Moore, that Lang was attacking, for in all but the last he recognized the genius, and something of the true artist; but against the exaggerated excesses of their less gifted followers, and the cynical intolerance of the critics who supported the new movement.

And he could not advocate always the literature of the past alone, but must suggest who, in his opinion at least, were treading in healthier, more desirable paths of literary art. Here his personal bias towards the romantic and the humorous made it not very easy for him to steer a controlled course. With Stevenson he was in reasonably sure waters, with Kipling and with Barrie he was at least still among the undoubtedly great. But the tragedy of the period, and of his crusade for the serious consideration of the more romantic fiction, was that no other writers of this type appeared who could be considered reasonably as of the same literary stature as Hardy and Henry James, or later as Galsworthy and Joseph Conrad and Arnold Bennett. Only with the prose romances of William Morris would Lang have found himself on sure ground (however rarefied the atmosphere), and here, unfortunately, his views on Morris's "Wardour Street" style of English were so strong as to make him apparently quite blind to the greatness of his contemporary's work. With Rider Haggard, Lang was on ground so treacherous that his praise of his friend's work came in time to be used as the most formidable cudgel in the hands of his adversaries. At a time when style was considered among the most important criteria of great literature—a period that produced Walter Pater, Stevenson and Kenneth Grahame, besides Lang himself—Haggard's style could seldom be described as more than adequate: when the delineation of psychologically true characters was growing in popular and critical demand, Haggard could only produce, save in rare instances, types—however suitable such characters may be to his peculiar turn of genius. Only for his astonishing powers of imagination and construction could Lang reasonably place Rider Haggard in the foremost ranks of prose literature—and these were precisely the qualities that the newer critics and novelists did not and would not recognize as of importance.

But otherwise Lang was unable to point to any writer who might be the leader of a new age of romantic fiction: there were story-tellers in abundance—excellent story-tellers, many of whom are not likely to be forgotten—Conan Doyle, A. E. W. Mason, Anthony Hope, Maurice Hewlett, Stanley Weyman, and the rest—all very well in their way, but not quite the founders of a school of fiction that should jeopardise the superiority of Henry James and Thomas Hardy.

Lang waged a losing battle in this campaign, though the day of Ragnarok is still to come. "Romance is permanent," he held, "It satisfies a normal and permanent human taste, a taste that survives through all the changing likes and dislikes of critics."[246] And it may be that this champion of lost causes that have proved victorious, may yet be on the winning side: for has not the "Catawampus of romance" raised its head again after nearly half a century—in the works of Mr. C. S. Lewis ?

In the matter of children's books—which follow the adult tastes, at a respectful distance—Lang may also come into his own again. The Fairy Books brought back fairyland to the nursery in the 'nineties, and flung wide the doors for Barrie and E. Nesbit and Kenneth Grahame. These also have known eclipse, but their night is not so dense, for children are not swayed by fashion as their elders are, and in any age the footsteps of many a child lead naturally and unavoidably to fairyland.

These things were the wider gifts of Andrew Lang to our literature, the labours for which little reward or recognition are accorded. Remembering for what he strove in his many million words of literary *causerie* and review, of introduction and notes explanatory, we can judge more fairly of his creative work, of what he set out to do and in how far he succeeded in doing it, and in how it was shaped or restricted by his personality and by the factors that influenced his mind.

"Nothing matters but the work done," was Lang's belief, "and that depends on a man's temperament and genius. To these he accommodates his 'æsthetic principles,' if he keeps such things, and does just what God gave him the power of doing."[247]

It is probably as a poet that Lang will take his highest place in literature; but how high a place it is impossible to say. Critics who were his contemporaries, such as George Saintsbury, William Canton, Richard Le Gallienne, Graham R. Thomson and W. P. Ker, would have it that he was one of the poets whose work endures; of *Ballads and Lyrics* W. P. Ker wrote "They were written in 1870, before the last great age of English poetry had come to an end, and they have their place in the House of Fame as surely as any poems of the greater masters"[248]; and a modern critic, Professor Blyth Webster of St. Andrews, writes that he has found " few first books of verse this side of *The Defence of Guinevere* to wear so well."[249]

That Lang's poetry is now so little known seems to be due (apart from the present trend of critical taste against most poetry of his type and period) to the lack of any standard collection. In 1923 his widow edited *The Poetical Works of Andrew Lang* in a limited edition in four volumes, beautifully got up and charmingly set forth—but sadly lacking in the essentials of a collected edition. Well over two hundred poems and verses are excluded or over-looked: even the volumes of verse collected by Lang in his lifetime are not reprinted in their entirety. Much of the excluded miscellaneous verse is trifling and ephemeral—but much is at his highest level either of serious poetry or of light verse. There is no attempt at chronology, and very little at any methodical arrangement—and, indeed, the book is for the Lang lover and not for the general reader. When a collected edition in a cheap and handy form (such as the Oxford edition of Austin Dobson) appears, poetry readers and students of literature will be able to form their own judgments. At present Lang is conveniently grouped as a poet with Henley, Dobson and Gosse—and is far less known than either of the first two. But his place in serious poetry is infinitely higher than that of Austin Dobson—and we may well place him higher also than Henley, in spite of that poet's few supreme lyrics.

Besides his poetry, Lang deserves to be remembered for his children's books. It is not likely that the fairy-tales which he edited for Longmans will ever be forgotten, but of his own original work it is not so easy to speak. The most famous and enduring books in children's literature are, on the whole, those which appeal to the adult reader as much or even more than to the child—*Alice*, *The Rose and the Ring*, *The Jungle Books*, *The Wind in the Willows*, *Winnie the Pooh*. Lang's stories have not the general attraction of these, for in all that he wrote he demanded, consciously or unconsciously, a certain fastidiousness of taste for a full appreciation. Although *The Gold of Fairnilee* is perhaps a better book than *Prince Prigio*, it is of a kind whose beauty is lost upon most children, and whose appeal only to the more poetical and imaginative feelings make it unlikely that many adult readers will trouble with it. In the case of *Prince Prigio*, however, the difference of appeal makes it easily popular with both sorts of reader. In this way it approaches more nearly to *Alice* or *The Rose and the Ring*, and gives much of the same kind of pleasure, at least to those of age mature: humour is the most unpredictable of literary gifts, but *Prince Prigio*, to any reader who is at all in harmony with Lang's variety of it, wears as well as any of its more famous rivals, delights as continuously as they, and leaves on our lips as many treasured quotations as any but *Alice*.

Of Lang's imaginative work, his fiction is the least successful and the least remembered. It is not probable that *The World's Desire* will be forgotten among younger readers, while Haggard endures. In after years we are apt to find it (as Professor Gordon said of Lang's *Helen of Troy*) "a sleeping beauty that was never awake": but it *is* a sleeping beauty for all that, even if its loveliness is the pale glamour of an unforgotten dream.

For *Parson Kelly*, too, there is room and to spare among the readers of *Brigadier Gerard* and *A Gentleman of France*, of *The Queen's Quair* and *Clementina*. But of Lang's more individual—and individualistic—fiction it is harder to speak. It is easy to see that the readers of "shilling shockers," even in its own day, did not appreciate *A Mark of Cain*, with its parodies of Homeric language and its chapter on the literary history of æronautics: it is unlikely that many readers of cheap fiction would like it any the better now. *The Disentanglers*, a far more satisfactory and a cleverer book, has just as narrow an appeal: it took ten years to exhaust the first two editions—and it has not been reprinted. And yet it is a very brilliant book, and it has its admirers not so far this side of idolatry.

In literary parody also Lang ought not to be forgotten: *Old Friends* is still fresh and amusing, and much of *In the Wrong Paradise* also. A collection of his parodies would be an attractive work, and a work provocative of much gentle laughter: for besides these two, there are some fifty examples in verse, many of which have never been reprinted from their original homes in forgotten papers and magazines; and there is "Dr. Johnson on the Links," besides *Pictures at Play* and *He*.

A collection or selection of Lang's essays would also be worth making, and besides their very real value as "human pleasure," would go far towards reinstating him as a critic of considerable importance.

The translations belong to a different branch of literature, but there, as in all his work, we find another side of Andrew Lang's greatness, his style. Writing in 1897 of the stylists of the previous ten years—a period that included Walter Pater and Robert Louis Stevenson, Sir Arthur Quiller-Couch gave his considered opinion that "the master of the best style in English prose" of this time was Andrew Lang. "His style is accurate, lucid, simple in the best sense; happy in illustration and allusion; familiar without a trace of vulgarity, for while not disdaining the full vocabulary and even the colloquialisms of his own age, it exercises its freedom on a basis of scholarship and within limits of good taste derived from scholarship. Thus it is at once modern (even modish at times), and pure—a difficult combination . . . I neither know nor care whether Mr. Lang's prose would be called 'classical' today; but as soon as he applies it to worthy subjects, it has the qualities which will make it classical tomorrow." And he went on to apply to Lang (from the point of view of style alone, of course) Henley's estimate of Thackeray's: " 'In his manner is the perfection of conversational writing. Graceful yet vigorous; adorably artificial yet incomparably sound; touched with modishness, yet informed with distinction; easily and happily rhythmical yet full of colour and quick with malice and with meaning; instinct with urbanity and instinct with charm—it is a type of high-bred English, a climax of literary art . . .' "[250]

As much, perhaps, as any other reason, it is the lack of any one acknowledged masterpiece that has prevented Lang from taking his due place in literature: "Andrew Lang," as Mrs. Lynn Linton once observed, "would be the greatest living writer, if only he had something to write about."

But I have tried to show that he left some half-dozen or a dozen works that, if not truly great, are yet treasures that should not be lost to us. The attraction of his writings may be a magic that works upon few readers: but speaking, for what it is worth, from my own experience, Andrew Lang's writings have in them a power of an astonishing durability: after more than twelve years as a constant reader of them, more than three of which years were spent in a specific study of these works, their charm has grown stronger rather than otherwise. His poetry, his fairy-stories, his fiction and his essays have been and remain constant companions—friends that grow dearer the better they are known.

Another touch of magic comes with them also, a dim, a cloudy, but a very dear personality, some poor realization of which I have striven to capture and pass on in these pages—which cannot better be concluded than in some words from the last letter I ever received from Andrew Lang's cousin and true friend, Mrs. MacCunn, who had been Florence Sellar:

"I am haunted by a slender, rather languid figure and a dear and familiar face, and the background of an old street leading to old ruined towers; or to the banks of a river among green hills, and to one in waders with a fishing rod . . ."

Epilogue

To J. B.

The poet of lost love and pale regret:
    Still 'neath the shadow of the Merton limes
    His spirit lingers; and the old, sweet chimes
Shed from the grey tower, bid us not forget
Youth's poet and youth's dream. His dreams are set
    With all the unreal day-spring of past times,
    A tender memory, touching but as rhymes
Heard in the yesterday, that haunt us yet.

Such shadows fade; but still the sad wind blows
    About our hearts, until his voice grows clear.
For we have walked together 'neath his trees,
And heard the chimes speak to us on the breeze
    Across the world of life: but, wandering here,
Surely we might have found the Singing Rose ?

Merton : June, 1946.

Key to Reference Numbers

1. Andrew and John Lang: *Highways and Byways in the Border*, 1913; pp 251-2.

2. "At the Sign of St. Paul's": *Illustrated London News*, 10th November 1906.

3. "At the Sign of St. Paul's": *Illustrated London News*, 7th March 1908.

4. Lang's Introduction to *The Works of Robert Louis Stevenson: Swanston Edition*, 1911; vol. i, page xiii.

5. *Poetical Works*, 1923; vol. iii, p. 37 (*Philadelphia Press*, 10th July 1892, etc.).

6. T. Craig-Brown: *The History of Selkirkshire*, 1886; vol. ii, p. 128, etc.

7. Sir Walter Scott: *The Antiquary* (*Border Edition*, note to vol. ii, p. 294—printed on pp. 310-312).

8. Lang's Introduction to *The Antiquary* (*Border Edition*, vol. i, p. xxxiii).

9. T. Craig-Brown: *The History of Selkirkshire*, 1886; vol. ii, pp. 149 and 166.

10. Quoted by Craig-Brown: vol. ii, p. 146.

11. Letter to the present writer from Miss Helen Harrison (daughter of Nellie Roberts).

12. E. M. Sellar: *Recollections and Impressions*, 1907; pp. 34-35.

13. *The Gold of Fairnilee*, 1888; pp. 17-24.

14. *Angling Sketches*, 1891; p. 141.

15. *Highways and Byways in the Border*, 1913; p. 245.

16. E. M. Sellar: *Recollections and Impressions*, 1907; p. 112.

17. *Angling Sketches*, 1891; pp. 10-13.

18. *Angling Sketches*, 1891; pp. 18 and 35.

19. "At the Sign of the Ship": *Longmans' Magazine*, July 1896.

20. Lang's Introduction to Stevenson's *A Child's Garden of Verses* (*Longmans' Pocket Library*), March 1907; p. ix.

21. *Adventures Among Books*, 1905; p. 5.

22. Lang's Introduction to Irene Maunder's *The Plain Princess*, 1905.

23. *Adventures Among Books*, 1905. (Various pages.)

24. "Literary Anodynes": *Princetown Review*, 1888. (Quoted in *The St. James's Gazette*, 17th September 1888.)

25. *Letters on Literature*, 1889; p. 183.

26. "A Dip in Criticism": *The Contemporary Review*, October 1888.

27. "At the Sign of the Ship": *Longmans' Magazine*, July 1896.

28. *Adventures Among Books*, 1905; p. 23.

29. "At the Sign of the Ship": *Longmans' Magazine*, July 1896.

30. "At the Sign of St. Paul's": *Illustrated London News*, 2nd October 1909.

31. Quoted by Sir D'Arcy Thompson: *Scots Magazine*, May 1944.

32. "The Boy": (*Adventures Among Books*; p. 301). *Cornhill Magazine*, March 1883.

33. Letter to Sir D'Arcy Thompson quoted in *Scots Magazine*, May 1944.

34. "The Teaching of Literature": *The Pilot*, 13th April 1901.

35. "At the Sign of the Ship": *Longmans' Magazine*, December 1898.

36. *Letters on Literature*, 1889; p. 45.

37. Lang's Review of Hallam Tennyson's *Life of Lord Tennyson*, in *Longmans' Magazine*, November 1897.

38. *Adventures Among Books*, 1905; pp. 15-16.

39. "Sour Classical Grapes": *The Pilot*, 22nd June 1901.

40. "Mr. Stevenson's New Novel *Catriona*": *Illustrated London News*, 16th September 1893.

41. "Enchanted Cigarettes": (*Adventures Among Books*; pp. 256-7); *The Idler*, February 1892.

42. "Old St. Leonard's Days": *Alma Mater's Mirror*, 1887; p. 7 *et seq.*

43. "Religio Loci": *Votiva Tabella* (St. Andrews), 1911; p. 412.

44. J. M. Anderson: *Library Bulletin of the University of St. Andrews*, October 1912.

45. J. M. Anderson: *Library Bulletin of the University of St. Andrews*, October 1912.

46. *University News Sheet* (St. Andrews), 29th March 1889. (Quoted by Salmond; p. 10.)

47. "Old St. Leonard's Days": *Alma Mater's Mirror*, 1887; p.7 *et seq.*

48. Allan Menzies: *College Echoes* (St. Andrews), October 1912.

49. *Adventures Among Books*, 1905; pp. 24-25.

50. "At the Sign of St. Paul's": *Illustrated London News*, 13th January 1906.

51. "Clevedon Church": *Poetical Works*, 1923; vol. i, p. 141. (*Century Magazine*, November 1886. *Grass of Parnassus*, 1888; p. 21.)

52. *Alfred Tennyson*, 1901; p. 72.

53. *The Life and Letters of John Gibson Lockhart*, 1897; vol. i, p.21.

54. Quoted by J. B. Salmond in *Andrew Lang and St. Andrews*, 1944; p. 13. The only extant volumes of the magazine contain eight numbers for 1863-4, three for (probably) 1867, and three for 1870.

55. *The Life and Letters of John Gibson Lockhart*, 1897; vol. i, p. 25.

56. Reminiscences contributed by Lang to R. J. Mackenzie's *Almond of Loretto*, 1905; pp. 38-39.

57. *Life and Letters of John Gibson Lockhart*, 1897; vol. i, pp. 32-33.

58. "Reminiscences of Balliol College": *English Illustrated Magazine*, November 1893.

59. "Coincidences": *Illustrated London News*, 22nd December 1894.

60. A. G. C. Liddell: *Notes from the Life of an Ordinary Mortal*, 1911; pp. 56-63.

61. Sir Frederick Pollock: *For My Grandson*, 1933; p.46.

62. "The Influence of Mr. Jowett": *Illustrated London News*, 10th August 1895.

63. "College Myths": *The Daily News*, 20th September 1895.

64. *Reminiscences of Lord Kilbracken*, 1931; pp. 61-62.

65. *Adventures Among Books*, 1905; p. 32.

66. "College Myths": *The Daily News*, 20th September 1895. See also "At the Sign of the Ship": *Longmans' Magazine*, July 1897.

67. "Literary Plagiarism": *Contemporary Review*, June 1887. The line from *Chastelard* runs: "Made of a red rose that has turned to white."

68. "At the Sign of the Ship": *Longmans' Magazine*, December 1899.

69. *Life of Sir Stafford Northcote*, 1890; vol. i, p. 11.

70. "On an Expensive Volume of Verse": *Poetical Works*, 1923.; vol. iii, p. 218. Privately printed with "Ode on a Distant Memory of Jane Eyre" by Clement Shorter, 1912.

71. "At the Sign of St. Paul's": *Illustrated London News*, 7th November 1908.

72. "Words of Comfort": *Illustrated London News*, 5th October 1895.

73. *The Mark of Cain*, 1886; pp. 28-29.

74. E. M. Sellar: *Recollections and Impressions*, 1907; pp. 24-25.

75. Louise Creighton: *Life and Letters of Mandell Creighton*, 1904; vol. i, pp. 46 and 67.

76. E. Arbuthnott Knox: *Reminiscences of an Octogenarian*, 1935; p. 86.

77. Professor Gilbert Murray (personal communication).

78. Professor H. W. Garrod: letter to the present writer, 23rd March 1944.

79. Mrs. F. A. MacCunn: (personal communication).

80. Sidney Colvin: *Memories and Notes*, 1921; pp. 118-119.

81. Robert Louis Stevenson: Letter of 1st February 1874. *Letters vol. i, p.* 139 (Tusitala Edition).

82. For Stevenson at Merton see *Adventures Among Books*; p. 44; and Graham Balfour, *Life of Robert Louis Stevenson*; vol. i, p. 126. For the visit to *Macbeth* see Balfour, i, 135; Rosaline Masson: *I can Remember R.L.S.* (Mrs. MacCunn's contribution), 1914. Also verified by word of mouth during a conversation with the late Mrs. F. A. MacCunn.

83. *Life and Letters of Mandell Creighton*, 1904; vol. i, p. 87.

84. "The Thames and Its Poetry": *The Magazine of Art*, September 1882.

85. *Oxford* (published 1879 but dated 1880). Cf. Preface, and pp. 55-56.

86. E. M. Sellar: *Recollections and Impressions*, 1907; p. 261.

87. "At the Sign of the Ship": *Longmans' Magazine*, May 1899.

88. A. Blyth Webster: *Andrew Lang's Poetry*: (Lang Lecture for 1937); p. 3.

89. Desmond MacCarthy: "Andrew Lang's Poetry": *Sunday Times*, 30th January 1938.

90. George Saintsbury: "Andrew Lang in the 'Seventies": *The Eighteen-Seventies*, 1929; pp. 81 and 83.

91. W. L. Courtney: "A Bibliographical Note on Andrew Lang": *The English Illustrated Magazine*, March 1904.

92. Kennedy Williamson: *W. E. Henley : A Memoir*, 1930; p. 72.

93. Sir Henry Lucy: *The Diary of a Journalist*; vol. iii, 1923; pp. 99-100.

94. Richard Whiteing: *My Harvest*, 1915; p. 273.

95. Richard Le Gallienne: *The Romantic 'Nineties*, 1926; p. 71.

96. W. Pett Ridge: *A Story Teller : Forty Years in London*, 1923; p. 10.

97. "The Art of Mark Twain": *Illustrated London News*, 14th February 1891.

98. "Epistle to Mr. Alexander Pope" (*St. James's Gazette*, 31st October 1885): *Letters to Dead Authors*, 1886; pp. 46-54. Not included in *Poetical Works* of 1923.

99. Desmond Chapman-Huston: *Sidney Low*, 1936; pp. 63-64.

100. "Ballade of Blue China": *Poetical Works*, 1923; vol. i, p. 197. (*Ballades in Blue China*, 1880; p. 49.)

101. "Cruelty to Poets": *Illustrated London News*, 28th October 1893.

102. "The Palace of Bric-à-Brac": *St. James's Gazette*, 26th August 1891. (Not in *Poetical Works*, 1923; incomplete version in *Rhymes à la Mode*, 1885; p. 97.)

103. *Alfred Tennyson :* 1901; p. 170.

104. "Mr. Stead Oracle": *Illustrated London News*, 28th October 1893.

105. W. H. Pollock's note in C. M. Falconer's *A New Friendship's Garland*, 1898.

106. "From a Scottish Workshop": *Illustrated London News*, 21st March 1896.

107. *Old Friends*, 1890; p. 3.

108. "A Pious Opinion": May Kendall's *Dreams to Sell*, 1887; p. 32. This poem is by Lang and May Kendall.

109. Lang's introduction to *La Mythologie* : Paris 1886, the French translation by Parmentier of Lang's article "Mythology" in the Ninth Edition of the *Encyclopædia Britannica*; vol. xvii, 1884.

110. *Adventures Among Books*, 1905; p. 37.

111. Soloman Reinach: "Andrew Lang": *Quarterly Review*, April 1913.

112. "Notes on Ghosts": *Forum*, December 1890.

113. "Ghosts up to Date": *Blackwood's Magazine*, January 1894.

114. "Human Personality After Death": *Monthly Review*, March 1903.

115. "From the Ghost's Point of View": *Time*, January 1885.

116. R. R. Marrett: *A Jersey Man at Oxford*, 1941; p. 169.

117. Samuel Butler: *Selection from Notebooks* (Traveller's Library Edition), 1930; p. 76.

118. "Notes on Books": *Cosmopolis*, January 1898.

119. Gilbert Murray: "Andrew Lang": *Quarterly Review*, April 1913.

120. W. E. Henley: Quoted in Cornford's *W. E. Henley*, 1913; pp. 72-73.

121. "Literary Fairy Tales": Lang's introduction to F. Van Eeden's *Little Johannes*, 1895.

122. E. M. Field: *The Child and his Book*, 1891; pp. 235 and 242.

123. "Literary Fairy Tales": Lang's introduction to F. Van Eeden's *Little Johannes*, 1895.

124. "Literary Fairy Tales": Lang's introduction to F. Van Eeden's *Little Johannes*, 1895.

125. Lang's Preface to *The Grey Fairy Book*, 1900; p. vii.

126. Lang's Preface to *The Lilac Fairy Book*, 1910; p. viii.

127. Lang's Preface to Irene Maunder's *The Plain Princess*, 1905.

128. Lang's Preface to *The Lilac Fairy Book*, 1910; p. vi.

129. "The Log-Rolliad": *College Echoes* (St. Andrews), 8th January 1891.

130. Letter from Lang to Rider Haggard; MS. at Ditchingham House, no date.

131. "Popular Poetry": *Wit and Wisdom*, 21st June 1890.

132. "Twilight on Tweed": *Poetical Works* of 1923, vol. i, p. 23. (*Ballads and Lyrics*, 1872.)

133. "Comedies of Shakespeare: vii": *Harper's Magazine*, April 1892.

134. "Argument for the Existence of a Brownie": *Illustrated London News*, 25th March 1893.

135. "At the Sign of the Ship": *Longmans' Magazine*, July 1889.

136. Letter from Lang to Haggard: MS. at Ditchingham House (n.d.).

137. "An Old House": *Illustrated London News*, 27th October, 1894.

138. *Angling Sketches*, 1891; p. 130.

139. "Advice to Young Authors": *College Echoes* (St. Andrews), 1st April 1907.

140. J. M. Barrie: *Address (to) The Royal Society of Literature*, 28th November 1912.

141. Memoir by Lang prefixed to *R. F. Murray : His Poems*, 1894; p. lxiii.

142. "Literary Fairy Tales": Lang's introduction to F. Van Eeden's *Little Johannes*, 1895.

143. "Modern Fairy Tales": *Illustrated London News*, 3rd December 1892.

144. "Over the Wall": first published in Lady Charnwood's *Call Back Yesterday*, 1938.

145. See *Poetical Works* of 1923; vol. i, p. 111; and vol. iii, p. 158.

146. "At the Sign of the Ship": *Longmans' Magazine*, December 1887.

147. "Romance and the Reverse": *St. James's Gazette*, 7th November 1888.

148. Letter (n.d.) from Lang to Haggard: *The Days of My Life*, 1926; vol. ii, p. 13.

149. Lang: "Editor's Introduction to Ivanhoe": *Border Edition of the Waverley Novels*, vol. xvi (*Ivanhoe*, vol. 1), pp. xvii and xix. April 1893.

150. Lang's Introduction to *The Works of Robert Louis Stevenson : Swanston Edition*, 1911; vol. i, p. xxx.

151. "Human Personality after Death": *Monthly Review*, March 1903.

152. "At the Sign of the Ship": *Longmans' Magazine*, November 1894.

153. "Dream as a Dramatist": *Illustrated London News*, 18th August 1894.

154. "Enchanted Cigarettes": *Adventures Among Books*, 1905; pp. 252-4.

155. "At the Sign of the Ship": *Longmans' Magazine*, February 1888.

156. Graham R. Thomson: Review of *Ban and Arrière Ban: Academy*, 2nd June 1894.

157. H. Rider Haggard: *The Days of My Life*, 1926 (written 1912); vol. i, p. 229.

158. "At the Sign of St. Paul's": *Illustrated London News*, 26th February 1910.

159. Letter (dated 1st May 1896) in *The Academy*, 9th May 1896.

160. "Romance and the Reverse": *St. James's Gazette*, 7th November 1888.

161. W. H. Pollock: Note vi in C. M. Falconer's *A New Friendship's Garland*, 1898

162. Letter from Lang to E. Nesbit: (n.d.) Quoted in Doris Langley Moore's *E. Nesbit*, 1933.

163. William Canton: "Mr. Lang as Poet": *Bookman*, August 1895.

164. "Comedies of Shakespeare: iii": *Harper's Magazine*, December 1890.

165. Lang's introduction to J. A. Farrer's *Literary Forgeries*, 1907; p. xv.

166. Horace Hutchinson: *Portraits of the 'Eighties*, 1920; p. 208.

167. "At the Sign of St. Paul's": *Illustrated London News*, 20th June 1908.

168. Letter from Lang, quoted in J. J. Jusserand: *What Me Befell*, 1933; p. 105.

169. "At the Sign of St. Paul's": *Illustrated London News*, 13th November 1909.

170. Alice King Stewart and Ella Christie: *A Long Look at Life*, 1940; chapter xvi.

171. Letter from Lang, quoted in W. Pett Ridge: *A Story Teller*, 1923; p. 10.

172. "At the Sign of the Ship": *Longmans' Magazine*, September 1899.

173. "Enchanted Cigarettes": *Adventures Among Books*, 1905; p. 255.

174. J. D. Mackie: *Andrew Lang and the House of Stuart* (Lecture), 1935; pp. 25-26.

175. *Letters of Henry James*, 1920; vol. i, p. 139 and vol. ii, p. 286.

176. Evan Charteris: *Life and Letters of Edmund Gosse*, 1931; pp. 335 and 344.

177. Lang's introduction to Lennox's *Memoir of George Douglas Brown*, 1903; p. 20.

178. "The Dreadful Trade": *The Scots Observer*, 16th February 1889.

179. A. C. Swinburne: *The Quarterly Review*, July 1902.

180. F. Anstey: *A Long Retrospect*, 1936; p. 334.

181. "Realism and Romance": *Contemporary Review*, November 1887.

182. "At the Sign of the Ship": *Longmans' Magazine*, January 1899.

183. "At the Sign of St. Paul's": *Illustrated London News*, 3rd August 1907.

184. "At the Sign of the Ship": *Longmans' Magazine*, September 1890.

185. "International Girlishness": *Murray's Magazine*, October 1888.

186. Review in *Cosmopolis*, January 1896.

187. "The Art of Mark Twain": *Illustrated London News*, 14th February 1891.

188. "At the Sign of the Ship": *Longmans' Magazine*, May 1891.

189. "Realism and Romance": *Contemporary Review*, November 1887.

190. "Mr. Buchanan's Young Men": *St. James's Gazette*, 10th April 1889.

191. "Literary Chronicle": *Cosmopolis*, November 1898.

192. "At the Sign of the Ship": *Longmans' Magazine*, January 1905.

193. Lang's introduction to Lennox's *Memoir of George Douglas Brown*, 1903; pp. 4-6.

194. "At the Sign of St. Paul's": *Illustrated London News*, 9th January 1909.

195. Article by Lang in *The Critic* (New York), quoted in *The Academy*, 1st September 1900.

196. "The Celtic Renaissance": *Blackwood's Magazine*, February 1897.

197. "The Science of Criticism": *The New Review*, May 1891.

198. H. Rider Haggard: *The Days of My Life*, 1926; vol. i, pp. 228-231, etc.

199. H. Cox and J. E. Chandler: *The House of Longman*, 1924; pp. 65-68.

200. Rosaline Masson: *Life of Robert Louis Stevenson*, 1923; p. 212.

201. Rosaline Masson: *I Can Remember R. L. Stevenson*, 1914; p. 80.

202. A. M. W. Stirling: *The Richmond Papers*, 1926; pp. 265-6.

203. Richard Le Gallienne: *The Romantic 'Nineties*, 1926; p. 71.

204. H. Rider Haggard: *The Days of My Life*, 1926; vol. i, p. 230.

205. E. V. Lucas: *Reading, Writing and Remembering*, 1932; p. 45.

206. *Old Friends*, 1890; p. 14.

207. "At the Sign of the Ship": *Longmans' Magazine*, December 1899.

208. Doris Langley Moore: *E. Nesbit : A Biography*, 1933; p. 176.

209. Lady Charnwood: *Call Back Yesterday*, 1938; pp. 271-276.

210. E. Christie and A. King Stewart: *A Long Look at Life*, 1940; chapter xvi.

211. Lord Kilbracken: *Reminiscences*, 1931; p. 122.

212. Anne Thackeray Ritchie: *Letters*, 1924; p. 208.

213. Garthorne Hardy: *Memoir*, 1910; vol. ii, p. 316.

214. Viola Meynell: *Life of Alice Meynell*, 1929; p. 246.

215. Martin Ross: quoted by G. H. Bushnell in "Andrew Lang at Fifty": *Scots Magazine*, March 1944.

216. Oliver Elton: *Memoir of F. Yorke Powell*, 1906; vol. i, p. 288.

217. Richard Le Gallienne: *The Romantic 'Nineties*, 1926; pp. 72-73.

218. Max Beerbohm: "Two Glimpses of Andrew Lang": *Life and Letters Today*, June 1928.

219. Richard Whiteing: *My Harvest*, 1915; pp. 272-4.

220. Evan Charteris: *Life and Letters of Edmund Gosse*, 1931; pp. 354-5.

221. E. Christie and A. King Stewart: *A Long Look at Life*, 1940; chapter xvi.

222. John Buchan: *Memory Hold-the-Door*, 1940; p. 91.

223. "Country Nights": *The Pilot*, 6th July 1901.

224. George Moore: "Mr. Andrew Lang as Critic": *The Saturday Review*, 5th December 1897.

225. Lang to Haggard: 20th October 1911. *The Days of My Life*; vol. ii, p. 74.

226. E. Christie and A. King Stewart: *A Long Look at Life*, 1940; chapter xvi.

227. George H. Bushnell: "Andrew Lang at Fifty": *Scots Magazine*, March 1944.

228. Horace Hutchinson: *Portraits of the 'Eighties*, 1920; p. 212.

229. "The Poet's Apology": *Murray's Magazine*, May 1890. (These verses never reprinted.)

230. See Roger Lancelyn Green: "Andrew Lang: Critic and Dickensian": *The Dickensian*, December 1944.

231. W. L. Courtney: *The Passing Hour*, 1925; p. 101.

232. "The Merton Professorship": *The Academy*, 20th June 1885.

233. Professor Gilbert Murray: reminiscences personally conveyed.

234. Laurie Magnus: *Herbert Warren of Magdalen*, 1932; p. 169.

235. Sir Herbert Maxwell: *Evening Memories*, 1938; p. 308.

236. "At the Sign of St. Paul's": *Illustrated London News*, 7th May 1910.

237. Sir Henry Lucy: *The Diary of a Journalist : Volume Three*, 1923; p. 100.

238. E. Christie and A. King Stewart: *A Long Look at Life*, 1940; chapter xvi.

239. Horace Hutchinson: *Portraits of the 'Eighties*, 1920; p. 211.

240. "The Dreadful Trade": *The Scots Observer*, 16th February 1889.

241. Richard Le Gallienne: "The Decline of Bookishness": *The Academy*, 2nd September 1899.

242. Ian Hamilton: "Andrew Lang": *The Times Literary Supplement*, 8th April 1944.

243. "At the Sign of the Ship": *Longmans' Magazine*, November 1899.

244. *Letters on Literature*, 1889; p. 41.

245. "At the Sign of the Ship": *Longmans' Magazine*, September 1898.

246. "At the Sign of the Ship": *Longmans' Magazine*, November 1904.

247. "General Essay on the Works of Charles Dickens": *Fortnightly Review*, December 1898. Also printed in the *Gadshill Edition of Dickens*, 1898; vol. xxiv, p. xxxiii.

248. W. P. Ker: "Commemorative Address on Andrew Lang," read before *The Royal Society of Literature* in 1912.

249. A. Blyth Webster: *Andrew Lang's Poetry* (Lang Lecture for 1937); p. 3.

250. A. T. Quiller-Couch: "From a Cornish Window": *Pall Mall Magazine*, July 1897.

Appendix A

The Odyssey Translations

The translation of the *Odyssey*, made by Andrew Lang in collaboration with S. H. Butcher and published in 1879, is one of the books by which Lang is most generally known, and was indeed described by the late Professor George Gordon as one of the formative books of its period. Lang had planned to make the translation alone, and was already working on it during his days at Merton, and in 1877 he caused to be printed privately his version of Book VI. This little book is one of the rarest of Lang's writings: it appeared in a pamphlet of sixteen pages (the last page being blank), bound in grey paper, with no title-page, no author's name, and no date; it is printed throughout with the "long s." The copy in the Bodleian belonged originally to Benjamin Jowett, and bears in the author's handwriting the words "From A. Lang." One notices with regret that the Master had not read it, for the pages were first "opened" by the present writer !

Butcher's share in the finished work was mainly, it seems that of the scholar; only slight changes seem to have been made, and their nature is well illustrated by a comparison of Lang's "Book VI" with the Sixth Book in the published translation.

The following passage is transcribed from the pamphlet as an example:

"So she spoke, but they had halted, and called each to the other, and they brought Odysseus to the sheltered place, and made him sit down, as Nausicca bade them, the daughter of Alcinous, high of heart. Beside him they laid a mantle, and a surcoat for raiment, and gave him soft olive oil in a golden cruse, and bade him wash in the streams of the river. Then, at that moment, Odysseus spoke among the maidens; saying: ' I pray you stand thus apart, while I myself wash the brine from my shoulders, and anoint me with olive oil, for truly oil is long a stranger to my skin. But in your sight I will not bathe, for I am ashamed to make me naked in the company of fair-tressed maidens.' Then they went apart and told all to their lady.

But with the river water Odysseus washed from his skin the salt scurf that covered and clothed his back and broad shoulders, and from his head he wiped the crusted brine of the barren sea. But when he had washed his whole body, and anointed him with olive oil, and had clad himself in the raiment that the maiden gave him, then Athene, the daughter of Zeus, made him greater and more mighty to behold, and from his head caused deep curling locks to flow, like the hyacinth flower. And as when some skilful man overlays gold upon silver—one that Hephæstus and Pallas have instructed in wisdom, and understanding, and cunning, to work goodly works—even so did Athene shed grace about his head and shoulders."

The same passage, as it appears in the published version by "Butcher and Lang" (edition of 1879, page 99) runs as follows:—

"So she spake, but they had halted, and called each to the other, and they brought Odysseus to the sheltered place, and made him sit down, as Nausicca bade them, the daughter of Alcinous, high of heart. Beside him they laid a mantle, and a doublet for raiment, and gave him soft olive oil in the golden cruse, and bade him wash in the streams of the river. Then goodly Odysseus spake among the maidens, saying: ' I pray you stand thus apart, while I myself wash the brine from my shoulders, and anoint me with olive oil, for truly oil is long a stranger to my skin. But in your sight I will not bathe, for I am ashamed to make me naked in the company of fair-tressed maidens.'

"Then they went apart and told all to their lady. But with the river water the goodly Odysseus washed from his skin the salt scurf that covered his back and broad shoulders, and from his back he washed the crusted brine of the barren sea. But when he had washed his whole body, and anointed him with olive oil, and had clad himself in the raiment that the maiden gave him, then Athene, the daughter of Zeus, made him greater and more mighty to behold, and from his head caused deep curling locks to flow, like the hyacinth flower. And as when some skilful man overlays gold upon silver—one that Hephæstus and Pallas Athene have taught all manner of craft, and full of grace is his handiwork—even so did Athene shed grace about his head and shoulders."

Appendix B

Andrew Lang's Prologue to "The World's Desire"
(*From the MS. in the Norwich Museum*)

"The great world was a little place in the days of the deeds that this tale is to tell. An isle of human life was the known world, begirt by lands of Faery, hemmed in by shadows, surrounded by untrodden lands and haunted by ghosts and gods.

"On one corner of the Mediterranean Sea the Sun shone clearly, shone upon Greeks and Egyptians, on the people of Sidon and the dwellers in the Islands. The rest of Earth was only mapped by fancy, being the home of visions and hopes, of desire and dread.

"He who from Greece sailed westward towards Sicily ventured on unknown waters, he trusted to touch at the havens of Giants or Man-eaters, or the shores that goddesses claimed for their own; he might dwell with the people of dreams, he was not far from the grey land where the poplars of Persephone grew, from the White Rock whence the souls wing their way to their own place, and the Ocean stream, that divides the dead from the living men.

"He who wandered northward reached a northern land, the realm of the Cimmerians who dwell in endless darkness, unvisited by the light of day.

"Eastward the wanderer might speedily come to the dancing place of Dawn, to the domain of King Aeetes the child of the Sun, in whose chamber the fleece of gold lay glimmering like the very sunlight.

"Southward an adventurous barque might win to the mouths of the sacred Nile and that mystic land where the war of gods and races was being obscurely fought; the veiled, the dread, the unseen Jehovah of the Chosen People was at awful strife with the dusky Egyptian deities, cat-headed, crocodile-tailed, Pasht and Ra and Amen, and the lord of the souls, Osiris.

"These were the days when Troy had fallen, when the heroes of Greece were driven into unheard of seas, when Israel was breaking her Egyptian bonds; days of tumults of many gods that have died with the men who worshipped them.

"All things were possible in a life whereof so little was understood; an adventure was not beyond hope to valiant warriors in the youth of time, believing themselves to be the children of gods and that the divine moved about them visibly on this side and on that.

"Concerning these days and these heroes the first and greatest of all poets sang, telling how Odysseus the son of Laertes of Ithaca (whom the Romans call Ulysses) bore his lot and took his share of sorrow on the sea and of the love of goddesses and of the hate of men.

"But the story of that Wanderer is left half told:

"The wide world knows how in youth he was one of the wooers of fair Helen, how for his oath's sake he fought to win her back under the walls of Troy, how on his homeward path he angered the Sea-god, and for ten long years was driven wandering even to the gates of Hell. Even when he had won home and had slain his enemies in his halls he might not rest, for the curse of the Sea-god remained on him. Then only he knew that he must carry the Sea-god's fame and worship even unto the land of men who had never heard of the sea nor tasted food seasoned with salt. From that far-off and unknown country he was to return, and from the sea was his own death to come—so much Odysseus knew, for so much the dead prophet had told him, but all the rest is hidden.

"So here we tell the ending of that tale, we tell of the last seafaring of Odysseus, of his latest battle, of his latest love, and the death that came upon him from the sea.

"Back to the Dawn of Time we look, with the dim eyes of the world's elder days, striving to see the sunlight gleam upon the golden helm and hauberk, and the fire of burning citadels glitter on points and blades of bronze.

"Wistfully we listen for a word out of that eager time, for a fragment of an ancient song, a murmur of grey tradition, a woman's name cried aloud through the din of battle; the clash of sword on shield, the hurtling flight of the shafts of sorrow.

"We listen and we look, and piecing together what we may, we tell of the ending of Odysseus."

Appendix C

Articles and Notes on Andrew Lang

The following is a list of the more important critical and biographical writings on Andrew Lang so far published. Besides separate articles, such books are noted as contain chapters or notes of particular interest. For shorter references see those quoted in the text.

1. AUTOBIOGRAPHICAL ARTICLES BY ANDREW LANG

Title	Publication	Date	
"ADVENTURES AMONG BOOKS"	*Scribner's Magazine*	Sept.-Nov. 1891	Reprinted in *Adventures Among Books* 1905; pp. 1-38
"A BORDER BOY-HOOD"	*Angling Sketches*	1891	Pp. 10-37
"OLD ST. LEONARD'S DAYS"	*Alma Mater's Mirror*	1887	Pp. 7-24 Reprinted in *Andrew Lang and St. Andrews*, 1944 pp. 36-42
"REMINISCENCES OF BALLIOL COLLEGE"	*English Illustrated Magazine*	Nov. 1893	

2. ARTICLES, PAMPHLETS AND MISCELLANEOUS REFERENCES

Author	Publication	Date	
GEORGE S. GORDON	*Dictionary of National Biography*		Article "Andrew Lang"
C. M. FALCONER	*Specimen of a Bibliography*	1889	Privately printed
J. SIMSON	*Andrew Lang a Gipsy*	1892	4-page pamphlet
C. M. FALCONER	*Bibliography of Andrew Lang*	1894	Specimen privately printed
WILLIAM CANTON	*The Bookman*	Aug. 1895	"Mr. Lang as a Poet"
A. T. QUILLER-COUCH	*Pall Mall Magazine*	July 1897	On Lang's Prose Style

Author	Publication	Date	
C. M. FALCONER	*A New Friendship's Garland*	1898	Privately printed
R. BROWN	*Semitic Influence in Hellenic Mythology, with Special Reference to the Works of Max Müller and Andrew Lang*	1898	
W. L. COURTNEY	*English Illustrated Magazine*	Mar. 1904	A Bibliographical Note on Andrew Lang"
T. D. WANLISS	*Scotland and Presbyterianism Vindicated. Being a Critical Review of the Third Volume of Mr. Lang's History*	1905	
ANDREW LANG	*Blackwood's Magazine*	Oct. 1905	"My History Vindicated" (an Answer to the above)
T. D. WANLISS	*The Muckrake in Scottish History, or Mr. Lang Recriticised*	1906	
E. M. SELLAR	*Recollections and Impressions*	1907	
G. K. CHESTERTON	*The Illustrated London News*	27th July 1912	"Andrew Lang"
ANONYMOUS	*Blackwood's Magazine*	Sept. 1912	"In Memoriam Andrew Lang"
J. CUMMING WALTERS	*The Dickensian*	Sept. 1912	"Andrew Lang and Dickens's Puzzle"
J. C. ANDERSON	*St. Andrews Library Bulletin*	1912	
ALLAN MENZIES	*College Echoes* (St. Andrews)	Oct. 1912	
GEORGE SAINTSBURY	*Oxford Magazine*	17th Oct. 1912	"Andrew Lang"
P. HUME BROWN	*Andrew Lang*	1912	*Proceedings of the British Academy Vol. V*

Author	Publication	Date	
W. P. KER J. M. BARRIE }	(Published 1913)		"Commemorative Addresses delivered before the Royal Society of Literature: 28th Nov. 1912"
R. S. RAIT GILBERT MURRAY SOLOMON REINACH J. J. MILLAR }	*The Quarterly Review*	April 1913	"Commemorative Articles"
EDMUND GOSSE	*Portraits and Sketches*	1913	"Andrew Lang."
G. G. GREENWOOD	*Is there a Shakespeare Problem? A Reply to J. M. Robertson and Andrew Lang*	1916	
HORACE HUTCHINSON	*Portraits of the 'Eighties*	1920	Pp. 208-217
SIDNEY COLVIN	*Memories and Notes*	1921	Pp. 117-119
GEORGE SAINTSBURY	*The Quarterly Review*	Oct. 1923	"Andrew Lang's Poetry"
H. RIDER HAGGARD	*The Days of My Life*	1926	(Written 1911-1912)
GEORGE SAINTSBURY	*The Eighteen-Seventies*	1929	"Andrew Lang in the Eighteen-Seventies"
MAX BEERBOHM	*Life and Letters*	June 1928	"Two Glimpses of Andrew Lang"
RICHARD LE GALLIENNE	*The Romantic 'Nineties*	1931	Pp. 71-73
SIR HERBERT MAXWELL	*Evening Memories*	1932	Pp. 216-219, etc.
LADY CHARNWOOD	*Call Back Yesterday*	1937	Pp. 271-277
MALCOLM ELWIN	*Old Gods Falling*	1939	Pp. 182-202
ELLA CHRISTIE AND ALICE KING STEWART	*A Long Look at Life*	1940	"Some Recollections of Andrew Lang and his wife" Chapter xvi.
FORREST REID	*Retrospective Adventures*	1941	"Andrew Lang and Longmans' Magazine." Pp. 15-25

Author	Publication	Date	
GEORGE H. BUSHNELL	*The Times Literary Supplement*	5th June 1943	"Notes on Andrew Lang"
ROGER LANCELYN GREEN	*The Times Literary Supplement*	17th July 1943	"More Notes on Andrew Lang"

3. THE ANDREW LANG LECTURES
Delivered at St. Andrews and published by
The Oxford University Press

Lecturer	Title	Date	
GEORGE GORDON	*Andrew Lang*	1927	
ALEXANDER SHEWAN	*Andrew Lang's Work for Homer*	1928	
R. R. MARRETT	*The Raw Material of Religion*	1929	
R. S. RAIT	*Andrew Lang as Historian*	1930	
LOUIS CAZIMIAN	*Andrew Lang and the Maid of France*	1931	
JOHN BUCHAN	*Andrew Lang and the Border*	1932	
H. J. C. GRIERSON	*Lang, Lockhart and Biography*	1933	
J. D. MACKIE	*Andrew Lang and the House of Stuart*	1934	
A BLYTH WEBSTER	*Andrew Lang's Poetry*	1937	(Also a few as yet unpublished lectures, by J. R. R. Tolkien, and others)

4. ARTICLES PUBLISHED DURING AND AFTER THE CENTENARY YEAR

Author	Publication	Date	
J. B. SALMOND	Introduction to *Andrew Lang and St. Andrews : A Centenary Anthology*	1944	St. Andrews University Press
GEORGE H. BUSHNELL	*Scots Magazine*	Mar. 1944	"Andrew Lang at Fifty"
W. M. PARKER	*Scots Magazine*	Mar. 1944	"Lang and Longmans"
J. D. MACKIE	*The Listener*	13th Apr. 1944	"Andrew Lang: the Man and the Writer"
ROGER LANCELYN GREEN	*The Oxford Magazine*	15th June 1944	"Andrew Lang at Oxford"
SIR D'ARCY THOMPSON	*The Scots Magazine*	May 1944	"Andrew and Pat"
ROGER LANCELYN GREEN	*English*	July 1944	"Andrew Lang: Poet and Romantic"
ROGER LANCELYN GREEN	*The Review of English Studies*	July 1944	"Andrew Lang and the Fairy-tale"
ROGER LANCELYN GREEN	*The Dickensian*	Dec. 1944	"Andrew Lang: Critic and Dickensian"
ROGER LANCELYN GREEN	*Scots Magazine*	Aug. 1945	" 'Dear Andrew' and 'Dear Louis' "

A Short-Title Bibliography of the Works of Andrew Lang

This bibliography includes books by Lang alone; by him in collaboration with others; translations by him alone or in collaboration; introductions and prefaces by him to books by others, and a few contributions to books by others. Reprints of selections or extracts from his books are not usually included. For his more important magazine articles see "Addenda to Bibliography."

Titles printed up to the left-hand margin indicate books or translations by Lang alone or in collaboration, or works in which his share exceeds a third of the whole book.

1863

ST. LEONARD'S MAGAZINE (with contributions by others).

1872

BALLADS AND LYRICS OF OLD FRANCE, AND OTHER POEMS.

1877

ARISTOTLE'S POLITICS—Bolland and Lang.
ODYSSEY BOOK VI (privately printed).

1878

THE FOLKLORE OF FRANCE. (Privately printed pamphlet) (Off-print from Folklore Record).

1879

THE ODYSSEY OF HOMER (with S. H. Butcher).
SPECIMENS OF A TRANSLATION OF THEOCRITUS. (Privately printed pamphlet).
OXFORD.

1880

XXII BALLADES IN BLUE CHINA.
THEOCRITUS, BION AND MOSCHUS.

1881

NOTES ON PICTURES BY MILLAIS (pamphlet of 30 pages).

THE LIBRARY.

XXXII BALLADES IN BLUE CHINA.

    INTRODUCTION to "The Poems of Edgar Allan Poe."

1882

THE BLACK THIEF. A Play. Privately printed.

HELEN OF TROY.

1883

THE ILIAD OF HOMER (with Walter Leaf and Ernest Myers).

1884

BALLADES AND VERSES VAIN (New York) edited by Austin Dobson.

THE PRINCESS NOBODY. A tale of Fairyland.

MUCH DARKER DAYS. By "A Huge Longway."

CUSTOM AND MYTH.

RHYMES A LA MODE.

    INTRODUCTION to *Molière's Les Precieuses Ridicules.*

    INTRODUCTION to Mrs. Hunt's translation of *Grimm's Household Tales.*

1885

THAT VERY MAB (Anonymous). (With May Kendall).

1886

LETTERS TO DEAD AUTHORS.

BOOKS AND BOOKMEN. American Edition with two extra essays.

LA MYTHOLOGIE (Paris). Article from *The Encyclopædia Britannica* vol. xvii.

THE MARK OF CAIN.

POLITICS OF ARISTOTLE. Introductory Essays.

LINES ON THE SHELLEY SOCIETY. Privately printed poem.

IN THE WRONG PARADISE and Other Stories.

BOOKS AND BOOKMEN. English Edition.

    CONTRIBUTION ("On Dogs") to *The New Amphion.*

1887

HE (Anonymous, with W. H. Pollock).

CUPID AND PSYCHE. Introductory Treatise 86 pages. ("Bibliothèque de Carabas.")

BOOKS AND BOOKMEN. Second Edition with one variant essay.

ALMÆ MATRES. 3-page pamphlet.

JOHNNY NUT AND THE GOLDEN GOOSE (from the French of Charles Deulin).

MYTH, RITUAL AND RELIGION. Two volumes.

AUCASSIN AND NICOLETE.

> OLD ST. LEONARD'S DAYS. Contribution to *Alma Mater's Mirror*.
>
> INTRODUCTION to Lamb's *Beauty and the Beast*.

1888

PERRAULT'S POPULAR TALES. Introductory Treatise 115 pages.

XXXII BALLADES IN BLUE CHINA. Enlarged Edition.

PICTURES AT PLAY. By Two Art Critics. (With W. E. Henley.)

THE GOLD OF FAIRNILEE.

GRASS OF PARNASSUS.

> INTRODUCTION to *Ballads of Books*.
>
> INTRODUCTION to *Border Ballads*.
>
> INTRODUCTION to Herodotus *Euterpe* ("Bibliothèque de Carabas").
>
> HISTORY OF CRICKET. Contribution to *Cricket*. Badminton Library.

1889

LETTERS ON LITERATURE.

THE DEAD LEMAN. From the French of Theophile Gautier, etc. (With Paul Sylvestre.)

LOST LEADERS.

PRINCE PRIGIO.

ODE TO GOLF. Privately printed.

> INTRODUCTION to *From my Verandah in New Guinea* by Romily.
>
> INTRODUCTION to *The Blue Fairy Book* (large paper only).
>
> PREFACE AND EDITING *The Blue Fairy Book*.

1890

HOW TO FAIL IN LITERATURE.

OLD FRIENDS. Essays in Epistolary Parody.

ETUDES TRADITIONNISTS (Paris). Essays from *The Saturday Review*, translated by H. Carnoy.

SIR STAFFORD NORTHCOTE: LIFE, LETTERS AND DIARIES. Two volumes.

THE WORLD'S DESIRE. (With H. Rider Haggard.)

> INTRODUCTION to Lamb's *Adventures of Ulysses*.
>
> INTRODUCTION to Kipling's *The Courting of Dinah Shadd*, etc. (New York).
>
> INTRODUCTION to H. L. Havell's translation of Longinus.
>
> INTRODUCTION to *The Red Fairy Book*. (Large paper only).

R

PREFACE AND EDITING—*The Red Fairy Book.*
INTRODUCTION to *The Strife of Love in a Dream.*
INTRODUCTION to Rae's *Song's and Verses.*
HISTORY OF GOLF. Contribution to *Golf.* Badminton Library.

1891

ESSAYS IN LITTLE.

ANGLING SKETCHES.

ON CALAIS SANDS. Poem with music.

CONTRIBUTION to *Famous Golf Links.*
INTRODUCTORY to Malory's *Morte d'Arthur* (Somers' Edition).
PREFACE AND EDITING—*The Blue Poetry Book.*
INTRODUCTION to *Elizabethan Songs* edited by E. H. Garrett.
INTRODUCTION to *Selected Poems of Robert Burns.*

1892

WILLIAM YOUNG SELLAR. A Brief Memoir. Privately printed.

GRASS OF PARNASSUS. First and Last Rhymes (with many additions).

A BATCH OF GOLFING PAPERS (With Others.)

INTRODUCTION to Sellars' *Roman Poets : Horace.*
PREFACE AND EDITING—*The Green Fairy Book.*
PICCADILLY. Contribution to *The Great Streets of the World.*

1892-1894. INTRODUCTIONS AND NOTES to *The Waverley Novels.*
Border Edition. In all 430 pages by Andrew Lang.

1893

HOMER AND THE EPIC.

KIRK'S SECRET COMMONWEALTH. Introductory Treatise 77 pages. ("Bibliothèque de Carabas.")

PRINCE RICARDO OF PANTOUFLIA.

ST. ANDREWS.

LETTERS TO DEAD AUTHORS. American Edition. (With Four Additional Letters never published in England).

THE TERCENTENARY OF IZAAK WALTON. Privately printed.

INTRODUCTION to Cox's *Cinderella Variants.*
INTRODUCTION to R. Duff's *Kings of Cricket.*
INTRODUCTION to Du Camp's *Theophile Gautier.*
PREFACE, CONTRIBUTION, EDITING *The True Story Book.*

1894

MEMOIR OF R. F. MURRAY. 62 pages. In *R. F. Murray : His Poems.*

BAN AND ARRIERE BAN. A Rally of Fugitive Rhymes.

COCK LANE AND COMMON SENSE.

INTRODUCTION to Scott's *Lyrics and Ballads.*

INTRODUCTION to Lever's *Harry Lorrequer* (U.S.A.).

PREFACE, EDITING—*The Yellow Fairy Book*.

INTRODUCTION to Van Eeden's *Little Johannes*.

1895

THE VOICES OF JEANNE D'ARC. Privately printed pamphlet.

MY OWN FAIRY BOOK.

INTRODUCTION to Scott's *Poetical Works*.

PREFACE, CONTRIBUTION, EDITING—*The Red True Story Book*.

INTRODUCTION to T. T. Stoddart's *The Death Wake*.

1896

A MONK OF FIFE.

THE LIFE AND LETTERS OF JOHN GIBSON LOCKHART. Two volumes.

INTRODUCTION to *Poems and Songs of Burns*.

INTRODUCTION to Parker's *Australian Legendary Tales*.

PREFACE, EDITING, *The Animal Story Book*.

INTRODUCTION to Roth's *Natives of Sarawak*.

INTRODUCTION to Walton's *Complete Angler*.

CONTRIBUTION to *The Poetry of Sport*. Badminton Library.

1897

PICKLE THE SPY.

MODERN MYTHOLOGY. A Reply to Max Müller.

THE BOOK OF DREAMS AND GHOSTS.

MIRACLES OF MADAME SAINT CATHERINE OF FIERBOIS. Translation from the French.

INTRODUCTION to *A Collection of Ballads*.

INTRODUCTION to E. About's *The King of the Mountains*.

PREFACE, EDITING—*The Pink Fairy Book*.

INTRODUCTION to Sybil Corbet's *Animal Land*.

INTRODUCTION to Scott's *The Lady of the Lake*.

INTRODUCTION, EDITING—*Selections from Wordsworth*.

INTRODUCTION to *The Nursery Rhyme Book*.

INTRODUCTION, EDITING—*The Highlands of Scotland in* 1750.

INTRODUCTIONS to the Gadshill Edition of the Works of Charles Dickens. 34 volumes.

1898

THE COMPANIONS OF PICKLE.

THE MAKING OF RELIGION.

WAITING ON THE GLESCA TRAIN ! Poem set to music by R. T. Boothby.

INTRODUCTION to Holmes' *Autocrat at the Breakfast Table*.

INTRODUCTION to Parker's *More Australian Legendary Tales*.

PREFACE, EDITING—*Arabian Nights' Entertainments*.

INTRODUCTION, EDITING —*Selections from Coleridge.*
INTRODUCTION to Shayton's *Pleasures of Literature.*

1899

HOMERIC HYMNS. Translations with Essays.
PARSON KELLY. (With A. E. W. Mason.)
MYTH, RITUAL AND RELIGION. Second edition, rewritten and enlarged.
    INTRODUCTION to Mackenzie's *Prophecies of the Braham Seer.*
    INTRODUCTION to Companetti's *Traditional Poetry of the Finns.*
    PREFACE, EDITING—*The Red Book of Animal Stories.*
    INTRODUCTION to Lamb's *Tales from Shakespeare.*

1900

A HISTORY OF SCOTLAND. Volume I.
PRINCE CHARLES EDWARD STUART.
NOTES AND NAMES IN BOOKS. Privately printed pamphlet (U.S.A.).
    PREFACE, EDITING—*The Grey Fairy Book.*
    INTRODUCTION to Brown's *Rab and His Friends, etc.*

1901

ALFRED TENNYSON.
THE MYSTERY OF MARY STUART.
MAGIC AND RELIGION.
    PREFACE to Nigel Oliphant's *Seige of the Legations in Peking.*
    PREFACE, EDITING—*The Violet Fairy Book.*

1902

A HISTORY OF SCOTLAND. Volume II.
JAMES VI AND THE GOWRIE MYSTERY.
THE DISENTANGLERS.
THE YOUNG RUTHVEN. Privately printed ballad.
    INTRODUCTION, EDITING—*The Gowrie Conspiracy : Confessions of Sprott.*
    INTRODUCTION to Victor Hugo's *Notre Dame.*
    PREFACE, EDITING—*The Book of Romance.*

1903

THE VALET'S TRAGEDY and other Studies in Secret History.
SOCIAL ORIGINS. With Primal Law by J. J. Atkinson.
THE STORY OF THE GOLDEN FLEECE.
LYRICS. Pirate Edition by Moscher (U.S.A.).
    MEMOIR—George Douglas Brown. *The House with the Green Shutters.*
    INTRODUCTION, EDITING—*Social England Illustrated.*
    INTRODUCTION to Dumas's *The Three Musketeers.*
    PREFACE, EDITING—*The Crimson Fairy Book.*

1904

A HISTORY OF SCOTLAND. Volume III.

HISTORICAL MYSTERIES.

NEW COLLECTED RHYMES.

> INTRODUCTION to Maitland's *Apology*.
> INTRODUCTION to Charles Elton's *William Shakespeare*.
> INTRODUCTION to Scott's *The Lady of the Lake*.
> PREFACE, EDITING—*The Brown Fairy Book*.
> INTRODUCTION to Robert Barclay's *Memoirs*.

1905

JOHN KNOX AND THE REFORMATION.

ADVENTURES AMONG BOOKS.

THE PUZZLE OF DICKENS'S LAST PLOT.

THE SECRET OF THE TOTEM.

THE CLYDE MYSTERY.

> INTRODUCTION to Irene Maunder's *The Plain Princess*.
> INTRODUCTION to Thomas's *Crystal Gazing*.
> INTRODUCTION to Scott's *Marmion*.
> INTRODUCTION to Scott's *The Lay of the Last Minstrel*
> PREFACE, EDITING—*The Red Book of Romance*.

1906

LIFE OF SIR WALTER SCOTT.

THE STORY OF JOAN OF ARC.

PORTRAITS AND JEWELS OF MARY STUART.

HOMER AND HIS AGE.

NEW AND OLD LETTERS TO DEAD AUTHORS.

> CONTRIBUTION to *Homes and Haunts of Famous Authors*.
> INTRODUCTION to Parker's *The Eahlayi Tribe*.
> PREFACE, EDITING—*The Orange Fairy Book*.

1907

A HISTORY OF SCOTLAND. Volume IV.

THE KING OVER THE WATER. (With Alice Shield.)

TALES OF A FAIRY COURT.

TALES OF TROY AND GREECE.

> INTRODUCTION to Stevenson's *A Child's Garden of Verses*.
> CONTRIBUTION to *The Poet's Country*.
> CONTRIBUTION to *Anthropological Essays*.
> INTRODUCTION to J. A. Farrer's *Literary Forgeries*.
> PREFACE, EDITING—*The Olive Fairy Book*.

RR

INTRODUCTION to Dumas's *My Memoirs*.

INTRODUCTION to *All's Well that Ends Well* (Caxton Shakespeare).

CONTRIBUTIONS to *The Union of* 1707.

1908

THE MAID OF FRANCE.

ORIGINS OF RELIGION.

ORIGINS OF TERMS OF HUMAN RELATIONSHIP. Pamphlet.

THREE POETS OF FRENCH BOHEMIA. Pirate Edition by Moscher of essay in *Dark Blue*, May 1871. (U.S.A.)

INTRODUCTION to School Edition of *Quentin Durward*.

EDITING—*Select Poems of Jean Ingelow*.

CONTRIBUTION to *Anthropology and the Classics*.

PREFACE, EDITING—*The Book of Princes and Princesses* (by Mrs. Lang).

INTRODUCTION to Alice Shield's *The Cardinal of York*.

1909

SIR GEORGE MACKENZIE OF ROSENHAUGH. His Life and Times.

LA VIE DE JEANNE D'ARC DE M. ANATOLE FRANCE. Not published in English. (Paris.)

INTRODUCTION to Robert Murray's *The Scarlet Gown*.

INTRODUCTION to Charles Murray's *Hamewith*.

PREFACE, EDITING—*The Red Book of Heroes* (by Mrs. Lang).

1910

THE WORLD OF HOMER.

SIR WALTER SCOTT AND THE BORDER MINSTRELSY.

DOES RIDICULE KILL ? Pirate Edition by Moscher of essay in *Morning Post*. (U.S.A.)

INTRODUCTION to E. Dagnell's *Folk Stories from Nigeria*.

INTRODUCTION to Charles Reade's *A Good Fight*.

PREFACE, EDITING—*The Lilac Fairy Book*.

1911

BALLADES AND RHYMES. New Introduction.

A SHORT HISTORY OF SCOTLAND.

METHOD IN THE STUDY OF TOTEMISM.

RELIGIO LOCI. Contribution to *Votiva Tabella*. St. Andrews.

INTRODUCTION to J. V. Morgan's *A Study in Nationality*.

INTRODUCTION to Swanston Edition of the *Works of R. L. Stevenson*.

PREFACE, EDITING—*All Sorts of Stories Book* (by Mrs. Lang.)

PRESIDENTIAL ADDRESS TO THE SOCIETY FOR PSYCHICAL RESEARCH.

1912

A HISTORY OF ENGLISH LITERATURE.

SHAKESPEARE, BACON, AND THE GREAT UNKNOWN.

BOOKS AND BOOKMEN. New Introduction.

ODE ON A DISTANT MEMORY OF JANE EYRE, etc. Privately printed poems edited by C. K. Shorter.

IN PRAISE OF FRUGALITY. Translated from Pope Leo XII. Poem, privately printed by "W.F.P. " Limited to 13 copies.

ODE TO THE OPENING CENTURY. Translated from Pope Leo XII. Privately printed poem. Limited to 13 copies.

INTRODUCTION to *The Annesley Case*.

INTRODUCTION to Barnett and Dale's *Anthology of English Prose*.

PREFACE, EDITING—*The Book of Saints and Heroes* (by Mrs. Lang).

1913

HIGHWAYS AND BYWAYS ON THE BORDER. (With John Lang.)

PREFACE to Mrs. Lang's *Men, Women and Minxes*.

EDITED—*The Strange Story Book* (by Mrs. Lang, including Preface).

1923

POETICAL WORKS. Four volumes. Edited by Mrs. Lang.

1932

CHRONICLES OF PANTOUFLIA. *Prince Prigio* and *Prince Ricardo*.

1944

ANDREW LANG AND ST. ANDREWS. A Centenary Anthology. Edited by J. B. Salmond.

Addenda to Bibliography

A selection of Lang's more important uncollected contributions to magazines

1. SERIES OF ESSAYS

AT THE SIGN OF THE SHIP: In *Longmans' Magazine*, monthly from January 1886 to October 1905. Approximately 1,920 quarto pages.

A SERIES OF MISCELLANEOUS ESSAYS in *The Illustrated London News*, weekly from 17th January 1891 to 29th February 1896. In all 250 essays of one column each (see selection below).

FROM A SCOTTISH WORKSHOP: in *The Illustrated London News*, weekly from 7th March 1896 to 2nd January 1897. In all 37 essays of one column each.

AT THE SIGN OF ST. PAUL'S: in *The Illustrated London News*, weekly from 4th November 1905 to 27th July 1912. In all 350 numbers of about one column each.

THE COMEDIES OF SHAKESPEARE: in *Harper's Monthly Magazine*, at irregular intervals between December 1889 and August 1895. A series of 14 essays.

LITERARY CHRONICLE: in *Cosmopolis*, at irregular intervals from January 1896 to November 1898, a series of "Notes on New Books," in all about 130 quarto pages.

BOOKS AND MEN: in *The Pilot*, weekly from 16th February to 2nd November 1901, in all 21 articles of about two columns each.

2. SINGLE ESSAYS (A Selection)

The Illustrated London News (250 Essays)

The Art of Mark Twain	14th February	1891
Border Memories	21st February	1891
A Prehistoric Review	28th March	1891
A School of Fiction	18th April	1891
Woman's Ways	13th June	1891
A View of Education in A.D. 3756	27th June	1891
The Country Quiet	25th July	1891
A New Shakespeare (Prose and Verse)	29th August	1891
Greek Magazine Poetry	5th September	1891
Arts and Crafts of Childhood	24th October	1891

Was Byron a Great Poet ? .. .. .. 21st November 1891
J. M. Barrie's "The Little Minister" .. 5th December 1891
The Teaching of English Literature .. 26th December 1891
Arbuthnot's Humour .. .. .. 5th March 1892
The Avengers of Romance .. .. .. 30th April 1892
Stray Cats .. .. 30th July 1892
An Unlucky Poet (Quintus Smyrnæus) .. 3rd August 1892
    Continuation .. .. 10th September 1892
Modern Fairy Tales .. .. 3rd December 1892
The Poetic Temperament .. .. .. 31st December 1892
Taste in Fiction .. .. 14th January 1893
An Argument for the Existence of a Brownie 25th March 1893
Giving Up Things .. .. 1st July 1893
The Tercentenary of Izaak Walton .. 5th August 1893
Mr. Stevenson's New Novel ("Catriona") .. 16th September 1893
An American at Oxford .. .. .. 7th October 1893
The Master of Balliol (Jowett) .. .. 14th October 1893
Irish Fairies .. .. 23rd December 1893
A Mysterious Monk (The Monk of Fife) .. 16th June 1894
Authors on Critics .. .. 13th October 1894
An Old Chair and an Old House .. .. 27th October 1894
Mr. R. L. Stevenson .. .. .. 5th January 1895
The Stage and Aristotle .. .. .. 2nd February 1895
Books We Have Stuck In .. .. .. 29th June 1895
Oxford in Fiction .. .. 21st December 1895

The Cornhill Magazine
French Peasant Songs .. .. .. May 1876
The Mystery of Lord Bateman .. .. February 1900
Examinations in Fiction .. .. .. January 1901
The Reading Public .. .. December 1901
Bibliomania .. .. July 1902
Border History v. Border Ballads .. .. January 1907
Irish Epics and Homer .. .. .. October 1908
Anti-Jacobite Conspiracies .. .. .. January 1909
Shakespeare or X ? .. .. September 1911

Fraser's Magazine
Rabelais and the Renaissance .. .. March 1870
The Kalevala .. .. June 1872
Gerard de Nerval .. .. May 1873
Carlyle's Reminiscences .. .. .. April 1881
The Philosophy of Mythology .. .. August 1881

A Dip in Criticism (on Haggard) .. .. October 1888
Wilkie Collins's Novels .. .. .. January 1890
Robert Browning .. .. July 1891
The Mimes of Herondas .. .. .. December 1891
The Young Men .. .. February 1894
Letters of Coleridge .. .. June 1895
Max Müller .. .. December 1900
Pre-animistic Religion .. .. .. May 1909

Forum
Books that Helped Me .. .. .. June 1887

Murray's Magazine
The Story of the Dead Wife .. .. April 1887
International Girlishness .. .. .. October 1888

Harper's Magazine
Sidney Smith .. .. November 1884
St. Andrews .. .. January 1890
Golf, Old and New .. .. .. June 1895

The Anglo-Saxon Review
Three Seeresses .. .. September 1900
Drawbacks of Certain Games .. .. December 1900

The Century Magazine
Matthew Arnold .. .. April 1882
Edinburgh Old Town .. .. .. January 1884

The Windsor Magazine
No Time for Reading .. .. .. January 1903

Good Words
Charlotte Brontë .. .. .. April 1889
Life in Homer's Time .. .. .. August 1891
Victorian English Literature .. .. February 1897

The North American Review
Unhappy Marriages in Fiction .. .. June 1889
Tendencies in Fiction .. .. .. August 1895
Genius in Children .. .. .. January 1897

Scribner's Magazine
Alexandre Dumas .. .. September 1889
Molière .. .. June 1891
Piccadilly .. .. August 1891

The Age of Homer .. .. 8th March 1879
Kaffir Folktales .. .. 9th September 1882
Anthropology and Ancient Literature .. 10th March 1883
Myths and Household Tales .. .. 7th February 1885
Letter: The Merton Professorship .. .. 20th June 1885
The Great Hare (Anthropological) .. 15th May 1886
The Metaphysics of Savages .. .. 21st January 1888
Letter: Odysseus and Helen .. .. 13th December 1890
Letter: Odysseus and the Cyclops .. 10th January 1891

The New Review
Mythology and the Old Testament .. August 1889
The Science of Criticism .. .. .. May 1891
(Five Book-Review Articles during .. .. 1892 and 1893)

The Monthly Review
Magic Mirrors and Crystal Gazing .. .. December 1901
Mrs. Gallup and Francis Bacon .. .. February 1902
Human Personality after Death .. .. March 1903

The Neolith
Neolithic Decadence .. .. February 1908

The Scots Observer
Literary Cadgers .. .. 1st December 1888
The Dreadful Trade .. .. 16th February 1889

Macmillan's Magazine
Giodano Bruno .. .. February 1871
The Aryan Races of Peru .. .. .. March 1873
Poetry and Politics .. .. December 1885
The Escape of Clementina Sobieska .. February 1895
A Generation of Vipers .. .. .. July 1898

The Athenæum
Helen in the Iliad and Odyssey .. .. 21st October 1882

The St. James's Gazette
Ballad Forgeries .. .. 2nd March 1888
Jules Lemaitre .. .. 12th October 1888
Romance and the Reverse .. .. .. 7th November 1888
Mr. Buchanan's Young Man .. .. 10th April 1889
Literature as a Trade... .. .. .. 22nd October 1890
An Unsolved Mystery (Sobieski Stuarts) .. 5th February 1892
An Appreciation of Tennyson .. .. 7th October 1892
The Yarn of the Black Hand .. .. 6th January 1894
The Contemplative Gentleman's Recreation 21st February 1894

The Magazine of Art

The Art of Savages	March and April	1882
The Thames and Its Poetry	May	1882
Dionysus' Sea Faring	July	1886

The National Review

Homer and the Higher Criticism	February	1892
A Critical Taboo	July	1892
The Song of Roland and the Iliad	October	1892

The Pilot (42 Essays)

Politics and Men of Letters	21st April	1900
Mysticism and Genius	23rd June	1900
Mary Stuart (Casket Letters)	28th July	1900
Lockhart and Scott	10th November	1900
A Note on Footnotes	16th February	1901
Criticising the Higher Criticism	9th March	1901
The Teaching of Literature	13th April	1901
Crummles and the Poetic Drama	8th June	1901
Sour Classical Grapes	22nd June	1901
Can Literature be Taught ?	29th June	1901
Country Nights	6th July	1901
The American Athlete	13th July	1901
The Unread Poet	27th July	1901
Toleration and Public Opinion	2nd November	1901
Biblical Lunar Heroes	18th January	1902
Presbyterian Saints and Miracles	5th July	1902
The Brontës and Other Matters	4th April	1903

The Daily News
The Morning Post
The Saturday Review

Many "leaders," articles and reviews that cannot now be identified, written mainly between the years 1875 and 1895.

The Encyclopædia Britannica
NINTH EDITION

Volume II	Apparitions	1875
III	Ballads	1875
IX	Family	1879
XVI	Molière	1883
XVII	Mythology	1884
	Names	1884
XIX	Prometheus	1885
XXIII	Tales	1888
	Theocritus	1888

TENTH EDITION (being volumes supplementary to the Ninth Edition)

Volume XXIX   Edmund Gurney   1902
       XXXII   Psychical Research   1902

ELEVENTH EDITION (including articles from the above editions re-written
or brought up to date)

Volume II   Apparitions   1910
   III   Ballads
    V   Casket Letters
  VII   Crystal Gazing
    X   Fairy
      Family
  XII   Edmund Gurney
 XIII   Hauntings
 XVI   James de la Cloche
XVIII   Molière
 XIX   Mythology   1911
      Name
 XXII   Poltergeist
      Prometheus
      Psychical Research
XXIV   Scotland (History)
      Second Sight
XXVI   Tale
XXVII   Totem

3. UNCOLLECTED POEMS AND VERSES

(Being a selection of those not included in the *Poetical Works* of 1923)

SIR LAUNCELOT: *St. Andrews University*
Magazine ..   ..   March   1863
DEI OTIOSI: *St. Andrews University Magazine* ..   November 1863
REASONS WHY THEY DON'T STAND FOR THE
POETRY PROFESSORSHIP: *Oxford Undergraduates'*
Journal ..   .. 6th March   1867
THREE POEMS FROM THE FRENCH OF THEOPHILE
GAUTIER: *Dark Blue*   ..   ..   March   1871
TRANSLATIONS FROM MURGER AND VILLION:
Dark Blue ..   ..   May   1871
THE MYSTERY OF QUEEN PERSEPHONE:
XXII Ballades in Blue China   1880
BALLADE OF RABBITS AND HARE: *XXXII Ballades*
in Blue China   1881
THE PALACE OF BRIC-A-BRAC: *St. James's Gazette* 26th August   1881
IDYLLS OF THE DADO: *The Pall Mall Gazette* 4th-11th January   1882

INDEX